BOOGIEMAN
(and his cat)
IN ANDALUCIA

Jim Mackie

A CIP catalogue record for this title is available from the British Library.

PRELUDE

When I was seven years of age, I was a fat, sweaty, obnoxious twat in a battleship grey school uniform, cap and round NHS specs.

That Christmas I got a present of a mouth organ. I cut my teeth on it until my dad told me I shouldn't chew it. I fiddled around with the wood and metal contraption, and the more I blew and sucked, the more saliva it accumulated.

I remember playing this foul, noxious mouthorgan in the back of my dad's car on the way home from visiting a depressing Scottish uncle - a tall, dour, moustached presbyterian who hated everything and everyone. If there was an annual Miserable Scotsman Competition, Uncle Finlay would have won it every year. He would visit our house unannounced, usually at night and usually when his wife had had enough of him for the week. He'd sit right on the edge of a lounge chair and spout off in a loud booming voice about how badly people had treated him that week. No wonder, I'd think.

This miserable individual was tolerated but pretty well detested by the whole family. However, I was told that he was an artistic type because he played the accordion. He was the only musician in our family, and this apparently made up for all his social failings. His wife once told us that he had been going to accordion lessons for years, but he never ever brought out an instrument at any of our regular Sunday family get-togethers.

For many years, this accordion was the subject of much debate - did he actually have one, or was it a figment of his perverted mind in order to endear us to him? I loved music, and just couldn't understand why he would never play his accordion for us.

During our visits to Uncle Finlay's house, the instrument stayed firmly in its box until I was a teenager. Then one Sunday after a family lunch, Uncle Finlay brought out his accordion and made a very decent attempt at some Scottish reels. That was the only time I ever heard him play. A few weeks later he keeled over and died of a heart attack.

I thought - what a waste of all those lessons! From a very early age I had always thought that music was in the air for sharing, and that entertaining other people was a good thing to do. My mother told me that I sang the 'Cuckoo Waltz' for anyone who would listen before I could talk. So when I played my mouth organ in the back of my dad's car in the days before car radios were common, I was just trying to provide entertainment. My mum and dad spotted this, and one day when we were out in the car they asked me if I was musical. I told them that I thought maybe I was, and launched into an approximate rendition of 'Scotland the Brave' on my mouthorgan in the back seat, drenching them with saliva in the process.

When I was eight, I read an article in a comic that a musical instrument could be made out of empty milk bottles by filling them up with water to different levels. For younger readers, I should explain that in the dim and distant past, milk was delivered to our homes in glass bottles by men called Ernie who drove electric milk floats. These would move about silently through the night, their eerie silence only broken by the clattering of the milk bottles deposited by the milkman on doorsteps in the black of night. Our kitchen larder was jammed full of empty milk bottles which hadn't been given back to the milkman "just in case". If there was a world shortage of milk bottles, then our family would be okay.

So, comic in hand, I followed the instructions. I took out eight bottles from the larder and started filling the first one with water, then tuned the rest to make a music scale. It's the first and last time in my life I have ever tuned an instrument using a kitchen tap. Then I got a big metal spoon and started working out how to bash 'Three Blind Mice' out of the milk bottles. After a lot of clanking and re-filling of the bottles, I had cracked it, and I remember how amazed my parents were at my crude instrument.

Later that night, after I had removed the milk bottles from the linoleum at the side of the lounge carpet and returned them to their rightful place at the bottom of the larder, my dad asked me:

"Jimmy, would you like to go to piano lessons?"

"Yes, I think so, but we don't have a piano, dad."

"Mr & Mrs Stewart next door have a piano, and I can ask them if they'd let you practice on theirs for a few weeks. If you take to it, we'll buy a piano. But I'm only going to buy one if you'll make the effort to learn"

"I'd rather play the guitar, dad."

"The guitar is not a proper musical instrument. You can only strum a guitar, but a piano is a proper musical instrument with lots of notes."

My dad had his own way of looking at things. Piano lessons it was, and their teacher of choice was Miss Beatrice McCorquindale of Seres Road, Glasgow, a bespectacled elderly spinster who smelt odd. I later found out it was mothballs. The same smell as when my granny took me to lunch at Bremner's department store in Glasgow. We always had mince and potatoes, which smelt great until you got the waft of an old lady going by in a fur coat. Not a pleasant combination.

Miss McCorquindale strongly disapproved of popular music. At my first lesson, she told me that the only pop song she had ever liked was 'Red Sails in the Sunset', then gave a nervous laugh, as if admitting that this was evidence that she had once been a wild child. It was hardly cutting edge stuff, but she told me sternly that she had no intention of teaching me to play any pop music.

After four weeks' lessons, which included pedantic stuff about how different the black keys were from the white ones, the only tune I was allowed to play was 'Three Blind Mice'. So, when I went over to our neighbour's house to practice, I sorted out 'Three Blind Mice' in a few minutes (my previous milk bottle experience no doubt helped). I then started to figure out how to play 'Red sails in the sunset' for Miss McCorquindale. My mum had a record of the Platters singing it, and it only had three chords.

One day a few weeks later our neighbour with the piano had a word with my dad.

"That piano teacher is amazing" she told him "She's already got Jimmy playing 'Red Sails in the Sunset' and 'Putting on the Style'.

My dad was horrified. He loved classical music, and he too regarded the pop tunes of the day as worthless tat. So he phoned Miss McCorquindale to complain, only to be told haughtily that she certainly hadn't taught me these songs, and that she didn't know anything about it. At my next lesson, she asked me to play the pop songs while tutting in disapproval and tossing her head in disgust, gassing me with mothballs in the process. So, at the age of eight, I had become an uncontrollable rebel, albeit a fat, sweaty one in a grey school uniform, cap and NHS specs.

That was the start of my musical discovery. My attitude was basically - sod 'Three Blind Mice', I want to have some fun playing what I want. I still have no idea how a tune in my head can find its way to my fingertips. If someone tells me a joke, I can't remember it the next day, but I've always been able to remember tunes. It's just the way my brain is wired. The piano keyboard has been my domain for the rest of my life.

I still really wanted to play the guitar, as you could pose and ponce about the stage with a guitar the way you never could with a piano. After I saw Chuck Berry in a film, I decided to ask for a plastic ukelele for my birthday. Ok, it didn't exactly pull the chicks, but at least I could get my wee fingers round the fretboard and strut about the school playground playing 'Five Foot Two, Eyes of Blue' on it while doing the Chuck Berry duckwalk. On the other hand, the piano was an altogether more static instrument which you had to sit down to play, and treat with reverence.

Or so I thought until I first saw Jerry Lee Lewis on a TV show. This man didn't just play the piano, he screamed "You shake my nerves and you rattle my brain". He had an incredible boogie left hand, and pummelled the upper keys of the piano with his right hand. In the middle of the song, he played the high notes with his feet while still playing this boogie left hand, then he got up, stood on top of the piano, leered at the audience and pointedly combed his hair. Wow! He did all this with a fierce passion and made a raw rocking sound I'd certainly never heard from Elvis or any of the other early rock stars.

Jerry Lee was my instant hero. I immediately went out and bought 'Great Balls of Fire' with my pocket money. This was a Brunswick label 78 rpm treasure, which hit me like a ton of bricks. I'd never heard that rolling boogie sound on a piano before. The flip side of the record was 'Mean Woman Blues' and that impressed me even more, and I thought it was simply brilliant how Jerry Lee controlled the volume of the music near the end of the song, bringing it right down, then screaming to bring the volume up to finish the song. What power! I was totally hooked, and I simply had to figure out how to do this sort of thing with a piano.

The night I bought the record, I brought it into the lounge to let my parents hear this amazing piano man, but my dad was less than impressed.

"It's a load of rubbish." he mocked "I'll tell you something, Jimmy. That's not real music. That fellow will be forgotten in a few months. He's no Al Jolson."

It went way past my dad. But as I write, Jerry Lee Lewis is still rockin' his life away. Maybe he'll die playing the piano. I probably will.

So from that day, my studies of the piano were concentrated mainly on boogie, blues and jazz piano players. My heroes are not those in the classical world. They are people like Jerry Lee, Albert Ammons, Oscar Peterson, Fats Domino, Little Richard, even Winifred Atwell (a great boogie player) - and the guy who gets to play with the world's top musicians and in my opinion has the best job in the world, Jools Holland.

Fast-forward nearly 50 years. My wife and I had brought up two cracking lads. They had left the family home to pursue their own lives. The cold, wet and miserable Scottish winters had got to our bones, and we had sold up one of our two businesses. We planned to spend our winters in a warmer climate. After 29 years of having to say "no" to most gigs, I was finally in a position to say "yes".

- - - - - - - - - - -

So now the fun can start.

It's not so much a story with a beginning, a middle and an end. It's basically a collection of anecdotes about my life and gigs as a piano man in Almería province of Andalucia. And a deranged cat who entered my life totally without my consent….

CHAPTER 1 - JANUARY

"You can't be serious! Are we supposed to eat them all?"

I looked at the bag of disturbingly large grapes in my hand. My wife Carrie opened her bag and inspected her booty. It was our first hogmanay in Spain since making the big move from Scotland.

We had just enjoyed a hugely satisfying 4-course meal with copious amounts of wine and liqueurs at a local restaurant in our village with Carrie's two sisters and a large enthusiastic bunch of our new friends, who were now even larger after the evening's repast. As we staggered noisily out of the restaurant, the buxom lady owner had stood at the door beaming, and had presented each couple with a complimentary bottle of cava and bags of grapes.

It was now two minutes to midnight, and we were standing in the nearby church square along with at least half the village.

Our neighbour John the Banjo had been away from Devon long enough in Spain to know the ropes. "You're supposed to eat a grape at each chime of twelve. Then wash 'em down with some cava. It's the tradition here at new year, folks. It's easy. You'll be fine".

John twitched his moustache as he reassured us. The slim, distinguished, white-bearded singer and banjo-playing naturist had a habit of doing this when he said or did something naughty. John prefers not to sing anything written after 1930, and when he occasionally breaks out and sings 'Hello Dolly' (a young upstart of a song, written a mere fifty-odd years ago) this twitch is very evident.

Midnight was now only moments away.

BONG.
Carrie and I each shoved a grape in our mouths and started to chew.
BONG.
A second grape. So far so good.
BONG.
Something's not quite right. Bung in a third grape anyway.
BONG.
Shoved in a fourth grape and found I had a lot of hard things in my mouth. Two coughs and a splutter from Carrie.
BONG.
Oh, bugg…. I was choking now too. These grapes had the most enormous pips, which we were clearly supposed to spit out between grapes.
BONG. BONG. BONG. BONG.

We both admitted defeat. We coughed, spluttered and spat out the enormous pips while providing great entertainment to the villagers around us.

Everyone hugged and kissed amidst greetings of "Feliz Fiestas" and "Happy New Year". It was a mild winter's night at the church square. Some young men from the village band had gathered to play a passable pasodoble, while spritely old senoras in radiant dresses and brand new hairdos shuffled around in each other's arms. From our vantage point looking down to the sea, we could see fireworks from towns and villages down to the coast. Just then, our own village's firework display lit up the entire valley for the next few minutes, and the stars in the clear night sky became less visible in the haze of smoke. I hugged Carrie, and she looked at me in a way she hadn't done since a hotel room in 1982. At long last we were on an adventure again. It was an unforgettable moment, and a reminder of why we had finally chosen as our new home this land that time forgot.

After the smoke died away, I collared John the Banjo as he stood beside his gorgeous wife, twitching his moustache.

"You sod, John. You never told us about the enormous pips."

"You never asked, Jim. All the grapes here are proper big and they come with proper big pips. You don't get none of these namby-pamby pokey little seedless grapes here."

"Do you and Josie manage to eat a grape at each chime of the bells?"

"Of course not!" laughed John. "Don't be daft, Jim. At our age, we'd probably choke to death. But the Spanish seem to manage it all right."

He was quite correct. I'd seen Spanish men and women of all ages pop sunflower seeds in their mouths, chew the seeds and spit out the husks in a matter of seconds. It was a staple of their diet here, as was eating raw broad beans straight out of the pod.

So began our first complete year living in Bédar village. I had moved here with my wife to spend our winters away from the cold and damp of Scotland. We were still finding our feet, and we were still finding pips in our mouths as we walked with the crowd down to the Bar El Paso a few hundred yards away.

As we neared the bar, we could hear that it was not exactly quiet and sedate. A Spanish duo was playing and there was the steady thud of a backing track. We pushed our way through the door, and I could see the duo - a dumpy blonde singing a Europop song with a disinterested scowl, and a tall, handsome hombre singing harmony while pretending to play not one but two stunt keyboards, in the accepted fashion in Spain - all the music being produced by karaoke backing tracks.

"Amigos!" cried Javier. The tall, good-looking son of the owner swept his long black hair from his face, raised a glass of amber liquid and shouted "Happy New Year."

The men and I fought our way to the bar for drinks. Our partners were swept on to the tiny dance area by the local women - mostly colourfully-dressed, well-upholstered senoras who were clearly out for a good time. I ended up on the sidelines with my friends, trying to drink my beer standing up, my drinking arm and my glass close to my chest.

After a while, a small, wizened Spaniard shimmied over to me and signalled that we should dance. He had a week's stubble on his face and was clearly way past his three score years and ten. Although I was a bit put out that this elderly caballero was the only person in the room who fancied dancing with me, he smiled at me in a seductive way with all three mustard-coloured teeth glinting in the fluorescent lighting. We ended up performing a sort of mock flamenco to the delight of the señoras, who promptly joined in.

I lay in bed at 4am, adrenalin still pumping, having left the festivities for an "early night". I recalled that New Year's Eve (or Hogmanay) in Scotland, where we come from, is a rather different affair. It's fraught with emotion. The last day of the year is spent reflecting, not just on the past twelve months, but on one's entire life, and what might have been if Scotland had been given half a chance by the English.

I used to hate New Year with a passion, as it was spent in this traditional maudlin reflection of happier times. To my mind, Scotland always seemed backward-looking. It's virtually a national pastime, often encouraged by documentaries on BBC Scotland showing ancient, soundless 8mm films of how steamers used to crowd the waters of the Clyde, how bracing holidays were taken at the stalag camps on the Ayrshire coast, and generally how good life used to be in the old days. This has probably been going on since time immemorial, and there is nothing your typical Scot enjoys more than a "wee greet" - shedding a tear on New Year's Eve for the good old days, before getting shit-faced and fighting drunk in the very first hours of the New Year.

I had spent the last 29 years having to curtail my musical activities in Scotland because my wife and I were working seven days a week running two businesses. If I was going to live most of the year in Spain, I had decided I needed a game plan. So I had decided I was simply going to say "Yes" to every opportunity which came my way to make music in Spain. "Yes" to every party invitation. "Yes" to every jam session. I needed to make up for a lot of lost time.

Lying in bed, I pondered for the first time how and why my wife and I had come to live in this weird and wonderful corner of Spain, where life was relished rather than endured. In my early morning stupor I finally figured out the catalyst, the one event which had led to our lives being changed forever.

It was because my wife's first two choices of hotel for her 40th birthday didn't have a room with a jacuzzi.

Simple as that.

Carrie had wanted a special romantic weekend for her 40th birthday, declining my offers of Paris, Prague and Prestwick, and eventually deciding that she'd like a luxury room in a nice hotel in the Lake District with a jacuzzi bath and a decent view. Back then in the early 90's, the internet wasn't the force it is now, so I had scoured the Sunday Times classifieds one typically wet and miserable Scottish Sunday, and came up with a short list of four Lake District hotels. I phoned all four hotels and asked them to send their brochures.

By the following weekend, three brochures had arrived and my wife inspected each in the same sniffy way that her mother used to inspect my cooking. She listed the hotels in her order of preference.

I phoned her first choice of hotel, which looked gorgeous with a view of Lake Windermere. They could offer a standard room, but not a superior room with a jacuzzi. It was the same story with her second choice of hotel, an imposing building of lakeland stone, on a hill and also with a lake view. Being the school half-term week in England (a week later than in Scotland) the Lake District was busy. I phoned the last hotel on our list, a country house hotel a few miles from Lake Windermere. Carrie wasn't too keen, as the only redeeming feature seemed to be the Bechstein grand piano in their music room. She didn't consider that to be anything like an adequate substitute for a lake view and a jacuzzi.

"Ello, Tall Oaks," the lady at the other end of the phone snapped in a broad Lancashire accent.

"Good afternoon. Does your hotel have a view of the lake?"

"Not yet."

"How do you mean?"

"Are you Scotch?"

"No. Scotch is a drink. Or an egg, I suppose."

"Eh?"

"I'm Scottish."

"Whatever you say, love. We've not long took over, like, and me 'usband has to wait until major whatsit next door and his snooty cow of a wife go on 'oliday next week before he can go in and saw chunks off their trees. Then we'll have a view of the lake. All right?"

This didn't sound like a boring, corporate 'otel chain. I pursued with interest.

"My wife and I are looking for two nights' bed and breakfast in a luxury double room with a jacuzzi." After I specified the dates, there was a few minutes' pause while she checked the diary and volubly argued over my request with her stroppy Lancastrian other half.

"We're very busy, but we can do the two nights you want. We'd have to give you the Oak room the first night, and Pine the second night. But only if you take dinner as well as bed and breakfast, like. We don't mind changing the rooms over for you, and you'll get to try two of our rooms. And Stan's coming that weekend."

Meeting 'Stan' was obviously too good an offer to refuse, so I booked and posted off our deposit cheque. Now there's a bit of pre-internet nostalgia for you, posting a cheque!

We duly turned up at Tall Oaks on the appointed Friday, checked out the lovely old lakeland house, and went down for dinner at seven o'clock. We were shown into the music room, all oak panelling and fancy plasterwork. Canapés and drinks arrived, all silver salvers and crystal glasses.

The menu was a challenge. As for the starters, 'Carpachio of bee' sounded fascinating. And we'd never before had salmon with 'creamed horse'. For me, 'Cannon of lamb' for my main course was irresistible. I hoped it would explode in my mouth the way 'canon' of lamb could never do.

Then we were escorted into the candlelit dining room and served a gloriously rich meal by Jimmy, a Scouse waiter who was unable to serve anything without laughing at his own jokes. One diner, a loud, annoying Irishman with a hyena wife kept winding Jimmy up by continually asking for a toothpick, and he persisted about this bloody toothpick until Jimmy finally brought a silver salver to the table with a dome on top. Jimmy removed the dome with a flourish, revealing a large metal crowbar. The dining room erupted in laughter, led of course by Jimmy.

After this meal, all candlelight, crystal, silver and stainless steel crowbar, we repaired to the music room, where Stan the Man was bellowing the Scottish song 'Caledonia' on a small stage next to the Bechstein grand piano, while knocking seven bells out of an innocent guitar. He was a tall thin Scotsman of indeterminate vintage, with an impressive Takamine acoustic guitar and dyed hair.

When Stan heard that Carrie and I were Scottish, he immediately launched into a magnificently loud version of 'Flower of Scotland'. His head quivered violently in an attempt to sing the song louder than any human being had ever done before without the benefit of a microphone. We took this as a great compliment, as we had just heard from the hotel owners that Stan was a legend. He would perform folk, pop and Neil Diamond songs at high velocity for hours on end, go to another gig and do the same, then go on to a night club and basically not go to bed for a couple of days or so. On the other hand, he had been known to sleep for nearly two days on the trot.

As an example of his 'legend' status, a few years earlier he had been given the keys to Lerwick, the capital of the Shetland Isles. The story goes that one year he performed there at the Uphellyaa Festival,

16

playing the evening gig from eight till twelve. The next band, coming all the way from Glasgow, were due on stage at midnight to perform until six in the morning, but they never turned up. So after his four-hour gig, Stan simply continued singing and playing his guitar until six in the morning - a ten-hour gig, his voice fortified by copius quantities of his favourite tipple - rum and blackcurrant.

There's an old-fashioned name for a bloke like Stan - he's not just a trooper, he's a real, genuine troubador. Like all Scots, he's made from girders. He's just one of the many musicians you'll meet later.

I made it known that I could play a bit of piano, and after Stan's usual set, he invited me up to see what I could do. For some reason, most likely to do with alcohol, Stan and I both decided to perform a Neil Diamond song which he hadn't sung for seventeen years and I'd never played in my life. We were flying on one wing all right, but I was used to that and the song went really well. We got a standing ovation from the guests. From that moment on, Carrie and I were to be as much a part of Tall Oaks as the grand piano.

We became regular visitors to this hotel, bringing our two sons at new year. We became like family to the delightfully eccentric owners. Carrie and I made many friends there, and every October we had a birthday bash, as many folk (including Trevor, the owner) had birthdays around the same week as my wife.

One October weekend a couple of years later the receptionist (known as secretary Anne) brought her boyfriend along. Brendan was a smart chap in his late thirties, and half Irish (I reckoned it was the top half - the half that talked). He was smart, slim and fairly good-looking, and could play a bit of guitar. We started to meet other musicians at the hotel. Stan sang with the other guys, I played piano, and Brendan just stood at the back playing a viciously emerald green guitar.

The next time we met Brendan, he was persuaded to sing a song - Van Morrison's 'Have I Told You Lately'. He kept turning up at gigs singing the same sodding song. I thought he had great potential to perform at gigs, but he needed to get some material organised. So we got together one weekend at our house in Scotland and practised loads of songs, Brendan singing and playing guitar, and me playing keyboards and harmonising unharmoniously.

He absorbed so much music that weekend that I called him 'The Musical Sanitary Towel'. He said he didn't like that name, period (sorry). Up yours, I thought (sorry again), so I had to find him another stage name. My first suggestion was 'Shane Martell'. He didn't dislike that as much as my second suggestion to use for any gigs in Sicily - 'Vinny (The Meatgrinder) Castelluccio'. He simply wanted to use his real name. But that October, he did his very first gig with me as the main attraction of the evening; he put on a great performance and was a runaway success.

Over the next few years we were invited to perform at weddings and other functions at Tall Oaks. I would drive down from Scotland with Carrie, and Brendan would drive up from Blackburn.

Brendan and I would invariably offer to sing the bride or groom's favourite romantic song for the first dance of the night. It's a tradition, of course, that the bride and groom have the first dance as it's their first as man and wife. One day I got a call from Brendan about the next wedding we were booked to perform.

"Jim, I've just had a call from the bridegroom-to-be. He's asked if we can play his fiancée's favourite song for their first dance on Saturday. It's an easy one, 'She's Every Woman' by Garth Brooks. I sort of know it."

"Oh, dear."

"Why do you say that, Jim?"

"Brendan, when you say you sort of know it, do you sort of know the chorus? Particularly the very last line."

"Why, is there a problem?"

"A rather big one. The last line goes 'When it comes down to temptation, she's on both sides of the fence'."

"Oh shit." Now he understood what I was on about.

"Maybe they think that a song about a woman who swings both ways is perfectly suited for their wedding. Their sexual preferences are none of my business. But if that's what they want, I can play it on the piano if you sing it."

"I might have a problem keeping a straight face at that line." Brendan giggled.

"No you won't. You're a true professional singer, except for your singing of course. Listen, can I suggest something which might help you get through this?"

"What's that?"

"When you sing the line about the woman being on both sides of the fence, can you wink at the bride?" Brendan gave out a loud hoot over the phone, which almost perforated my eardrum. "Better still, we'll both wink." Another hoot.

"Jim, you're sick."

"Not as sick as you'll be on Saturday."

We struggled to keep straight faces all through that wedding until a fight broke out near the end of the evening. It ended with the bridegroom having the best man's head in an armlock. Maybe the best man had said something about the song.

The last time Brendan and I played together in the UK was at a wedding in London where the son of the couple who owned Tall Oaks was to wed a girl from a seriously rich family. The bride's father had set the wedding budget at 300 grand, but I was told it had gone over by 50 grand or so, and we all know how easily that can happen! There was even a professional choir at the ceremony. The reception was at the Dorchester Hotel, and as we walked in a harpist and a string quartet were playing in the reception area. Brendan and I had been asked to sing a couple of songs at the interval while the band took a break.

The band booked for the reception dance turned out to be a crack ten-piece soul band comprising seasoned session musicians and a coloured girl singer who didn't really need a microphone. They were truly shit-hot. Brendan and I had a word while they were performing. He had decided against singing, as he reckoned that we had absolutely no chance against that lot.

Anyway, the interval came and the best man announced us. Brendan was now hiding in the toilet, too nervous to go on, but a couple of rugby players pulled him out and we made our way gingerly towards the stage.

"I'm really not sure about this, Jim." Brendan muttered several times.

I asked if I could use their piano. The band were clearly a bit sceptical about what a wild Scotsman might do to their nice piano, but they obliged. Most of the 300 or so guests were well-oiled by this time, and seemed to be on our side. We started our first song, a rocking old New Orleans number called 'Brickyard Blues'. Brendan got right into the song and totally nailed it, lifted by the audience clapping along to the beat. We got a huge cheer at the end. They were shouting for more, and on our second song the band's drummer and bass player sat in and helped us along - an unexpected mark of respect. By our third song, more of the band were in, and the place was really rocking. Brendan and I got the biggest cheer of the night. It was a sensational feeling.

The wedding was a great success, but sadly the marriage was a dismal failure and ended less than a year later. The bride was scarily bulimic, just skin and bone, and I thought it was a big mistake for her to turn up at her wedding without any breasts.

Fast forward five years, and Brendan and his partner Anne badly wanted to get out of their home town of Blackburn. They tried to buy a pub, but things didn't work out for them. Brendan and Anne took this as their cue to get out of the UK, and one Sunday morning out of the blue I got a phone call from Anne.

"Jim, we've been offered a house in Almería, and we've decided to emigrate."

"Almería? Are you sure? Have you visited Almería? 'Cos we have."

"Yea, yea, I know, but we're not going down south where you went with all these polythene greenhouses. We're going to Northern Almería, the Levante area. It's a protected area. We're buying a do-er up-er near Huercal Overa. It's a shell with a disused pig barn and it's right next to a small pig farm, so we'll be sorted for pork chops. The village is about an hour inland, and nowhere near the fancy coastal resorts."

This from a woman who frequented luxury hotels and owned a fortune in posh frocks.

So, Almería?

Carrie and I had visited Almería province with our boys in October 1989. The province is located between Malaga and Benidorm, and it has over 120 miles of coastline. I had picked up a really cheap deal on a week's holiday in Almerimar, a holiday resort consisting of two high-rise hotels and a small marina for boats with nowhere to go. Our only entertainment was a Spanish band at our high-rise hotel on the Saturday night. One night we went on a bus trip to a mountain bar, which served chicken with grease and chips. The entertainment was cringing sub X-Factor stuff, performed of course by the holiday reps.

After a few days I gave up trying to find things to do locally, and hired a car with the intention of driving up to see Granada. However, after hiring the car I was advised that the road was dangerous and not to go as we may not survive the trip (this was in the days before Spain got billions of lovely EU money to build its motorway infrastructure).

The only other place to go was the resort of Roquetas de Mar, and the only way to get there from Almerimar was via a complex of poorly-maintained back-roads through acres and acres of commercial polythene greenhouses full of tomatoes, cucumbers and peppers. The roads were so God-awful that one day I hit a pothole and destroyed a tyre. Anyway, it was worth the trip to Roquetas, because they had a few restaurants there, which were a welcome change from our hotel's nightly buffet of stale fish, chicken legs, chips and salad.

So we had not the remotest idea why Brendan and Anne wanted to move to Almería of all places, particularly to a ruin next to a pig farm.

A year after they had moved there, we decided to visit in early January, mainly to take a week off from the hard Scottish winter at a time of crushing hangovers when no-one was interested in doing business. I called Brendan to find out if we could stay with them.

"Jim, the house is only half-finished," Brendan explained. "We've only got one bedroom and a bathroom of sorts, and the stairs up to our lounge are not installed yet. You could sleep upstairs if you don't mind using my ladders, but you'd need to bring sleeping bags."

"Thanks mate, but it's a holiday we need, not an assault course."

Our boys were staying with family over new year, so Carrie and I booked a package deal at beach apartments about half an hour away from their village, and we flew out on New Years' Day. Our accommodation was a beach club on Vera Playa.

We had rented a car at the airport, and it took us over two hours to find our beach apartment complex, as there were no signs. We went to bed tired, hungry and angry, and we wondered what kind of place we'd come to.

The next day the sun was out, so we walked down to the beach for a look around. There were a few bars and restaurants open, even in early January, and folk walking around in tee-shirts and jumpers. They certainly wouldn't be doing that in Scotland. We noted a total lack of any high-rise buildings. In fact, in this area of Almería province, called the Levante, no high-rise buildings are permitted, so the area has kept its charm. The population density is low, the roads are excellent and there is little traffic. Not even a traffic light - we had to go to the old Vera town to find one of these (actually, there are two traffic lights there).

When we arrived at the lovely old town of Vera, we had a lunch of three tapas between us along with three beers, a coffee and a large bowl of lovely rustic bread. We had been in a corporate tapas restaurant in Edinburgh a week or so previously, and roughly the same amount of food and drink had cost me over twenty quid. So when I got the bill for just under six euros from the waiter in the Spanish bar, I told him that he must have made a mistake. But no, it seemed that the tapas were complimentary with the drinks. Six euros went a long way around here, and later that week we found even better value.

The next day we decided to drive up to see Brendan and Anne.

"I'll meet you when you come off the motorway," said Brendan when I phoned him to arrange our visit.

We drove up the motorway for about half an hour and came off at the specified junction. Brendan was leaning out of the window of an ancient, dusty Range Rover, grinning from ear to ear, and wearing red sunglasses and a pair of yellow shorts. This was early January, mind. We followed him up the hill past a sleepy town, then turned off left down a track, then along a dusty rambla (dried-up river bed) for a bit, then along another track scrabbling along on the side of a hill. Then we drove through a narrow gap between some houses, down a hill and along another rambla. Finally, we turned left and up a hill past some derelict houses until we could smell the pig farm.

I parked the car in front of an old ruin. Across the road was their house in all its grey unfinished glory. I walked over to Brendan.

"You'll be safe here," I told him with a big smile. "The assassins will never find you in this place."

Now I can't remember how many parties, gigs, lunches and dinners we attended that week, but it was a lot. And there seemed to be musicians and artists around every corner. We had visited Spain many times in the past, but we'd never before encountered so many interesting characters and met so many charming Spanish locals. We flew back to Scotland in a sort of daze, and contemplated the remainder of our winter. For the next four months our neighbours would drive home from work, dive from their cars into their houses to avoid the freezing cold, rain, snow, howling gales etc. We usually wouldn't see much of our neighbours until Spring began and they started to appear in their gardens, usually around early May.

For some years, we'd been looking for a warm place to spend our winters. We'd gone on a few cruises, visiting places like Malta (full of scrapyards and unfinished paint jobs), Tenerife (wildly over-developed), Corsica (lovely but hard work to get anywhere), Estonia (Estonians are just weird), Cyprus (can't put toilet paper down the toilet - yeuch), Italy (full of sweaty, noisy Italians), Greece (full of sweaty, noisy Greeks) and France (everything they say about the French is true). Brendan's village didn't really compare at all favourably to anything we'd seen so far, but he and Anne seemed very happy and settled.

A year later we returned for another week in early January. Once again it would make the hard Scottish winter a week shorter. This time Brendan and Anne insisted we stay with them, as they had now completed the conversion of their pig barn into bedrooms. It was a lovely conversion in the Spanish rustica style, though I do prefer an en-suite toilet to be separated from the bedroom by a wall and a door rather than just an archway. We decided to get out of their hair during the day, and drive around the area in our rental car.

One day we decided to check out some property for sale nearer the coast, and we decided to drive up to Bédar, a white hillside village which we'd seen in a magazine and sounded enchanting. It's about halfway up the Sierra de los Filabres mountain range. I drove past a couple of bars and decided to follow the sign for the village centre. Carrie suggested we walk, but you know how it is when sometimes you just prefer to take the car - you just never know if you might arrive during that fiesta when they throw tomatoes at you. It's always safer in a car. You can close the windows. We were used to closed car windows in Scotland.

We headed a hundred yards or so up the Calle Mayor (Main Street) and discovered that this was a single-track winding switchback road paved with decorative red bricks, and lined on both sides with houses and shops. I was sure it was a one-way street, but a couple of hundred yards up the road the calor gas lorry came round a corner and the driver sat in his cab, folded his arms and looked at me. This clearly meant that he wasn't for reversing his lorry back round the corner of the narrow main street. I didn't blame him. So I reversed our rental car the hundred yards or so back to the entrance to the main street, pursued within inches by the lorry which was clearly on a desperate mission. Now we were back where we started.

"Just park the car and we'll walk," instructed my wife.

"But we don't know how far we'll have to walk," I argued. "Besides, I'm sure we can park at the village centre and use that as a base to see the place".

So I set off again down the main street, and this time I had a clear run to the village centre. Only I must have missed a turning, as we were now at a triangular-shaped dead-end in front of someone's garage. And behind us was a car containing the owner of the garage who seemed keen to put his car inside it. Reversing was not an option, so the only thing to do was to turn the car around. As I reversed, there was a scream in my ear.

"You're going to hit that wall !"

Carrie got out and helped me turn the small car around. This involved a nine-point turn in front of this garage, while the owner of the garage patiently waited for me to complete turning our car. When that was done, it was clear that there wasn't enough room for both cars to pass, so I had to reverse to let the other car pass. I decided to make my way out again to the entrance to the village and park there.

"This place is impossible," I snarled. "There's no bloody way I would ever want to live here. It's way too difficult. I'm driving out now and we can find somewhere civilised with proper roads."

Just over a year later we moved into that village. And into the weirdest house in the village.

Talk about deja vu.... Our house in Scotland had been an old building, built in 1821 with a long stone frontage. There were eight rooms in it when we bought it in the late seventies, and as it was so old, some of the ceiling and door frame heights were fairly low. The previous owner, who lived across the road, had bought the disused shell of the house plus the land from Lanarkshire Council for just £80 in the late 1960s. He planned to knock it down to improve his view over the Avon Valley. But then he discovered that he could rebuild it for a lot less than the cost of demolishing it. We brought our two sons up in this rambling, frustrating, odd-shaped house, and by the time they were teenagers they were rather taller than the doorways. Most children suffer from colds and flu and the like. Ours suffered a lot from concussion.

So if we were going to buy a house in Spain, we certainly didn't want such a weird house again. And we certainly wanted to downsize. But we both agreed that we wanted a house in a village, not in a housing development. Carrie and I are village people (not the original Village People, of course, and I've never been able to do that blasted YMCA sign thing with my arms). We loved the village way of life, where just about everyone knows you. We loved the little things, like the old ladies who'd look out for our boys on the way back from school. If they got into trouble, we'd soon know.

So we had a good idea about what we were looking for, but we vowed never to buy such a weird and unusual house again. That was until we met Frances on one of our trips over to Almería, which were now becoming more regular. Frances was an estate agent friend of someone we had met. She had heard that we were looking to buy somewhere to spend the winter.

"Have you seen property in Mojacar?" she enquired.

Mojacar is the main coastal resort, a sprawling, low-rise, friendly place frequented by strident eastenders, retired lonely spinsters, hippies with camper vans, Germans, Dutch and hordes of Spanish families during summer. It's one of the few resorts in Europe where you can drive along the main road right next to the sea. Benidorm it ain't.

"Yes, we've seen property in Mojacar, but we've heard it's too busy in summer and rather quiet in winter," Carrie replied.

"We have some apartments for sale in a gated development on Vera Playa," Frances suggested.

"No thank you." My turn to get a word in. "We don't want to live in a stalag in winter."

"Oh, yes, I see what you mean." Frances was becoming a bit dejected trying to find what we wanted.

"Tell you what. We have a cracking villa for sale up in Bédar village. A beautiful house ready to move into, and it doesn't need anything."

I looked at the schedule for the villa and quickly put it down again.

"Sorry, it's way too expensive. Anyway, we've been up to Bédar, and I can't be doing with the roads." I explained the problems we had experienced on our aborted visit.

"I know what you mean, but you'd get used to them, and the village itself is just lovely. Very friendly, lots of Spanish who mix with the British folk and the other nationalities who live there. It's been voted one of the top twenty places to live in Spain. And there's a real buzz about the place, even in winter. Why don't you go and have another look. I live only a couple of villages away, if you want to view some property in the area."

So I reluctantly drove up the following afternoon, and parked the car in the car park next to the cemetery. It was a proper car park, with trees and bench seats. Not just a park for cars, but somewhere to chill out, take the weight off, and enjoy the stunning view down to the coast. Somehow I hadn't noticed it on our last visit. We were in no rush, so we had a look round the cemetery, and discovered that to die before you hit your eighties seemed an early exit. As Spain was an extremely poor country when these señors and señoras grew up, they were very likely to have been Spanish peasants with only a few pesetas to rub together.

Then we walked around the village.

"Hola," said a coiffured Spanish señora, as she stepped down from the hairdressers.

"Hola," said a group of schoolkids on their way to band practice.

"Buenos Tardes" (good afternoon) said a man in black. Not Johnny Cash, but a stooped and elderly Spanish caballero, a good three feet shorter than the original man in black.

"Hola. Buenos Tardes," said Clara, proprietress of the village supermarket Superclara as we popped in for a look. It wasn't so much a supermarket as a small Aladdin's cave. It was jam-packed with everything from oranges to souvenirs, from a selection of local sausages to a selection of paint. Clara served a couple of elderly señoras while carrying on at least three simultaneous conversations inside with other señoras, plus another conversation with a young man outside. She then marked up their purchases in a jotter. You could get tick in this shop, something we hadn't seen since the late sixties. Try asking for that in Sainsbury's.

We walked around the fairly steep narrow roads of the village, passing whitewashed terraced houses, most covered in brightly-coloured bouganvillea shrubs. The Spanish people love flowers, and in Bédar they had used every available space around their homes, even small holes in the ground, to grow plants. Ceramic pots with even more plants were also in profusion. The village was mostly picture-postcard material, although there were a few houses needing work, which only added to the feeling that this was a living Spanish village and not a sterile tourist trap.

There were several little squares in the village, and when we had nearly reached the highest point, we stopped and sat on a bench in the shade of a gnarled old olive tree.

We walked along to a little square with a statue in the centre, a tribute to local miners of years gone by. Then we went over to some railings at the end of the square. From there we could see a huge section of the coastline of the Levante area - the towns of Los Gallardos, Turre, Garrucha, Mojacar Playa, and guarding them all like a benevolent fortress, the town where Walt Disney was allegedly born, and the town which was responsible for bringing musicians and artists to the area - Mojacar Pueblo. The backdrop was the stunning Sierra Cabrera mountain range, and even on a January afternoon, the shadows of the sun highlighted the detail on the hills.

We stopped off at the charming Bar El Paso for a beer. As we sat outside on white plastic chairs and rested our drinks on a white table, a football suddenly thudded against my chair, swiftly followed by its young owner, Nicholas. Swiftly followed by Nicholas' dad Joseph.

"I do apologise for my son." A tall, bearded American in sandals and a dark brown cape stood over us, like Jesus shepherding his flock. "You know, we're allowed to hit our children here." He looked pointedly at his wayward son, then winked at us.

We got talking. He told us he was a chef from New Jersey, and that he and his German wife Anna owned a restaurant up the hill. It turned out that their restaurant was the only business in the village not owned by a Spanish family. We had walked all round Bédar and not seen La Fuente restaurant, so we made it our mission to pay for our drinks and drive round looking for Joseph's restaurant.

We followed Joseph's directions and drove into his cark park just as he was walking up the driveway with his lad. Although his restaurant was closed for the siesta, he opened up, got us drinks, sat us down on the terrace with the sun on our backs, and gave us a couple of menus to ponder. Carrie and I had wanted to go somewhere special before flying back to Scotland to endure the four remaining months of winter. We looked over the railings at the magnificent view down to the sea, then we looked at each other. I booked a table for two for that Friday.

Joseph asked if we liked his menu, and I asked him about his herb-crusted lamb and his home-grown ice cream made with fruit from the restaurant garden.

"I grow all the herbs and fruit myself. Come see my garden".

We followed him out, past a fragrant curry plant, and he showed us his herb garden, then took us down some steps to where he grew Chinese gooseberries, star fruit and raspberries. We walked past a lemon tree and a Seville orange tree on our way back to finish our drinks. Bédar was clearly a place where people gave you the time of day, something we had increasingly missed in Scotland for a number of years.

Came Friday, and I drove up in the half-light and parked our hire car in the car park, then we headed towards the main door of the restaurant. We were followed in by a swarthy young man with a battered Spanish guitar slung round his shoulder. As we were shown to our table, the young man, Estoban (Spanish for Steven) sat himself down next to the bar and proceeded to play some flamenco on his battered instrument.

A little while later another guitarist appeared, and set up next to Estoban. Yet another Spaniard came in and did hand-claps on the off-beat. They sang a very long and involved Flamenco song, then seeing our enthusiastic applause, Estoban came over to our table, introduced himself and explained the meaning of the song in broken English (which, incidentally, is precisely the way the Scots profess to like the English).

"The words of the song mean it's true I killed your sister and wiped out her entire family with a machete, but it's because I'm consumed with love for you." Estoban was dead serious.

Some more couples came into the restaurant and there was quite a buzz about the place. We enjoyed a truly excellent meal. Joseph's herb-crusted lamb was excellent, and his mango and star-fruit ice cream was simply fantastic. At the end of our meal, Joseph came over for a chat.

"Do you live locally?"

"We're only over for a week." Joseph's face fell. "We fly back to Scotland on Sunday. But we've had a great evening, and we've even been talking tonight about maybe buying a house in Bédar."

Joseph chatted for a while, then went to talk to a group of people at the next table. We couldn't believe we'd just had such a fantastic meal, virtually all home-grown and home-made.

Then I heard a woman's voice in my ear. "Excuse me. I hope you don't mind, but we overheard you telling Joseph that you might be thinking of buying a house in Bédar."

I turned round to face the attractive brunette from the next table. "I'm Barbara. If you'd like to come over and join my husband and I at our table, we'd be glad to tell you about the village."

I didn't need to be asked twice. I ordered another bottle of wine and we found out a lot more about the village from the couple to the background din of Estoban and his friends wailing away in increasingly loud voices. Barbara sported a jovial husband, a generously-proportioned open-faced chap called Colin, who smiled constantly throughout and seemed in his element. We talked about the area, and we seemed to share the same ideals. They laughed a lot, and seemed very happy and contented. They told us all about the village - its bars and restaurants, its shops, some of the local characters, and some of the houses which they had viewed before they decided to buy the one on the next hill. Colin and Barbara have since become very good friends.

"Excuse me," I suddenly announced to our new friends, "but I'd really like to play a blues now."

Carrie shook her head. She knew I'd been itching to play. I walked over to Estoban and his mates and asked if I could borrow a guitar. They looked stunned, as if this had never ever happened before. I explained again using rather more sign language. Then it sunk in and my idea was welcomed as if it was the best idea ever in the history of the universe. A guitar was enthusiastically placed around my neck while the sozzled group of musicians looked on in reverent anticipation.

I managed to knock out a simple blues on Estoban's guitar. Not exactly Clapton, but it was the best a piano man could do without a piano. I finished, got a decent bit of applause and gave back the guitar.

"Fuckin' ell. Fuckin' ell." announced Estoban to the restaurant. "Fuckin' ell man. Muy bueno. Fuckin' ell. I mean fuckin' ell, man." He hugged me like a long-lost brother and his mates ordered me up a brandy.

When I was on my third brandy, Joseph came round with some complimentary shot glasses of lemon liqueur for a nightcap. To cut a long story short, we had entered the Fuente restaurant at 7-45pm and we disembarked at 1-15am.

We stepped outside the restaurant and although my senses were impaired by the alcohol, my breath was simply taken away by the awesome view of the Levante area seemingly lit up by fairy lights, and framed by the unpolluted crystal clear sky full of stars. As we walked to the car park and said goodnight to Colin and Barbara, the mish-mash of traditional white houses forming Bédar village twinkled in the warm glow of the street lights. A few frogs croaked in the pool where the women had gathered to wash their clothes in days gone by.

I sighed. Then Carrie sighed too, and gave out an "mmm" as I gave her the car keys. After five years of searching, it looked like we were home and dry.

The next job was to find a house in the Bédar area. The Spanish had been selling off houses to Brits for the past few years, the only problem being that most of them needed work to make them habitable. We had seen a couple of such houses advertised at decent prices for those who could do a bit of refurbishment work. There was only one problem with that idea.

I'm rubbish at DIY.

If you enjoy books where the author leaves behind a busy sophisticated city life to move abroad, buy a hovel and renovate it into a rustic jewel with his bare hands, you'd be in safer hands elsewhere.

My mission for what remains of my life is to spend as little of it as possible doing drudgery, and as much time as possible playing useful boogie piano and partying. There's never been a chance in hell that I'd follow in the footsteps of those eminent folk before me who've emigrated to foreign lands and rebuilt crumbling wrecks with their own hands. My hands are no good for anything except playing piano and maybe the odd bit of sensual massage.

The big house in Scotland which I mentioned previously was a great family home, but we had bought it from a builder not called Bob, whose slogan seemed to be "Can we fix it? No we bloody can't." The day we moved into the house, I was hanging up some clothes in a built-in wardrobe, when I cut my hand on the sharp end of a nail which was sticking out on the inside of the wardrobe. The place was more lethal than Gordon Ramsay's mouth.

My first DIY task at our house in Scotland was some basic joinery - sorting some loose floorboards on the upper landing. It was a source of annoyance to me that these creaked every time someone got up in the middle of the night to go to the loo (usually me). So I invested in a large hammer and some nice long nails, lifted the carpet and proceeded to nail down the loose floorboards.

Two days later, Carrie noticed water seeping down the lounge walls, and called the local plumber. He discovered that I had not only nailed down the loose floorboards, I had also nailed a central heating water pipe, which had sprung a leak. The plumber had to drain the tank and all the radiators, lift the carpet, then the floorboards, weld the hole, then nail the floorboards back down, put the carpet back down, refill and fire up the central heating system again. It cost my wife £180 to have all this done, rather more than it would have cost to get a joiner to fix the floorboards down in the first place. Sadly, this was not the only instance of her having to pay a tradesman to repair what I had fixed.

For instance, there was the time I decided to paint the fireplace in the lounge. This was a grey and depressingly black monster constructed from bricks manufactured by the Friday Afternoon Brick Company. I thought it would brighten up the lounge if I painted the fireplace white. Once I had finished, our lounge certainly looked a lot brighter, and I had cleverly used only a couple of litres out of a large 10-litre paint pot. As I stepped back to admire my work, my heel knocked against something, and the remaining 8 litres of paint found their way onto the deep red Wilton carpet. This was a reversal of fortune from the incident in our previous home when the best part of a gallon of my home-made red wine found its way onto the cream dining room carpet.

I'm not good with carpets. Or glass shelves laden with crystal decanters and glasses (you couldn't imagine our dining room floor after that one). And my attempt in the '80s to put down flooring in the loft of our first brand-new house resulted in what my wife calls 'The Frank Spencer Incident'. I was very lucky not to seriously damage my wedding tackle when my left leg burst through the plasterboard and my tender parts hit a floor joist. Ouch!

I wasn't good with mirrors either. Some years after ruining the lounge carpet, we had the lounge refurbished and a new fireplace fitted. It was a cracker - natural stone with an inglenook and a wrought-iron Spanish grate. All it needed was a tasteful mirror above it. So we'd gone out one day and bought a lovely big gold-framed mirror about three feet high. I put this up in the lounge the following Saturday afternoon. A friend advised me to put the screws in the wall with wee plasticky things called rawlplugs to prevent the screws coming loose, but these needed a big hole so they would fit into the wall, and the fixing seemed a bit loose to me.

Well, the rawlplugs didn't help at all, and the crash came in the early hours of Sunday morning. Next morning we cleared the debris. A few days later we bought a second mirror, similar to the first one but lighter. Not light enough, unfortunately. But at least it stayed on the wall longer than the first one, presumably because I had put parcel tape over the screws to help hold them onto the wall. The second mirror departed the wall of its own accord the following afternoon. The third mirror was put up by our local plumber, whom my wife once again trusted to do the job properly, and it was still there on the wall leering at me when we sold the house.

So I definitely wouldn't be planning to rebuild a crumbling wreck like my friend Brendan did. It would have to be a finished house, maybe needing a lick of non-drip paint, but not much more. I'll not bore you with the tedious details of our house search, but fair to say we spent many weeks looking, and left no doormat unturned. Some houses were out in the campo (the Spanish countryside) and many were reached by perilous roads so steep that a funicular railway would have been the safest method of access. On the other hand, if we had wanted to buy a house with a driveway like a rocket-launching pad, there were plenty for sale with this facility.

Village houses within the narrow streets were sometimes

impressive until we asked about the outdoor space. This usually consisted of a doorstep. But we had seen one nice house with a 'For Sale' sign right on the perimeter of the village, set back and up a private lane. We reckoned it must have had great views, but it was sold before the estate agent could get it on his books. It was probably out of our price range in any case.

One Thursday morning, an estate agent who had shown us several houses without success, phoned me excitedly.

"Mr Mackie, we've just had a new instruction which looks interesting. It's a brand new villa with 10,000 square metres of land. The house is not finished yet, but the owner is prepared to finish it at a discount price."

A discount? Needless to say, this had an irresistible appeal for an impecunious Scotsman....

CHAPTER 2 - FEBRUARY

We met the estate agent in the car park in Bédar. She was a nice girl and very helpful, and eager to show us the villa with lots of land.

She drove us along an attractive country road, then up a hill, then onto a dirt track leading up to another dirt track along the sheer face of a steep hill. Through clouds of sand kicked up by her car's wheels, we watched stones fall over the edge as we drove along. It was a bit like being in an Indiana Jones film without the noisy background orchestra. Carrie sang 'She'll be comin' round the mountain' while we hung on for dear life.

At the end of this terrifying dirt track was what looked like a vomit-covered wedding cake. It was the shell of an ochre-coloured house. Not just any ochre-coloured house, but a round ochre-coloured house with a smaller round ochre-coloured upstairs section. And a matching ochre-coloured flat roof. The windows weren't round, but they were a rich ochre colour. If you don't know what an ochre colour looks like, it's basically mustard. Back in the '70's Austin used this colour for many of their Allegro cars. We owned an Allegro years ago, and the mustard paint contrasted really well with the darker colour of the rust.

We stepped inside the villa and discovered that the interior was just as round as the exterior. In Spain, new homes are often sold without kitchens, to give the buyers their own choice of kitchen units. We had absolutely no idea how we could fit a kitchen into this house. The upstairs bedroom was similarly round. Sure, you could fit a normal bed against the wall, but the bedside cabinets would be in a very odd position.

"Oh, you'd need hand-built furniture here," was the agent's answer. "You'd have to allow quite a bit on top for that. That's probably why the price has been reduced."

"Never in a million years." Said Carrie. "This house doesn't make any sense at all. We could never invite friends over for a meal, especially in winter. We might lose a few off the mountain."

As the agent dejectedly drove us down the hill again, she turned round to look at me, as her little car lurched and thumped around the bends.

"What houses have you seen?"

"Oh, dozens. Just about everything in the Bédar area, except for an abandoned chemist's shop and a brick goat shed."

"Have you seen the big house up the private lane near the municipal pool?" she continued.

"The local agent in Bédar village told us about it the last time we were over, but we never got a chance. It was sold before it went on the market."

"I think the seller may have another house nearby for sale. I know her pretty well. Do you want me to ask her?"

This sounded interesting, and as I looked at Carrie, she nodded and said "Yes, we'd really like to have a look."

The estate agent drove us down the dirt track with a sheer drop on the left hand side. She was talking to us and fiddling with her mobile phone to find her friend's phone number, while my hair turned white in the back seat. But we got a result. Yes, the house had been sold, but the offer had fallen through just the previous day as the potential buyers couldn't raise the money, and now it was up for sale again. There had been no time for an estate agent to re-market the house, and yes we could come and see it in an hour or so.

We popped into a local bar for coffee and tapas. An hour later we were on the doorstep. Right away, I saw that it had huge outside terracing, perfect for outdoor parties. The seller opened the door, a petite and charming Irish lady called Fiona. Before we entered the

34

house, I asked her about the terracing.

"Oh, we had our wedding reception there," she replied. "Nearly a hundred guests and the local Blues Brothers band. It was a great party." Right there and then, even before setting foot inside, I pondered the idea of more great parties to follow.

We stepped inside, and right away I saw that the huge lounge would also be perfect for parties. The house was vast, on three floors, with nooks and crannies galore. The first floor had an enormous bedroom and a gym (which I wouldn't be needing) bigger than the lounge in our house in Scotland. And the top floor was a self-contained studio, not entirely unsuitable for a musician like myself. But if I asked you to design a house on a hillside, I guarantee you wouldn't come up with anything like this one. It was truly weird and it had actually more floor space than the Scottish pile we had just sold. The floor space needed sorting out - there were actually only two bedrooms although there was ample space for at least five, and the kitchen needed replacing.

We were taken to a rear terrace which looked on to the village just up the hill from the villa. I looked across the road and saw a large swimming pool.

That's the municipal pool," said Fiona. "It's open every summer. Anyone can use it and the local children have a great time."

Directly underneath the pool was a basement with windows and large double doors. I asked what it was used for.

"It's a tanatorio," Fiona explained.

"A tanning salon? In southern Spain?"

"No, a tanatorio is a funeral parlour." Fiona laughed. "It's not a crematorium, just somewhere to say goodbye to loved ones. It's not used much as people don't tend to die here very often."

This was too good to refuse. If I popped my clogs during a hot summer down here, my friends and relatives could pop across the road to say their farewells to me, then nip upstairs to the pool for a refreshing swim. I thought this was a fantastic idea, and it was certainly something I'd never found in the UK.

There and then, we made the lady an offer, which was accepted. We e-mailed our elder son some photos, and he sent us a message back saying that our attempt at downsizing in Spain had clearly been a miserable failure. He then asked when he could come over and "see the place."

Our house search had taken several weeks. Rather than fly back and forward to Scotland, we rented an apartment on the glorious El Cortijo

Grande golf valley for a few weeks until we could move into our house in Bédar. This is an enchanted time-warp valley where nothing has been built for over 20 years. It's like something out of "The Sound of Music", especially when the goat-herd comes around accompanied by the sound of the tinkling bells on the necks of his animals. Sadly, the Irish company who currently own the estate do not have a history of being honest with the property owners, and they have absolutely no idea how to promote this jewel.

In the seventies when the old village of El Cortijo Grande valley was developed and plush houses built around the perimeter, an airfield was built nearby with a control tower. Before the motorways were built, it took several hours to get from Almería's airport to El Cortijo Grande by road, so the best-heeled property owners would jump on a small plane to take them to the valley. The airfield is still there, and was used during the making of the first Indiana Jones movie. The plane dogfight scenes were filmed in the valley, and legend has it that Steven Spielberg got put out of the valley when oil from the old planes leaked and nearly caused a bush fire.

Anyway, the next thing we needed in Spain was a car. We planned to spend the winter in the area, and it made sense to buy rather than rent a car. So we visited some showrooms, and found disappointing specimens, cars often presented with a thick covering of dust, presumably to hide the scratches and dings. Second-hand cars hold their value well in Spain. They don't rust (well, not properly into holes like they do in Scotland) and decent cars are always sought after.

We scoured the classifieds, and went to view several strange cars in sickening colours which the dealers had obviously refused point blank to trade-in. Even my wife, not usually that fussy about cars, drew the line at driving a Hyundai in lurid pink or a Citroen in metallic vomit (sorry folks, I have a thing about vomit and I even wrote a sickly song about it).

One day I spotted an interesting classified advert for an old two-door Mercedes coupe. It was low and sleek in a sensible silver colour, loaded with goodies, and most importantly it had an automatic gearbox. This meant that my wife could drive the car without hurtling my back into spasm every time she changed gear. It looked interesting, so I arranged to call one Saturday afternoon to view the car. Carrie didn't see any point as she believed the car would be much too big for our needs. But I was optimistic that it wouldn't be a wasted journey. My wife calls me depressingly optimistic....

As we pulled up outside a modern bungalow in a street of identikit houses, Carrie tutted and shook her head at the sleek and beautiful coupe in the driveway.

"That car is totally impractical," was her reaction. "It's far too big for what we need, and it only has two doors."

"A door for me and a door for you," I explained in return for a scowl from my beloved.

The sellers were a youngish couple, pleasant but dim, and they were giving up their Spanish carpet fitting business and moving back to the UK in only a few days' time, so they wanted rid of the car urgently. Their attempt at selling the car had been as successful as their carpet-fitting business (everyone has tiled floors in southern Spain), and the price had come down to an irresistible level as far as I was concerned.

The car had clearly been well cared for, so I had a closer look. The first thing I did was to measure the boot and declare it perfect for what I needed. I had worked out that my full-size 88-key stage piano would fit into the boot in its protective case, and my two amplifiers would fit behind the piano. My smaller synthesizer keyboard would fit on top of the amplifiers, and my piano stool, speaker stands and other odds and ends would sit on top of my piano case. All my gear would fit into the boot, under lock and key and out of sight. The car's boot was perfectly dimensioned for my needs, and the plush velour and walnut interior wasn't bad either.

But the clincher for me was a clever button on the dashboard. If the rear headrest blocked your rear view when parking, this button solved all your problems. It operated a small motor which dropped down the two rear headrests for better visibility. A brilliant device! The only downside was when you needed the rear headrests up again for passengers. This involved opening one of the two huge side doors, clambering onto the back seat, pulling up each headrest from the parcel shelf and slotting them back into place again. For me, this was a minor drawback for having that extremely useful button on the dashboard.

I reckoned that although the car was fifteen years old, with the odd bump and scrape, it was a great buy, so I chanced my arm and made them a sensible offer - well, sensible from my point of view. The sellers tried half-heartedly to get me to raise my offer, until I asked if anyone else was coming to see the car. They quietly shook their heads, looked at each other resignedly, and accepted my offer with a sigh.

It was only after we had paid a deposit and were halfway home that Carrie asked whether a rear parking sensor (the thing that bleeps when you are about to reverse into a wall) would have been a lot more useful.

"No, of course it wouldn't have been more useful, because that car is tougher than any wall. And you don't get a button on the dashboard with a rear parking sensor. It's a no-brainer."

Carrie shook her head and laughed. "You never said a truer word."

The boogiewagon has acquired a few more bumps and scrapes on the narrow streets around here, but it still behaves impeccably. It purrs me along to gigs in restful silence - and it never misses a beat. Unlike some drummers I've worked with.

Now that we were more or less living in Spain full-time, I started to go to jam nights, and there were quite a few of those. My friend Brendan introduced me to some local musicians. One night, Carrie and I went down to a hotel in Vera where a jazz jam night was in progress. I met some of the local musicians there, strictly jazz guys, playing the usual old jazz standards plus a few bossa novas.

Professional jazz musicians often regard themselves as cutting-edge performers with a disdain for other types of music. They often appear with pony-tails and strange clothes, to present an image of cool, and they play far-out music, often their own compositions. Amateur jazz musicians, on the other hand, have the pony-tails and stuff to look cool, but they are usually stuck in a world of mainly 1930's and 40's show tunes which they play in jazz style. I'm talking old tunes like 'You Go To My Head' (no, you don't) or 'S'wonderful' (s'not). Occasionally they will stray into early trad jazz tunes and 'modern' bossa novas from the early '60s. You might get some 'be-bop' which is much, much duller than it sounds, and you could cripple yourself trying to dance to it.

But they mainly concentrate on playing interminable versions of hackneyed material like 'Fly Me To The Moon', 'The Girl From Ipanema' and 'Summertime', in which every single instrument gets a long and dreary solo. You'd be especially unlucky if a bongo player turned up on the night as he'd probably want to take a solo. Amateur folk musicians are cutting-edge by comparison. Sorry for the rant; must be my time of the month already.

The jam session was not a lot of fun. The hotel itself was the corporate sterile type, and the cocktail bar where the jam was held was easy to find. You simply walked through the hotel's sliding glass main doors, walked past reception, and turned left at the shrine. Now, a shrine was not something I had ever found in a Glasgow hotel, where such a feature would have inevitably been as smashed as most Glaswegians by the first Saturday night. But it was a really nice brightly coloured shrine, if you like that sort of thing next to a posh cocktail bar run by snooty waiters in black jackets and bow ties.

One night we went with a friend and his wife who'd flown over for a few days. The jam was due to start at 9pm, and we arrived bang on time to find a Spanish football match blaring on the plasma TV on the wall. It was being watched by four customers and three staff. There was a white grand piano tucked away at the side of the bar which the staff were supposed to have moved in readiness for the evening's gig.

I ordered beers for Carrie and myself, at double the price of the local bars. It seemed that it was costing the musicians dear to drive to the gig and give their services free. Not even a complimentary drink in sight from the management, who had the temerity to advertise the jam night while not paying the performers with even one lousy drink.

Customers and musicians began to arrive for the jam night, but it couldn't start until the staff had seen the end of the Spanish football match on the TV. So a few of the musicians got together to move the piano into position. The jazz eventually started at half past ten, once the football match had finished.

The band set up and began to play. It was all pretty predictable 1930's jazz material, and it didn't exactly swing. The drummer seemed to follow the guitarist, who seemed to know hundreds of fancy jazz chords, clearly a highly educated player but without any idea of how to swing. He was in constant competition with the rest of the band in trying to hit the right beat, and the tunes generally finished rather faster than they had started. Our friends David and Katie were puzzled by the stodgy time-keeping, and at one point, Katie leaned over to me and looked me straight in the eye.

"Jim, do you think it would help the guitar player if I was to tap the tempo for him on the arm of my chair?"

I nearly choked on my expensive beer. Katie had no musical training, but she was a big Rat Pack fan, so she knew that music from the jazz era was intended to swing rather than trudge along.

Near the end of the evening, the pianist called for Lena to come up and sing. After some mock persuasion, a short blonde lady of not a few years made her way towards the band. Every man and his dog sing Gershwin's 'Summertime' around here. Most jazz musicians or singers play this simple two-verse lullaby in a funky style, believing this to be far-out and cutting edge (it's definitely my time of the month). However, this particular blonde lady sang it sweetly in the traditional manner. But she had muddled the words. A line like 'You're gonna spread your wings and the cotton is nigh' was an interesting take on the original.

People started to yawn and look at their watches. Lena sang Cole Porter's 'Every time we say goodbye', and people took this as their cue to say their goodbyes and leave the hotel. Her performance wasn't exactly scintillating, and I later confided in my friend Brendan "I'll certainly never work with that woman". They say never say never, and I'd never, never disagree, as I had to eat my words a few weeks later.

Over the winter we had visited quite a few restaurants, and one night we decided to drive back up to Bédar to try somewhere new to eat. Friends had told us we must try the food at Bar El Rincon, run on a very casual basis by a swarthy Spaniard called Tomaso (Tommy to the villagers), his charming wife Maria and their son Julio. Upon entering his bar, Tomaso welcomed us by muttering "digame" ("tell me") between his teeth while keeping a large and moistening cigar alight despite his copious saliva. His unsmiling appearance and severe moustache would have made him ideal for a part in 'The Good, The Bad and The Ugly'. I'm sure he's the fellow who mouths "I speet on your grave, hombre" out of sync with the English overdub.

I had been warned that there is no menu, and the cost of the food and drink would be purely arbitrary, dependent on Tomaso's mood and the success or otherwise of the night. A bottle of house wine can cost ten euros, but usually it's no more than five. Sometimes drinks cost nothing at all, as coffee will sometimes be dispensed gratis, and Tomaso will wave away any attempt at payment. Sometimes he'll bring out a plate of complimentary tapas or chipitos (small liqueur glasses). He's really a kind soul.

Once seated in the big square restaurant area on this, our first night, Tomaso came over to the table and announced the choice of menu through the remains of his cigar. For the plato primer (first course) we were offered a mixed salad. And that summed up the choice of first course. For the plato segundo (second course) Tomaso chewed on his cigar for a moment then announced Pollo, Cerdo, Chuleton de Cordero, Emperador or Ternera - Chicken, Pork, Lamb chops, Swordfish or Beefsteak. I ordered a salad to share, plus lamb chops for myself. Carrie ordered lomo (pork tenderloin).

When it arrived, the mixed salad starter was enough to feed four. It included tuna, sweetcorn, lettuce, tomato, olives, capers, pickled onions and cucumber. My lamb chops numbered eight, and Carrie had to deal with seven slices of grilled pork. Both dishes came with a huge pile of chips - not just to please the Brits, but because the Andalucians are usually not interested in cooking fresh vegetables.

We met a few of the locals that night, and decided to return soon.

When we returned to Bar El Rincon the following week, there was already piped music playing throughout the building. After Tomaso had switched the restaurant lights on and found us a table, he turned on the television and turned the volume up so we could hear the football match on the screen. We were told that this sort of treatment showed that we had been accepted into the community - the Spanish love noise when they go out, preferably several bands playing at once and several conversations going at the same time, so we were indeed privileged.

We had been to a few Spanish lessons, so when Tomaso came to the table to take our order, I decided to try out my newly-acquired language skills. Carrie and I fancied sampling the fish this time.

"Quiero algo piscina," I announced.

"Que?" Tomaso answered with a look similar to Manuel from Fawlty Towers.

"Quiero algo piscina," I repeated louder and slower.

"Que? Que?"

Tomaso still had no idea what I wanted, so I puffed up my cheeks and opened and close my mouth to simulate a fish's breathing. It was no good. He shrugged and inhaled deeply of his noxious, saliva-drenched cigar.

"We'd better show him what we want in writing. Is the dictionary handy?" I asked Carrie. Her handbag was usually stocked with all of life's essentials, from our childrens' baby teeth to clothes pegs - and she absolutely always has emergency sachets of ketchup. She waded through the debris and eventually produced a English-Spanish dictionary from the depths of her black leather tardis. She looked up the word 'piscina' then burst out laughing.

"You've just told Tomaso that you'd like some swimming pool."

"Ah. That'll be why he looked puzzled then. Any idea how I tell him that I'd like some fish?"

"Quiero algo pescado."

I knew it began with a "P".... Anyway, as it was a Sunday night they didn't have any fish, so Tomaso suggested steak as a suitable alternative. To avoid any more confusion, we both agreed. After battling the enormous mixed salad, we contemplated the plates which followed, proudly held aloft by Tomaso. Each contained an enormous rib-eye steak which spilled over the large oval plates. There was no room on the plates for the chips beside the steaks, so Maria had simply piled them on top of the steaks.

"Poco hecho o bien hecho?" Tomaso asked us before putting down the plates on the table. He waited while we mentally scratched our heads.

Then Carrie figured it out.

"He's asking who wants rare and who wants well done."

Tomaso had never asked us when he took the order. We hadn't known we had a choice. Maria had cooked both steaks, then told her husband to ask us who would like the well-done steak and who would like the rare one. Presumably it all made sense to them. Carrie picked the well-done steak and I was happy with the rare. I couldn't remember ever having had a tastier or better value steak dinner anywhere.

After our meal, some of the locals recognised us and invited us to have a drink and chew the fat with them. It was getting on for two in the morning when we left the place to return to our rented house, having made several new acquaintances in Bédar village in advance of our move – some British, some Spanish, two Dutch ladies, a French girl and a German couple.

We spent the rest of the winter exploring the area. One Sunday afternoon we went to the Bread Festival at the charming hillside town of Lubrin. The village brass band played enthusiastically while a statue of San Sebastian was taken from the church and paraded through the streets. The locals threw rings of bread to the crowds from the balconies of the houses. Hanging bread rings up on the kitchen was believed to bring good luck in the coming year, as long as you didn't try to eat the stuff. We tried to catch as many bread rings as possible, but we were no match for the Spanish youths who dived for the stuff like world cup goalkeepers.

Spanish families had set up long tables in Lubrin's main square and had brought picnic food. We found a small table and I fetched us some drinks and tapas. The Spanish family at the next table were getting ready to leave, and offered us some of their food as they were wrapping up. This is typical of the kindness of the Spanish people here when it comes to food. It may be to do with the fact that during the Spanish Civil War, the people of Almería suffered terrible starvation.

One day in February we drove down to the Cabo de Gato, the national park. It was just over half an hour's drive away. We found wonderful roads almost totally devoid of traffic and lovely fishing villages with little rowing boats parked up on the beach.

At the charming little seaside town of Agua Amarga we found a sheltered cove and dipped our feet in the Med for a while before sunbathing on the sand, not something we'd ever done in Scotland in February. Then we found a cafe in the square for lunch, where we shared the most wonderful tortilla - a large potato and egg omelette oozing garlic and onion with a soft gooey centre. A masterpiece of culinary skill for six euros.

Then on to Rodalquilar, where we walked around a charming botanic garden in the warm sun, with only the twitter of birds to break the peace. On the side of a hill we found an abandoned gold mine which had been run by a British company up to the beginning of the 20th century. We passed windmills and viewing points of the stunning coastline until we ended up at La Isleta de Moro, a wee village with a tranquil bay and small fishing boats bobbing up and down in the water. This was like something out of the Greek islands, and we came to the conclusion that Almería was quite clearly a fantastic winter destination which had been woefully undersold.

We discovered that part of David Lean's movie 'Lawrence of Arabia' had been filmed in Carboneras, and there was a hotel called El Dorado in the town where lots of major movie stars had stayed when filming in the area. All the Spaghetti Westerns had been made down in Almería's desert region of Tabernas, and Sean Connery had made a movie with Brigitte Bardot. Part of Connery's last Bond movie 'Never Say Never Again' had been filmed at the huge Alcazaba fortress in Almería city.

Another day in February we went to the big parade at the Aguilas Carnival, in which over four thousand people took part. Aguilas is a town about 40 minutes' drive away in the neighbouring province of Murcia. We'd seen this 2-week long event advertised, and we fancied seeing the big parade on the closing Saturday night.

When we arrived at the outskirts of town, the local police directed us to a car park and we walked the half-mile or so to the town centre. It was just after 6pm, and the procession had just started. There were literally hundreds of decorated and motorised floats, surrounded by dancers dressed in fabulous costumes, and featuring everything from a huge Eiffel Tower to the Torrevieja Gay Club. I couldn't begin to describe what they were wearing. One float had young children on waltzers. All the floats had drivers sitting in a compartment near the front, and taps in the back dispensing refreshing drinks.

We had to leave shortly after 9pm due to hunger pangs, but on our way out we walked back up the procession and discovered dozens of floats in a back street still to join the procession. It turned out that we should have allowed at least four hours for the big parade, and we could have bought a seat in one of the dozens of tiered stands facing the road where the procession went down.

One night when we had actually stayed in to watch TV, I had just locked up and was making my way back into the lounge of our rented townhouse, when Carrie looked up from her paper.

"It says here that Mo and the Moments are playing at Los Corderos on Valentine's Night."

"Who are Mo and the Moments? Can't say I've heard of them."

My dearest had seen an advert for a Valentine's night dinner dance with a live 4-piece band at a hilltop village not far away. She hadn't heard of the band either, but thought they sounded rather romantic. Live bands are fairly rare in these days of karaoke backing tracks, and most venues don't have the turnover or profit margin to support more than a solo singer or maybe a duo at a push. So a fancy meal at a posh village restaurant with a live band sounded like a real treat for Valentine's night.

The next day I phoned the restaurant and booked a table for two.

We had visited the village in question some months ago when we were looking to buy a house. It had a couple of bar/restaurants, and it was more or less exclusively well-heeled British territory, full of the type of architect-designed villas often inhabited by retired majors and their coiffured wives.

On the afternoon of Valentine's day, Carrie went to her appointment to get her hair cut, dyed and permed, which took hours of course. It was raining, so I was unable to improve my fading looks by topping up my tan. Later on, we got poshed up. I put on my best jacket for the occasion. Carrie was resplendent in her new hair-do and a light blue posh frock, and weighed down with an appropriate supply of bling.

I drove us up to the hilltop restaurant in the grand old Mercedes. It was pitch dark when we arrived. Being in unfamiliar territory, I had no idea where to park. Carrie spotted a sign saying 'Restaurant Car Park' so we figured that would be the best place to leave the car. The old car's wheels crunched through the gravel. There was only one other car in the car park, so I had no problem finding a space.

Before we got out, I mentioned to Carrie that the car park might get busier, so I'd better turn the car for an easy exit. Big mistake. The tyres were fairly new with loads of tread, but they just wouldn't grip the gravel surface. Before I knew it, the beast had sunk six inches into the gravel.

Now, six inches of gravel may seem over-generous as a surface for a car park, but this was only the surface. Beneath the surface lay common soil, which the day's rain had turned to mud. I found this out when I got out of the car and heard a squelching noise coming from my shoes. A great start to a romantic evening.

We trudged over to the restaurant, walked through the door and, as expected, found that our feet were covered in mud. I explained the problem to the receptionist.

"Oh, don't worry about that." The chubby English lass smiled and reassured us. "It happens all the time. I'll show you to your table, and the manager will get some of the lads to push your car out afterwards."

We ordered food and wine from the menu. Our starters arrived within seconds - a salad was thrust at my place setting, dull and without any dressing. No wine. Then the band started up in the next room with a Bob Dylan song 'I Shall Be Released'. Perhaps not quite the most appropriate song for romantic couples, I thought. The song was subtly enhanced by the singer's German accent which made 'I Shall Be Released' sound like a commandant's order. The drummer didn't require amplification. His style was simply to play every single drum and cymbal as loudly as humanly possible.

Two minutes later, there was a power cut and the music stopped. All except the drummer, who hammered on in the candlelight until the bitter end of the song some minutes later. He played so loudly that he probably hadn't realised that the rest of the band had stopped.

Power was restored, and the band resumed their Valentine's night music. Their next song was another Bob Dylan number 'Mr Tambourine Man' - the one about LSD. Then we were treated to 'All Along The Watchtower' - again by Bob Dylan.

We chugged our way through our salads, then the band struck up 'Like A Rolling Stone'. This is truly one of the greatest songs ever written about hatred and loathing. It's about a renowned model down on her luck and on the streets, with the venomous chorus in which Dylan spits out the line "How does it feel to be on your own?" A great song, sure, and I was one of the first in the queue to buy the single when it exploded onto the charts back in 1965.

"I know you like this song," Carrie said "but do you think this is the right music for Valentine's night?"

"Depends on how much you detest your partner, I suppose." I got the glare I expected. "Look, when I phoned to book, they told me the band played different types of music, so I just assumed that would include some romantic songs."

Dylan has written many romantic songs, but none were on the band's set list that night. Anyway, the next song was entirely different - 'Desolation Row' by - you've guessed it - Bob Dylan. The song descibes a lynching and hanging of three men following their rape of a woman. Thankfully, Carrie wasn't as familiar with the song as I was, and the singer's Germanic screaming masked most of the lyrics.

The wine eventually arrived with our main course of Beef Wellington, served without any sauce to counter the dryness of the meat and pastry. We were treated to a change of composer, as the band closed their Boys' Big Bob Dylan Song Book and started on their Rolling Stones songbook. 'Paint it black' was the band's raucous version of Mick and Keith's song about a bereavement. As Carrie and I chomped our way through our main courses, the band struck up the Stones' great song about a Memphis prostitute 'Honky Tonk Women'. This was followed by 'Brown Sugar', a real Valentine's night treat in which Mick and Keith's song lyrics magically weave together the subjects of interracial sex, cunnilingus, heroin use, slave rape and sado-masochism.

Dessert in the form of a dry slice of cheesecake arrived to the tune of 'I Can't Get No Satisfaction', at which point my lady wife looked at my dejected face, and could no longer deal sensibly with her Valentine night's entertainment. She dissolved under the table into a giggling mess.

Thank goodness she saw the funny side, or at least she did until she saw the bill. We had been charged for items we had not ordered or received, and getting that sorted took quite a while, during which time the band had closed their Rolling Stones songbook and started on Chuck Berry. While Carrie stood over me with a red pen in her hand, I eventually settled the amended bill. We left our table to the strains of that perennial Chuck Berry favourite 'No Particular Place To Go', in which the fellow can't get out of his car's safety belt to enjoy a bit of action with his girlfriend. This caused even more giggles from my other half.

I asked the receptionist again what we should do about our car. This was perhaps not the best point in the evening for her to shrug disinterestedly. So I took her aside and described to her in precise detail the events so far of our romantic Valentine's night. I more or less suggested that she should get off her fat arse and arrange to get my car back from their sodding useless car park. She said nothing, but called the manager over.

A few minutes later he and three other heavies followed us out to the restaurant's car park. Carrie stood under an arch to keep dry while the manager, a stylish Italian gent resplendent in light blue suit and contrasting dark blue scarf, confidently took the wheel of the Mercedes. He gave me a look which clearly meant "Watch this, fool". A few seconds later he had managed to sink the car much further into the gravel and mud than a mere rookie like myself had managed to achieve.

He got out in a fury, and shouted at his minions to bring planks of wood. When these arrived, he angrily jammed them under the rear wheels of the car, to absolutely no avail. The car refused to budge. Then he spotted a plastic sack, and tried to use this to engage the wheels. A total waste of time.

More waiters were summoned from the restaurant, and with eight of them pushing and pulling, my old Mercedes eventually rose from the gravel. It was quite majestic, rather like seeing Ursula Andress emerge from the water onto the beach in that James Bond film.

Nearly half an hour after starting to extract the car from the car park, the manager contemplated his wet and muddy suit and grudgingly wished us "Buenos noches".

We drove off down the steep, narrow road. Some cars were coming uphill, very likely carrying happy couples home after enjoying their Valentine's evening at places we wished we'd been. Progress home was slow, but by now we were past caring. Then a large refuse truck came up behind us - they are out every night of the week down here. Everything was fine until after a mile or so, when we had to stop as the recycling truck was trying to get up the hill. So there we were, sandwiched between two refuse trucks on an unlit single-track road.

I groaned when I spotted three cars coming up the hill behind the recycling truck. There was only a driver on his own in this truck, and naturally he wasn't for reversing. The only solution was for our car and the truck behind us to reverse up the hill to a passing place. I remembered seeing one a hundred yards or so back up the hill.

One of the lads jumped down from the truck behind us, and guided the driver back up the hill to the passing place. Carrie wasn't yet ready to drive the big Mercedes, so I was behind the wheel. She had to get out and guide me to reverse back up the hill to the passing place.

When we left the restaurant car park it had been drizzling, but by the time my wife had guided me to the passing place, it had turned to heavy rain. The recycling truck managed to slide up the hill past our car with inches to spare, followed by the other cars. Then Carrie was able to return to the car. But by now, and in spite of the umbrella which goes with her everywhere, the rain had turned the top of her light blue dress a much darker shade of blue. And her expensive hair-do resembled her appearance after a morning shower.

When we eventually got back to the house, it was past midnight, but I was eager to make up for our disastrous Valentine's evening.

"Would you care for some more entertainment tonight?" I grinned and winked at her as we stepped through the front door.

"No thank you. Just a hair dryer, a very large gin and tonic, and a hot water bottle. In that order please."

Isn't it funny how easily some women lose their romantic streak?

CHAPTER 3 - MARCH

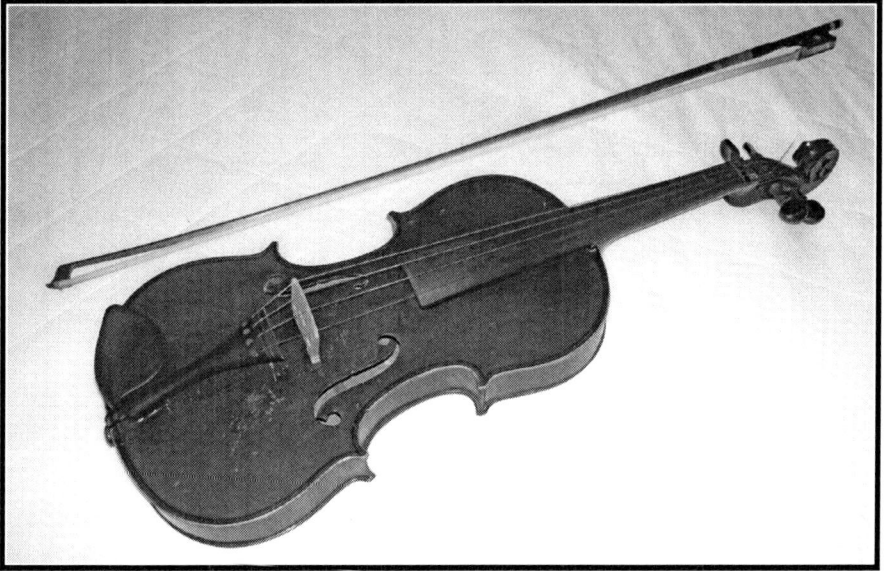

It was now March, and we had moved into our Spanish villa. I had booked a local removal man to pick up our furniture and boxes from storage in Scotland. A few days after we picked up the keys, it was delivered.

One morning I was dreaming about wrapping Roy Orbison in clingfilm. I had been reading a book about this very subject - it's an amazing novel by a guy with a surname which is the German equivalent of 'hairbrush'. In my dream I had completely wrapped Roy Orbison in clingfilm and was just starting to spit-roast his wife when I awoke to the sound of a knock on the door. It had gone 10am and I had reluctantly come to the end of my lie-in after a bit of a party the night before.

I fumbled for my specs, donned a dressing gown and shambled down the stairs. As I threw back the huge bolts on our substantial front door, I found my next door neighbour Fiona standing on the step with a big Irish smile on her face.

"Hi, Jim. Are you settling in ok?" Without waiting for an answer, she continued. "Remember you said that you and Carrie wanted to get involved in local events? Well, Easter is coming up, and the local church is raising funds for a new virgin."

"How do you mean, Fiona?" My voice was an octave or so deeper than usual, and my eyes blinked back the sunlight.

"Every village here has its tableaus, which they bring out at religious occasions and fiestas. They're wooden statues on plinths which the men parade round the streets. It's a great honour to be one of the pall bearers for a holy icon."

"I'm afraid I have a bad back." Fiona ignored my excuse and continued.

"Bédar's Virgin Mary got terminally damaged at last year's Easter parade, and the church is raising funds for a new tableau. They need to raise twenty thousand euros."

"Must be a bloody big virgin for that kind of money."

Fiona ignored my comment and continued her tale.

"Pedro closed his summer bar near the town hall a couple of years ago, but he's opening it again for the summer to host dances to raise money for a new virgin. I'd heard that you're a musician and I was wondering if you'd be interested in helping out." Fiona then produced another sweet Irish smile.

My immediate thought was, is any virgin really worth twenty thousand euros, but then I realised it was a great way to introduce myself to the village, so I jumped in.

"I know a couple of singers around here, so I'm sure we can knock up a dance one weekend."

"Fantastic. How soon can you arrange it, Jim? The carpenter who's making the tableau has finished it ahead of schedule, but he says we can have it if we give him what we've got and pay the balance when we've raised the funds."

Business is conducted in an atmosphere of old-fashioned trust and respect down here.

"We could try for a Saturday before the end of the month," I suggested.

John the Banjo was up for it, as was Bruce, a local sax player. John said he would sing some old-time trad jazz songs with his banjo, and Bruce said he hadn't played for a while but he offered to vamp along as best he could. I also enlisted the help of a local bagpipe player, who John told me was Scottish Jim number one. Apparently I was Scottish Jim number two, but John quietly confided to me that if Scottish Jim number one popped his clogs before me, I'd get promoted.

We needed a singer, and I didn't fancy the job. Back in the early seventies I played with a dinner dance band. We had a good singer

50

who also played bass, and a competent drummer. I played piano and sang a bit of harmony along with the singer, and I always joined the drummer in making chicken noises during the last waltz at every gig, the song Andy Williams always closed his shows with - 'May Each Day'. That song is perfect for making chicken noises to, and I have no idea why Andy Williams never tried it. Try it yourself sometime if you get a chance and tell me I'm wrong. Sorry to digress a bit, but it's important advice.

Anyway, one night we were playing a dance at a hotel in Paisley and our singer had laryngitis, so he sent along a non-singing replacement bass guitarist and the drummer volunteered me to sing. I was pleased that my vocalizing of some easy swing numbers attracted polite applause, but slow waltzes are much harder to hack as you have to find the right note and hold it. After what I thought was a touching rendition of 'Edelweiss', this rough-looking fellow came up from the audience with a serious face on.

"Listen son, you're a good pianist and we're really enjoying your playing…." His voice became quieter and rather plaintive. "….but could you PLEASE not sing."

I smiled at him and told him not to worry, it wouldn't happen again. And it didn't. It was hard to get over such a plaintive plea from a listener clearly in some discomfort, and that was the start and finish of my career as a solo vocalist.

So, I tried to figure out who I could approach to sing at the fund-raiser. It was to be a Saturday night, and it's always difficult to find a decent performer who isn't working on a Saturday night. I remembered that someone had told me that Lena, whom I had met in February, lived near Bédar. It was the woman I swore I'd never work with. When I 'phoned her to ask if she would sing at the fund-raiser, she kindly agreed straight away and we arranged to meet to try out a few songs.

Musically, I'll have a bash at anything from Mozart to New Orleans blues. Within half an hour, I had worked out a rough set list which included some easy jazz to get the music going, then some bluesy songs like 'Kansas City' on which Bruce could join us on sax. But I knew that there would be Spanish people at the dance in addition to the Brits. I wanted to try performing some latino music using backing tracks which I knew I could write myself using the fantastic synthesizer in the spare room. We needed songs which would appeal to everyone, so I included songs like 'Amor', 'La Bamba', 'Besame

51

Mucho' and 'Bambaleo' which the Spanish and the British would all know. I set to work and sorted out an act.

The night of the dance came a couple of weeks later, and we set up in the open-air bar. Nearly a hundred people turned up for the first proper gig I had ever performed at in Spain. I opened with some piano music, then John came on to play some great old banjo standards. Bruce did a couple of really good sax solos, then before I knew it, my watch showed that it was 11 o'clock and time for our final set of latino music.

Lena and I kicked off with my easy samba arrangement of 'Quando, Quando, Quando' and by the end of the song the floor of the bar was heaving with dancers. By the time we got to 'La Bamba' twenty minutes later, lots more Spanish folk had turned up, having heard the music from their homes. A bunch of Spanish girls were shaking their booties inches in front of my keyboards. Fair inspirational it was, to quote a Scottish expression.

By midnight we had run out of material and finished to a wonderful reception. It was unforgettable for me, and Lena and I vowed to work again. It wasn't long before we came up with some more ideas and gingerly worked our way into the local music scene, trying not to step on the toes of the established performers.

My wife Carrie is very understanding of my need to be involved in music. When I'm involved in a project like a new song or recording, my mind is not particularly where she wants it to be. At such times much of what the poor girl tells me will go in one ear and out the other. She doesn't play an instrument or sing, although she can certainly hold a note. Her preferred note when she screams at me is a top B flat, and she can hold that particular note extremely well.

Being the musical tart that I am, my tastes change from day to day. I might put on my favourite doo-wop CD when I'm cooking dinner, then watch a Mahler symphony on BBC4 later. I enjoy blues, opera, pop, some country & western, jazz of which Louis Armstrong would approve, ska & bluebeat, Mozart, fifties rock & roll. My CD collection includes Arcade Fire, Lang-Lang, Jake Bugg, Gerry Rafferty, Pavarotti, Oscar Peterson and Jim Reeves.

As far as I'm concerned, the only thing of importance in music is that it must be good and original.

I cannot abide doleful reggae drowned in echo or rave music, or indeed any of the repetitive music forms which can only be savoured while on drugs. Nor do I enjoy being shouted and sworn at by large

American gentlemen. I have not the remotest idea what Brits have in common with gansta rap. For the uninitiated, this often means taking an old song like Sting's 'Every Breath You Take' and talking over it about a favourite gangsta rapper who has been killed in a drive-by shooting. You leave out the interesting key change in the middle section as this might upset those whose addled brains can only understand songs with three chords. It's not exactly musical development. It may appeal to the backward and drug-addled in American society. It has no relevance whatsoever for drug-free Brits so it doesn't appeal to me.

The conductor and founder of major orchestras, Sir Thomas Beecham, was once sent a music score by a young composer. He gave it the once-over and returned it to the composer with the comment "Your score is good and original. That is to say, the original parts are not good, and the good parts are not original". Nearly a century later, not much has changed.

Rant over.

One morning in March I got a phone call from a fellow called Ed who asked me to call into his Cellar Club in Vera. He'd heard that I played piano, and was looking for someone to host jam nights. Not to sit around eating bread and jam, mind, although it's not a bad idea, but a gig where musicians jam with each other. I arranged to pop in the following Wednesday afternoon.

Ed told me that his club was below a shop at the edge of a Spanish town about 20 minutes' drive from our village, and that the basement area had previously been used for storage. On the day we had arranged, I parked my car then found a withered poster for the club at the side of the shop. There was no sign on the wall to let folk know that a music café existed there, only the remains of this poster. Seems that the signwriter had let the owners down and hadn't delivered the sign in time for the opening night.

I walked down a flight of stairs, then down a ramp to the bar area within, where there were white plastic patio tables and chairs on one side, and a bar area on the other.

Once I had checked things out, I took my piano down and set it up. I played some requests for Ed and he didn't take long to sit me down and talk business. And what a fascinating character he turned out to be! An approachable chap with a face like a balding leprechaun, talking fifteen to the dozen and changing the subject every few minutes. Turns out he had been an entrepreneur for many years. He had spent some time in Brazil, where he was kidnapped twice. When he settled in Spain he had this idea of starting up a venue to provide top-notch entertainment for the local residents.

Ed told me that he had gone back for a visit to the UK, went to an auction and bought the entire contents of a traditional pub which had closed down, tables, chairs, drapes, pictures, the lot. He wanted to provide an authentic English pub atmosphere for his new venture where we were now seated. But one thing wasn't quite right. We were sitting on white plastic chairs at a white plastic table.

"Oh, that'" laughed Ed. "I had the contents of the pub put in a container to be shipped out here. But the container got lost in transit, and I had to go and buy some cheap furniture so I could open in time."

So for the grand opening, the 'authentic English pub' look consisted of white plastic tables and chairs in a windowless basement with no curtains to dampen the hollow acoustics. This was the first indication that Ed was not the luckiest fellow I had ever met. I should have got the message there and then, but he was such a fascinating bloke that after chatting for over two hours, I was in with both feet.

To run the Cellar Club and provide the patrons with food and drink, Ed had engaged a very pretty but somewhat intense young lady. She ran the food and drink side of the business in a tight-fitting blouse and skirt and with tight-lipped precision. Ed found a chef who had the ability to deep-fry anything he could find in a freezer. So, the Cellar Club was ready to rumble with white plastic furniture and absolutely no sound deadening. In fact, the acoustics were the standard of a concrete cowshed.

What a start ! On the positive side, there was no sign above the door to attract critics.

Ed wanted me to provide a house band at the Cellar Club, and host fortnightly jazz and blues jam nights. He wanted to emulate a pub in London which had a professional house band and only allowed seasoned jazz musicians on stage with them. The only problem was that the Cellar Club wasn't bang in the business end of the world's biggest cities. It was in a small town in a backwater of Andalucia.

Ed's other plan was to make the Cellar Club renowned for the best Saturday night entertainment in the area. His plan was book quality tribute acts from the UK, fly them in, provide transport to and from the airport, and provide accommodation for them.

At the club, there was a sizeable stage with a small dressing room. Ed had a fantastic PA system installed - four large speakers, one on each corner wall, an on-stage mixer plus radio microphones and stands. In one corner he had a raised sound booth, with a sound desk plus the main amplifier and mixer. This is the kind of set-up you'd expect to find in a theatre. But the Cellar Club was not what you would call a large venue - it could seat around eighty at a pinch, but they could never provide meals for that many, partly because there were only enough plates and cutlery for fifty-six. So spending over £1000 on each tribute act from the UK to play a one night stand at a small venue was never going to be a money-maker.

Ed's luck with these tribute acts was not great. He flew in a Ronan Keating tribute act from London (no, I don't know why either) and he had to arrange to pick him up from Alicante airport, over 2 hours away. He drove the singer to a local hotel, treated him to an expensive meal that night, and they agreed to meet the following morning to do a sound check. The singer only sang a few words at the sound check and said that the sound was fine.

Came the evening, the audience arrived, all thirty four of them, tickets were taken at the door, dinner with wine was served, then the lights dimmed for Ronan Keating. His CD of backing music started up, dry ice wafted over the stage, and the star of the show strolled out from the shadows to polite applause. He croaked a few lines, stopped his backing track and announced to the audience that he was very sorry but he couldn't sing due to a really bad throat.

The audience weren't best pleased. Neither was Ed - he'd paid top dollar in advance for the act, plus the flights, meals and accommodation. And he could hardly charge his thirty four disappointed customers for their dinner and wine.

Ed had no back-up act, so the only thing he could do was offer the audience a refund or a ticket for the next show & dinner the following Saturday - a Rod Stewart tribute act. Most folk accepted the tickets. Ed flew in the Rod Stewart copyist from the UK. It's possible that he didn't know that there was a local Rod Stewart tribute act, less than ten miles down the road.

So, everything was arranged for the Saturday. Taking into account the 30-odd folk who'd bought tickets for the Rod Stewart act, plus the folk who had been given free tickets after the fiasco of the last show, it was shaping up to be a good night. Unfortunately, Ed got a phone call two days before the show to say that the Rod Stewart act couldn't make the flight as he had 'flu. So, two cancelled shows in a row.

Not to worry, the jazz and blues jam night was on the next

Wednesday, and had been well promoted, so we expected a decent audience that night.

When I arrived that night with my music gear, the building was shut up and no lights were on. Strange, I thought, because no-one had phoned me to say the gig had been cancelled.

Just then, Ed appeared from round the corner. The venue's electricity had fused, not inside the building, but at the electricity company's box on the wall outside. The only people with access to this box were the electricity company. Thinking on his feet, Ed immediately decided to break into this outside box, so hammers and chisels were procured and a bunch of heavies set about the box. Power was restored and the gig went ahead.

Ed had kindly offered the house band free tickets to any of the Saturday shows. He told me about this great act, a lady called Marian who impersonated twenty different acts, and in the process did seventeen costume changes.

"She's fantastic, Jim. She's flying over from London for the show and you've got to see her. Come along with your wife on Saturday. Your friends Tom and Julie are coming too, and I'm sure you'll have a great night."

Tom Lee is a good friend of mine, an experienced band singer who came down regularly to the jam nights - he's a big man, a real blues shouter, great at rock and roll, and the perfect front man for jam sessions. A big-hearted guy but with a half-hearted beard. He's exactly two weeks younger than me and the big sod reminds me of this every year during the two weeks after my birthday.

On the Saturday we were given a table, and although we didn't expect it, we were given a meal of sausages and chips in a basket, the same as the folk who had bought tickets. There were only about a couple of dozen other folk in the audience. Some of them had won tickets on a local radio show, and it seemed that we were there to make up the numbers.

After the meal, the lights dimmed, the backing music started up, and a large woman sporting an enormous blonde wig appeared from the back of the room and bounded onto the stage. Marian began her act with a medley of two great rousing songs from the First World War – 'Pack Up Your Troubles' followed by 'It's A Long Way To Tipperary'. We all looked at each other.

"What the hell's going on?" I whispered to Tom. His rolling eyes told me that he had no idea either.

We thought maybe Marian had the wrong backing tape - the one for care homes. During her medley, Marian took her radio microphone out to the audience and thrust it at the mouths of some unsuspecting people. Tom made the mistake of making eye contact with her, so he had the mike thrust in his face and was forced to sing the whole of the second part of 'Tipperary'. With a face like thunder. He got some applause from the audience. Although I told him he sang it really well, he's never included the song in his act.

The next part of Marian's act was to go round the audience with the radio mike and ask them all where they came from.

"Is there anyone here from Hertfordshire?" No takers.

"Is there anyone here from Yorkshire?" No takers.

"Is there anyone here from Wales?" No luck there either.

"Anyone here from the north?" Bottom of the barrel.

Marian thrust her microphone in several faces in the audience to ask where they were from. It was wonderfully excruciating. It filled ten interminable minutes and we cringed quietly while being thankful that she wasn't singing any more songs from the Great War.

Marian returned to the stage, put on some dramatic music, then disappeared into the tiny dressing room next to the stage. On the backing tape, the announcement came that Dame Shirley Bassey was about to make a special guest appearance, and out Marian came wearing a blue spangly dress with splits on the side, and sporting dark make-up and a black nylon wig. Just like the real Dame Shirley only in a size 18. Once again, she went out to the audience, and assaulted us with her version of 'Big Spender', rather louder than Dame Shirley's version. She laid a cellulite-ridden leg on the knee of several men in the audience, causing some of the older gents to groan visibly.

By the time Marian got to what she presumably believed was an amusing impersonation of Tina Turner, exposing yet more leg cellulite, the cringe-ometer had gone off the scale. By the interval, we all discussed how we could get out before she returned for the second part of the show.

"I think Brendan's on at the camp site tonight," offered Tom.

"I'll phone his missus and check," I replied without hesitation.

Sure enough, my friend and saviour was singing there. I had a word with Ed and thanked him for the evening's entertainment, but told him that we had to go and see Brendan about some gigs.

"You didn't like Marian, did you?" Oh dear, he'd twigged.

"Well, I thought she had a good voice."

"Listen Jim, your face was a picture. I always know what you're thinking when you get singers on at the jam nights. I can tell when you think they're crap. I can see it in your eyes, mate. And I could tell Tom didn't enjoy singing Tipperary. Marian's very popular though." I looked round the sparse audience for evidence of her popularity.

"Sorry, Ed, maybe she's just not my kind of thing."

"Come down next Saturday, Jim. I've got a fellow coming who does Buddy Holly. He's been before and he went down a storm. He tells Buddy Holly's life story and sings all his hits."

"Thanks, Ed, that's much more up my street." We slunk out quietly to go see Brendan's gig.

The following Saturday, Carrie and I went down with Tom and Julie to see the Buddy Holly act. I share the opinion of many, many others that Buddy Holly was an absolute genius, and I've never lost my love for his music since saving my pocket money to buy those magical Coral label 78s around the time my age hit double figures. Buddy's music never seems to age. He was the first singer-songwriter, and the first performer ever to form the classic four-piece rock band of lead guitar, rhythm guitar, bass and drums. This is the format still used well over fifty years later by most rock bands.

Carrie and I have seen the 'Buddy' musical four times over a period of some years. That's no great boast. I met a fellow at one of my gigs who had seen it seventeen times. For people like me who grew up with Buddy Holly's songs, it seems to me that no other performer's songs have been so well-loved.

At the Cellar Club the following week, the show was much better attended, and once the sausages and chips had been downed, there was a real air of anticipation.

The Buddy Holly tribute act was brilliant, despite being at least a foot shorter than Buddy Holly. He sang well, played great guitar and was a real old-fashioned pro. He was so slick, he'd obviously done this for years and years, but he still performed the great songs with passion, as if he was singing them for the first time. He also looked quite a bit older than Buddy Holly in his prime.

I spoke to him after the show, on the way out to his van. I thanked him for his show, and he was happy to talk to me awhile about Buddy Holly. He told me that he'd been to Lubbock in Texas to visit Buddy's home town, and visited his grave. He proudly told me that he was born in 1938, the same year Buddy Holly was born.

Buddy Holly was 21 when he died in that plane crash in February

1959. I did the maths; the tribute act was well over 70. No matter, he was a worthy tribute to the great man.

The fortnightly jam nights were fun. I'd got a house band together - a trio comprising me on piano, a great double bass player called Robin, and my friend Graeme on guitar. That's all Ed could afford after losing fortunes on the tribute acts. I compèred the jams and followed Ed's wishes to allow only 'proper' musicians up on stage with us. Well, most of the time anyway. The jam nights were a fair old success despite the dire acoustics. If you can imagine a cosy jazz trio playing in a swimming baths, you'll have a fair idea what it sounded like. However, once proper wooden tables and chairs were procured a few weeks later, the place looked a lot more homely. Once curtains had been put up to absorb the echo, the acoustics improved no end.

My friend Graeme was a loyal supporter of the jam nights. He's a good guitarist, and can pick up the chords of just about any tune. He's no fun to watch when he's playing jazz, as his face goes into contortions trying to fit in clever chords. He's much more at home playing blues. Graeme's only problem is that he's unreasonably tall, and when he falls over, he usually breaks a bone somewhere. So he's not always fit to play.

John the Banjo was also a regular supporter of the jams. He'd usually come early and check the sound, tune his banjo and set up a music stand with his chords and song lyrics. The audience loved his old trad songs, and I worked like a trooper to play stride piano along with him - not easy if, like me, you're not blessed with big hands.

Most nights we had Robin on bass, Graeme on guitar, me on electric piano, and whoever else turned up. We'd kick off the evening with some swing and blues numbers, then invite musicians to jam with us. Sometimes John's pal Terry would come along with his clarinet, and we'd play some old trad jazz tunes which always got the audience's feet tapping. I loved playing with these guys; to me, it was in the true spirit of what the father of jazz, Louis Armstrong, believed jazz should be all about – fun dance music.

At the interval one jam night, two young Spanish lads popped in with electric guitars. Ed knew them, but I had never met them. Turned out they were twins from the nearby fishing port of Garrucha. Francisco is dark-haired and quite serious. Pedro is a tousle-haired hombre, usually with a big smile on his face. They speak perfect English, and are simply two of the nicest lads you could ever wish to meet.

"Ah Jim," said Pedro "We have heard all about you and your piano. The musicians here call you the highlandboogieman."

"Actually, Pedro, I call myself that. The musicians here often call me something much more Anglo-Saxon." He didn't understand. "Anyway, I've heard about you guys. I'm really looking forward to you jamming with us."

I kicked off the band with a simple 12-bar blues, and after a couple of minutes I signalled to Fran to do a solo. What he produced was an amazing display of guitar artistry which blew the likes of Santana completely out of the water. I'd not been expecting that. Then he signalled to Pedro to do a solo, and he was simply mind-blowing, producing complex runs up the fretboard which I could only gasp at. I got both lads to play simultaneously to finish the blues in style, and they got a tremendous cheer from the audience. This was totally world-class guitar-playing, from two young guys from a fishing village. I wondered where they had learned to play like that. Pedro explained.

"Our father is an artist who loves the guitar, and he sent us both to classical guitar lessons when we were very young."

"So you're both classically trained?"

"Oh yes, Jim, we only play rock and blues for fun."

You could have fooled me. Fran and Pedro's stage name for their rock gigs is 'Mas Que Dos' which means 'More Than Two'. However, if you book them for a gig, you may find that only the two of them will turn up. In the UK, Trading Standards would have something to say about that. Anyway, they certainly sound like far more than two!

One singer was not so great. He was a really nice guy, quite tall with frizzy asylum hair, who's tried to sell himself as everything from a BBC show singer to a rock god. Unfortunately, his success has never matched his enthusiasm. He had to change his stage name a few times, as venues would never re-book him once he'd played a gig. So he kept trying to find new places to play, or places where they didn't know his current stage name. I heard that he moved to Tenerife to try the market there. To save him any embarrassment, we'll call him Steven. That's not his real stage name, unless of course he's changed it again by the time you read this.

On the jam night in question, Steven came up to the stage and instructed me to start with 'Satin Doll' in C, then 'It Don't Mean A Thing' in D minor. I played the standard intro to Satin Doll in the key of C, and he started singing in A flat. I played on for a couple of verses, hoping he would find his key, but seeing some of the audience pull faces, I abandoned ship and stopped playing. Steven realised that he had given me the wrong key, so I asked him to sing a snatch of the song to help me find his key. The song went much better at the second attempt. He wanted to go straight into 'It don't mean a thing' and that went well until the end of the final middle section, when he simply stopped singing and smiled at the audience while I played the last verse and finished the song. Way beyond weird.

One day a few weeks later, Steven phoned asking me to play for him on a gig. He had suffered a rejection when some musicians told him they had decided not to do a gig with him. I wouldn't play the gig either, as it required three rehearsals plus the Sunday gig, all bloody miles away in the next province and for less money than it would have cost me in petrol. But I invited him down to the Cellar Club for the jam night. I suggested that he sing a song simply, just with my piano and without any histrionics, to show the audience that he could really sing. I thought that this would maybe restore his confidence.

Came the night and he decided upon 'Over the Rainbow'. The first verse went pretty well, he was bang on key. Then at the middle section 'Someday I'll wish upon a star', he took his radio mike and stepped down into the audience, waving his arms about and contorting his face in stagey mock passion. Maybe he never saw the horrified faces of the audience, but by the end of the song he had wrung out every morcel of ham and fake drama from the song. I've always found Judy Garland hammy and over-dramatic, but she simply wasn't in Steven's league.

Later that night, my friend Tom Lee told me that he and his wife had gone to see Steven's show at a hotel down in Mojacar.

"He was due to start at nine. We arrived at the hotel just after nine to find the audience waiting for his show, and he was just starting to set up."

Tom is a top band performer, a real pro, and he looked genuinely puzzled that a professional singer could mess his audience about like this.

"Anyway, when he started to sing to his backing tracks, he did this sort of gurning at the audience. He looked demented, that's the only word I can use to describe it. His singing would have been okay if it wasn't for all this contrived hamming-up, as if he'd been to stage school. Then he told the audience about this Spanish singer he liked, and told the audience that he'd like to do a tribute to her. So he put on a CD of the singer, and stood beside his speaker listening to the song."

I was puzzled. "You mean he didn't sing along with the record?"

"No, he just stood there grinning at the audience while they listened to this record. It was the weirdest thing I've ever seen at a gig, and God knows I've done a few gigs in my time, Jim."

Just then, Ed came up to me. I asked him what he thought of Steven as a performer.

"Christ, I'd never book that twat. He wants to do some shows on Sunday nights, but I'm not paying him. He wants to charge at the door, so I've told him he can use the room and we might sell some drinks and a few dinners. But I don't expect much of an audience, and I don't expect him to be here for long. Everyone knows he's crap."

Steven's shows didn't last long, and Ed told me that his third and final show attracted only four paying customers.

At least he wasn't as bad as old Alfie. A short, rough-looking guy on the wrong side of seventy, Alfie had been a professional singer, working with bands in his heyday, now holidaying in the area. Ed introduced Alfie to me at the interval one jam night, and I got practically the full story of his singing career. Alfie told me that he'd sung in variety shows for years and performed in summer season variety shows at holiday resorts. But variety had totally died a death by the mid-seventies, and he hadn't sung much since then. He was a regular at the Cellar Club, and had his own table. One night he came over and asked me if he could come up and sing a few numbers.

"Do you know San Francisco?" he asked. Now I don't know how many times I've played 'I Left My Heart In San Francisco', but it's got to be several hundred. In the seventies when my band played a lot of wedding receptions, there would always be some wedding guest who wanted to sing it. They were usually sozzled old duffers who couldn't hold a note if it was nailed to the ends of their fingers. They usually got such a cheer for getting to the big high note at the end of 'San Francisco' that they had to sing a second song. It was invariably 'Don't Laugh At Me 'Cos I'm A fool', a turgid, self-pitying song made famous by Norman Wisdom.

Came the moment, and Alfie struggled onto the little stage. Like a true amateur he thumped the microphone then blew into it to make sure it was working (he'd clearly read the book 'How To Destroy a Microphone in One Easy Lesson'). He started singing 'The loveliness of Paris' in E flat and by the next line 'is somehow sadly gay' he'd gone up to the key of F. Trying to follow Alfie was like trying to follow an escaped helium balloon in a hurricane. By the time he got to the chorus, 'I left my heart' which starts low, he had arrived in the key of G. By 'the morning fog' in the middle of the song he was back in E flat. For the last line of the song, Alfie chose the key of C, as it was lower than the rest and made a nice change, and of course it made the last high note much easier to hit.

I asked Alfie if he had anything in mind for a second song.

"Do you know 'Don't Laugh At Me', the Norman Wisdom number?" Oh, I knew it all right.

After a smattering of applause (probably directed at me for my heroic attempt at trying to find the same key as Alfie), he announced that he would sing 'Don't Laugh At Me' in B flat, and could I give him an intro on the piano.

I gave him the most obvious intro possible into B flat - the type of intro which pianists always give for 'Happy Birthday to You' which never ever fails.

It failed, and he started singing in F sharp. I can't recall much more of the precise details of that performance, but I followed Alfie's example and kept changing key all through the song. He wasn't at all fazed by it. Indeed, on some lines we both landed on the same key, so my efforts were a pretty fair success. By the end of the song I could indeed confirm that Alfie did sing in variety.

One jam night at the club, Carrie and I arrived with friends, and Ed came over to me as we walked through the door.

"Jim, I've arranged a little treat for Alfie. It's his birthday, and I've got something special for him. Keep it under your hat, but Elvis is in the building."

Ed had bought a huge birthday cake, and had arranged for it to be delivered to the Cellar Club. Candles were duly lit, and the cake was brought out, a rectangular monster of a thing. After dinner, everyone in the audience got a slice of cake.

Then the lights dimmed, and a backing tape started. We heard the theme from the film '2001: A Space Odyssey' start up - the classical piece which Elvis used in Vegas to herald his entrance to the stage. An announcement on the tape informed us that Elvis was in the building, then this old hunched chap made his way to the stage, doing mock karate chops. He was clearly of advanced years, and somewhat more rotund than The King in his final days. He was resplendent in a white jump suit, a cheap plastic wig and a pair of sunglasses from a pound shop, his red face sweating profusely by the time he got to the stage.

The introductory music stopped and a backing track started up in the form of a quickstep of 'I Got Rhythm' with a cheesy theatre organ sound. I couldn't remember this being an Elvis hit. The wee hunched fellow greeted us with a "Thangyou vary much" and a "Yea baby" then launched into the Goons' 'Ying Tong Song' to the total consternation of the audience. He sang the song once, there was an organ break on the backing track which sounded like a £20 Christmas keyboard purchased for a despised child, then Elvis finished the song to tumultuous applause.

There was a short break while Elvis picked up his violin and checked it was in tune (it wasn't), then a military backing track started up and the familiar strains of the Dambusters March began. Elvis went up to the microphone and played violin to the backing track. I say played, it was more like two cats having a slanging match. Anyway, the audience went wild for it, and by the end of the tune they were waving their arms around pretending to be aeroplanes. Elvis said "Thangyou vary much" and left the stage to cheers and whoops. His bizarre act got the kind of reception most performers dream about.

After the show, I recognised the fellow without his Elvis gear, and went up to him to ask what his act was all about.

"Listen, son, I do Elvis for parties. They love it here. In Aiberdeen, I got laughed AT. Aye. Fuckin' plebs. Here, they laugh WITH me."

I was intrigued by my fellow Scot. "So where did you get the idea of Elvis doing the Ying Tong Song and the Dambusters March?"

"Oh, I never liked Elvis. I hated his fuckin' songs and the way he sang them. 'Return to Spender' an' a' that shite. I much preferred Kenneth McKellar. He always performed in the kilt, you know. A great tenor voice tac. You're frae Scotland, son. Did ye ever hear him singin' 'Rothesay Bay?'

"Elvis?" I was beginning to lose the plot.

"Nae, ya eejit. Kenneth McKellar. Listen, I had the great privilege of hearin' him sing it at the Oban Highland Games in 1958 I think, no' lang after the record came oot, so dinnae fuck wi' me sonny, right? They had the junior highland dancin', then the competition fur the best Angus cattle, then the singin'. Calum Kennedy was on first, an' he was guid, aye ah'll gie him that all right, then it was Jimmy Logan's girl Sally. Christ she had great tits, but when Kenneth McKellar came on, he had the lassies greetin'. He was fuckin' brilliant!"

"So you preferred Kenneth McKellar to Elvis?"

"Nae contest, son. But McKellar was never the same in his later years. Ye ken, sometimes he would perform without the kilt, in some kind o' suit. Whit a let-down. Billy Connolly wore the kilt you know, when I saw him at the Glasgow Pavilion in 1975, but I'm sure it wis jist fur a joke. Did ye see Connolly on TV the ither week wearin' some kind o' Egyptian claes? A smock kinda thing. Fuckin' poncy wanker."

"But why the Dambusters March?"

"I usually do it at Valentine's Night and it always goes down a bomb."

"Oh, very funny." I don't think he intended the joke. "But do romantic couples not find it offensive?"

"Dae they fuck! They love it. Think aboot it lad, whit could be more romantic than a moonlight bombin' mission o'er Germany?"

Sadly, the Cellar Club is closed now, following a rising sewage problem which I couldn't even begin to describe. Like many others, I miss it greatly.

The last time I heard Ed, he was hosting a phone-in one Thursday night on his radio show. Unfortunately, he seemed to be alone in the studio, and the sound wasn't properly set up. Listeners could hear the callers, but the callers couldn't hear Ed. Everyone who phoned in got the same treatment.

"Hello caller. Can you hear me?"

Silence.

"Hello. Hello. HELLO. HELLO. CAN YOU HEAR ME?"

Nothing. A click as the caller disconnected.

"We'll try the next caller. Hello caller. Can you hear me? Hello? HELLO? HELLO?"

Click.

Ed announced that he would play a record and try to sort out the phone problem. I could tell that this was shaping up to be interesting radio, so I set up my tape recorder to record the next section of the show. The following is a transcript from my recording and might give you an insight into Ed's dogged optimism in the face of continuing bad luck.

"Hello. Hello. Hello caller. HELLO. HELLO. CAN YOU HEAR ME? HELLO. HELLO."

"Hello," from the caller. "Can you hear me?"

"HELLO," from Ed. "Are you there, caller? I can't hear you."

"Can you hear me, Ed?"

"Hello. Hello. Hello. Hello. HELLO. HELLO. HELLO. HELLO, HELLO. Can you hear me?"

"I can only hear you on the radio."

"You need to switch off your radio or we'll get feedback on the mike."

"Okay, I've switched it off."

"HELLO, CALLER. CAN YOU HEAR ME NOW?" Screamed Ed.

Silence.

"Hello. Hello. HELLO. HELLO. HELLO. HELLO. HELLO. HELLO. HELLO. I can't hear anything. Hello. Hello. HELLO. HELLO. HELLO. HELLO. HELLO. HELLO. HELLO. HELLO. Nothing. I'm on tonight from seven through till ten. So you've still got more than two and a half hours to tell me what you think about what's happening out there. I'm sure I'll get to the bottom of the problem."

I don't know if Ed ever did. This one-sided phone-in went on for about half an hour, until my wife eventually decided that shouting at people on the radio was not her choice of entertainment for a Thursday night. We ended the evening watching David Dimbleby host 'Question Time'.

For me, the entertainment value of the legendary BBC programme was not a patch on the perfect radio phone-in show.

CHAPTER 4 - APRIL

One morning, a few weeks after we had moved in, there was a noise at the front door. It sounded rather like an unsavoury child being strangled. I went to the door and before I could open it, a black animal climbed up to the glass, gave me a dirty look and wailed at me in the manner of Kate Bush singing "Wuthering Heights". It was a cat, and when I took a closer look I saw that it was a handsome yet scrawny beast.

I didn't want a cat. I wanted to live my life in freedom to go out for as many late nights as I wanted, and I didn't want to have to stop enjoying myself in order to attend to an animal's needs. I really didn't want a cat.

"Sod off," I told the wailing Kate Bush tribute act. I went upstairs to get showered and dressed.

Well, the cat didn't sod off. It hung around the front porch and from the hallway I could hear it muttering under its breath and intermittently wailing. We ignored it and tried to get on with our lives. Later that day, the cat gave up and went on its way.

When I came down one morning a few days later, Carrie was sitting at the table with a coffee, tapping her right foot in a disapproving manner. By her look, she had obviously heard the cat again.

"It's not going away. It's started scratching at the door to get in. What are you going to do about it?" She enquired testily. (Like most households, everything untoward which happens in our house is the man's fault).

"I think It's Carlos' cat, come back looking for him." I explained. "The noisy male cat. But it's stick thin and looks as if it's been living wild. If we give him some food, he'll probably go away."

Carlos was our neighbour who had lived two doors away. He was Welsh (obviously) and of the same scrawny build as his cat. He was a really nice guy who shook my hand each time we met, and always called me "mate", as if he couldn't ever remember my name. To be fair, he called everyone "mate", including his mother. He was a vegetarian with a permanent look of desperation on his face. His cat was also vegetarian, not through choice of course, and the poor beast would apparently howl at doors around the village looking for a reasonably acceptable alternative to his daily ration of tofu and beans or whatever.

Carlos had an even more scrawny girlfriend, and when she dumped him for a fat Spaniard with a well-endowed bank balance, he decided to move back to Wales to tend his broken heart. He had two cats, imaginatively named "Mate" and "Mate's Mate", and it appeared that "Mate's Mate" was stalking us.

Both cats had been taken in by a lady further up the village when he left. When I say "taken in", she didn't allow cats into her home, but fed them and kept them in her back yard. This was clearly not an acceptable standard of accommodation for "Mate's Mate", so he had returned to his old stamping ground to stamp on the ground and demand better quality accommodation and meals.

However, I wasn't prepared to have anything to do with the cat.

"You give it some food if you want. It might shut the thing up. I don't want a cat," I told Carrie.

I went off to the kitchen for a second cup of tea.

"I don't want a bloody cat," I muttered to anyone listening.

I wouldn't have minded a dog, as they're so optimistic and loyal. But my lifestyle as a musician would have made it impossible to give proper attention to a dog. Hopefully we would never have been stuck with a dog like Oscar. He was a cute white West Highland Terror, the pick of the litter (or so we thought) when our beloved Stanzi had pups at our home in Scotland. We sold three of the pups to very good homes, and kept the cutest one for ourselves.

Oscar grew up to be a complete moron. I'm absolutely convinced that there are food mixers with more intelligent insides than Oscar had. For example, whenever the doorbell rang, he would yelp excitedly then bound upstairs into the bathroom, tip over the basket of dirty washing, select a pair of Carrie's silky knickers, panting in excitement, then belt downstairs at the speed of sound. With the knickers in his mouth, he'd then jump up at the visitor, weeing on them in his excitement. The gas man preferred to leave a card telling us to read our own sodding meter.

For a small dog, Oscar had a huge appetite - dog biscuits, chicken, scones, diaries, lampshades, pipe lagging, plasterboard (nice and crunchy). He was always chewing something, including on one winter's night his mother's rear right leg. She was sound asleep inside the hearth of our roaring coal fire at the time, and her white coat had begun to singe and turn brown. It took on an aroma which Oscar obviously found appetising. Probably the same kind of aroma when French farmers burn live sheep.

Oscar was often doubly incontintent into the bargain, and visitors to our home were frequently greeted with the refreshing smell of Domestos. Sadly, when he began to chew on one of our children, we had to give our Westie away to a strictly adult household whom we made well aware of Oscar's problem. So I had no intention of risking another impossible animal.

I finished my cup of tea. Carrie then delved into the fridge, produced a left-over pork chop, and asked me to cut it up. I used my chopper (not that one) to dice the pork into small cubes, then put the pork into an old bowl. I opened the front door and left it on the doorstep.

"I don't want a bloody cat," I repeated plaintively that night as I turned out my bedside light.

Next morning I was soundly dreaming of my new business venture called Rastahairian. I don't really keep a diary, but I do note down my dreams. To appear in public as a fully-paid-up Rastafarian in the style of Bob Marley, a chap obviously needs dreadlocks. In my dream, Rastafarian gentlemen lacking much in the way of hair needed a little help. So my business would provide dreadlock hair extensions for follically-challenged Rastafarians.

In my dream, the ideal situation for such a business was a former cafe in Stranraer in southern Scotland, as that was the port for the ferry from Larne. That way, we would catch the Irish Rastafarian trade coming off the ferry. I was at a bank looking for a start-up business loan. My tall, dark, handsome but balding bank manager kept saying "really?" very patronisingly, and seemed unimpressed with my venture. I was just about to fit him with sample dreadlocks when an urgent wail brought me back to the real world.

"Waaaaaaaaaahhh. Waaaaaaaaaaaaaaahh."

Carrie woke up at the same time as me. "Where's that coming from?" she asked drowsily.

"I think it's the terrace," I croaked. "I'll bet it's that sodding cat looking for food."

"I'll go down and give it some."

"No, I'll go," I volunteered.

"Mmm-uh." Carrie turned over and went back to sleep.

I switched on my bedside light and screwed my eyes to see the alarm clock. It was 6-45 am. Not a time of day with which a musician like myself is overly familiar.

In my half-awake stupor I figured that the only way to finish our night's sleep in peace was to let the cat in, feed it, then lock it in a room far enough away from our bedroom so that we could get some peace. Letting the cat in was the easy bit. I simply opened the terrace door and he bounded into the lounge, complaining loudly.

Finding suitable food wasn't quite so easy, but I found some raw sausages in the fridge, and that did the trick. Our local Spanish sausages don't contain all that filler like cereal and re-processed fat you get in certain British sausages - they're mostly pork, so they went down rather well with an enforced vegetarian cat. I found an old blanket, shoved the sausages and the cat into the downstairs loo, closed the door and went back to bed.

But the deed was done. I had let the cat into the house. To my eternal shame, I had finally given in to sharing my life with a nagging presence (and not for the first time….).

Things would never be the same again.

"What did you do with the cat?" Carrie asked as I came back to bed.

"I fed him and locked him in the downstairs loo with an old blanket so we can get some peace. I'll let him out when we get up. I still don't want a bloody cat. I just want peace."

"Did you put the toilet lid down?"

"No. He might want a drink of water."

"Could you get ME one, Jim? And could you get it from the fridge please."

I put the cat out in the morning and left him some food and water, but I made it clear to him that he wasn't allowed in the house.

My plan failed miserably, and to my shame the cat had taken up residence within a week or two. He had already established a routine.He would rise in the morning and loudly demand service. A large plateful of cat biscuits, thankyou, followed by milk. If the plateful of cat biscuits was insufficient, we would get complaints. He seldom drank water from his bowl, favouring our bedroom en-suite toilet or the swimming pool.

One day I was in the kitchen and the cat was sleeping on a sofa bed at the top of our main stairs. I thought I'd get his dinner ready by removing the crinkly wrapping from some crab sticks, which were his special favourite. All of a sudden there was this scrabbling sound as he dived downstairs yelling at the top of his voice. In our lounge at that time we had laminate flooring, fitted in their wisdom by the previous owners. This smooth shiny plastic surface is not much use for braking purposes. The cat raced into the lounge, lost his grip and skidded along the shiny surface on his way to the kitchen before loudly crashing into the drinks cabinet. This didn't faze him one bit, and he screamed at me for his treat. There was nothing wrong with his hearing - he'd recognized the sound of the wrapper being taken off the crab stick from upstairs.

"We need to give him a name," Carrie suggested one day. "He's black, got a loud voice and dives about, so what about Sammy?"

"Why Sammy?"

"After Sammy Davis junior." At least she hadn't suggested Sambo, so I agreed. Sammy it was.

"We've still no idea if he'll stay. And I still don't want a sodding cat," I pointed out.

"Listen, Jim, for someone who doesn't want a cat, you treat him like royalty. I think he's in love with you."

I winced. But it was true that I gave Sammy regular treats to build him up, and he was certainly becoming less scrawny with each passing day. When we sat down at night to watch TV, Sammy would immediately jump onto my lap, nudge his nose against mine, then lie back in my arms so I could cradle him like a baby, while he gazed up lovingly into my eyes and purred loudly. It certainly didn't look as if he was about to seek alternative accommodation. To be honest, I found it oddly pleasing to have a male admirer, especially one with such attractive whiskers.

Everything is an adventure down here in Spain. The first time I went for a haircut it was a totally new experience. This was a couple of weeks after we had moved over. We had been at the Friday market in Turre getting our fruit and veg, when I spotted a barber's shop behind a stall selling what I can only describe as traditional ladies' nightwear. Flanellette is still big business here, as is Winceyette. Full-body nightgowns are grandly displayed in the full range of floral designs, mainly in soft pink with red roses. My granny used to wear stuff like that, and you can still buy it in Almería.

Anyway, the day in question was windy. As I made my way along the narrow passage past the clothes stall to the barber's shop, I had to dodge assorted bras of every imaginable size and colour flapping about in the wind. Just behind our favourite vegetable stall was Señor Morales's barber's shop, with the door open for all to view the proceedings.

As I gingerly entered the shop, it was clear that the shop was actually the front room in someone's home. The giveaway was the settee and coffee table in one corner of the room, and the photos of children dressed in flamenco costumes. An elderly Spanish gent in frayed red braces appeared to be arguing with the proprietor about money before leaving.

After a lot of angry shouting, the customer suddenly hugged Señor Morales and left. I was then summoned to the barber's chair by the proprietor, a beaming, ageing caballero of generous proportions with worryingly thick spectacles. Señor Morales never asked me what I wanted. He simply took his time circling the barber's chair to inspect my hair, then he sniffed loudly and produced a voluminous grey cape the size of a decorator's dust sheet, which he placed around my neck. He then went to the back of the room to sharpen his razor, and called over to me.

"Bebida?"

"Perdone?" I replied. I thought he was asking me if I wanted a drink.

"Bebida? Vino, cerveza, agua?"

"No gracias." I had understood correctly. This was the first time in my life I had ever been offered a drink at a barber's shop. But then it was the first time I had attempted a haircut in Spain.

Señor Morales commenced his performance - that's the only word for it. Since being a wee boy in Scotland, I had been accustomed to sitting still in the barber's chair and the barber moving around me as he cut my hair. In his salon, Señor Morales stood stock still while he whisked me around from side to side in a revolving chair. It was a bit like being on one of the rides at Alton Towers.

I could hear a baby crying in the back shop, then a woman's voice, then what seemed like a Spanish lullaby being sung by an older woman. The lullaby ended with both women singing. Señor Morales shouted loudly to Natalia in the back room for a report on progress with getting the baby to sleep. His wife came out to the front shop and admonished him for making all that noise, then a woman who may have been his daughter came out and gave him the same treatment. Señor Morales shrugged and looked at me for support. I shrugged in solidarity, and he patted the side of my face in appreciation.

The performance ended with a cut-throat razor scraping my fine neck hair, perilously close to my ears. My eyebrows were swiftly trimmed. The cape was removed from my person, then some kind of powder was cermoniously puffed out and applied to my neck. Natalia was summoned back to provide a critique of the work carried out on my bonce, and the compliments flowed. At least I think they did, as I was still not up to speed with the Spanish when they rabbit excitedly. By now, I just wanted out of the shop before the rest of Señor Morales's family were called upon for their views on my haircut.

I handed over the requested five euros. Perhaps the one euro tip was taking the whole thing too far. I doubt that a single euro has seldom caused so much excitement in Spain, and I eventually managed to leave the shop despite further attempts by Señor Morales to ply me with drink. Carrie was waiting outside the shop for me, and once it was discovered that she was my wife, Señor Morales asked her to wait a moment while his daughter was dispatched to the kitchen. She returned with a jar of home-made jam and presented it to my astonished wife.

A few weeks later, when a further visit to the barber's was way overdue and I became tired of comments about my disgusting straggly hair, I decided to walk up to the village and try my luck at the local hairdresser in Bédar village. The shop is run by Isabel, the daughter of Clara, who runs the Superclara supermarket next door to her daughter's premises.

As I opened the door of Isabel's premises, I heard a small voice say in Spanish "Hola. Would you like to play?"

Isabel was busy with a lady customer, and she appeared to be applying a pint or two of foul-smelling dark dye to the Señora's hair.

Many Señoras in this area have chunky and colourful hair in rich hues. Spanish women detest having grey hair, and the preferred colour of choice seems to be Mahogany Cuprinol.

"Cinco minutos," called Isabel from the source of the putrid smell.

A wait of five minutes was clearly over-optimistic. No problem, her daughter Laura was happy to look after me until her mummy was finished with the customer. She took my hand and led me to a low table where a bright green plastic tea set awaited. I spent the first fifteen minutes of my first-ever visit to the village hairdresser having an imaginary tea-party with a two year old Spanish toddler. It was simply enchanting. I had very little idea of her language, and she had absolutely no idea of mine, but it didn't stop us having a serious discussion over imaginary tea and scones. Laura may have thought we were having Spanish coffee and cake, but for me it was definitely Scottish tea and scones.

I was rather sorry when her mum summoned me to the barber's chair. But young Laura kept an eye on me throughout. Once her mum had finished cutting what remained of my hair in my requested style of Pierce Brosnan (I wish…), I was hers again and we finished our tea party.

As I prepared to leave the shop, I took the hand of the Spanish lady with the mahogany hair and introduced myself as Pierce Brosnan, to the Señora's total consternation and Isabel's unbridled hilarity. I think Laura arranged for us to meet again at the same time the following week. I confess that I stood her up for a tall and curvaceous solicitor in a mini skirt, and I just hope Laura has forgiven me by now.

Recently I've been going to our friend Gail's place for my haircuts. My wife comes with me to supervise and the visit usually takes around three hours. Which is around half the time Carrie takes when she has her hair done at Gail's. I have around a tenth of Carrie's hair, so answers on a postcard please.

We became friendly with Gail and her husband Grenville before we moved to Almería. In these days they had a great social life and went to some local gigs, which is where we met Gail and Gren. They have since become the best kind of friends anyone could ever wish for. They're from Halifax in Yorkshire, so they share the same careful attitude towards money as the Scots, only more so.

Gail and Gren now live in Cariatiz, a village about twenty minutes away from us. They bought the house as a single-storey ruin, and Gren and his builder friend Pip literally raised the roof and rebuilt it into a charming two-storey country retreat. Gail is a lovely lady who always greets us with big smiles and big hugs. She's what I would describe as a 'smiley lady'. Her husband Gren is more reserved, and is not so good with the big hugs thing. He has done a fair bit of building work for us, and as an ex-mechanic he looks after our cars. He's pedantically honest, and I would trust either of them with my wife's life.

A typical visit to get my hair cut at Gail's place always begins with a knock on their stable door followed by wailing and barking from three dogs of varying sizes but fairly equal volume. I love dogs and look forward to an enthusiastic welcome, but I'm always under strict instructions not to encourage them. I'm told to ignore them. It never works, and I'm always pulled to the floor by three lunatic canines scrabbling for my attention and tugging off chunks of my hair. Ideally, this should qualify me for a discount on my haircut, but we're dealing with Yorkshire folk here.

Two of their dogs are young and enthusiastic yellow mongrels, Little and Large, and their third dog is an elderly and blind Jack Russell bitch who has not the remotest idea what's going on but doggedly (sorry) joins in the barking mayhem anyway. All the while Gail is manically laughing her head off. It's like going to a mad auntie's house.

Gail has an enthusiasm for life which I've seldom found in many other human beings. She has a similarly smiley but rather more mental younger sister, Sally, who comes over from Yorkshire a couple of times a year, mainly to sunbathe and support the local vineyards. Both Gail and Sally are great fun.

So I got my hair cut in good time for Easter, as per the instructions from my other half.

The day before Easter Sunday I was in Garrucha, putting down some piano on Francisco's CD. Fran is the guitarist I met at the Cellar Club in March, and he was recording songs in a style similar to Enrique Iglesias. This is a style which involves a regular "bleuch" sound leading up to a note, reminiscent of a someone about to vomit. Listen to some of Enrique's lines on 'Hero' and tell me I'm wrong.

After the recording session, I packed up my gear and the lads gave me a hand to carry it all back to my car. I had just locked the last piece of equipment in the boot when Pedro put his arm around me and looked me straight in the eye.

"Jim, we would like you to meet our father. Will you come round to our church and meet him?"

"Pedro, I would be delighted to meet your father. But it's after seven and Carrie is cooking a nice dinner for us, so I wouldn't be able to stay long."

"Please come, Jim. We have told our father about you, and he would be honoured to meet you."

Well, how could I refuse? I followed the twins round the corner and up a side street to their church. They knocked at the door of the church hall and we all trooped in. It was Easter, and what greeted us around the large hall were huge tableaus of characters from the Easter story, like Jesus and the Virgin Mary. Bur pride of place went to the Easter feast - two lengths of trestle tables, each at least 30 feet long, groaning with home-made delicacies, plus side tables of huge hams. Pedro explained that there would shortly be a church service, and the feast would start afterwards.

The twins introduced me to their father, a quiet man with a long grey beard, whom I had seen before at art exhibitions. It turned out he was a highly-revered artist, and a gentle soul who was obviously very proud of his twin sons. I said a few words in Spanish to their father, and he kindly pretended to understand what I was on about. He took me to see the inside of his church, and the décor was certainly pretty impressive.

As we walked back into the church hall, Fran came over to me. "Jim, you must try some tapas before you go. They are made by the women of our church. Try this bacalao with raw fava beans. I think you'll like it."

He found a plate and put a chunk of the salt cod on it along with a raw broad bean pod. I tried the combination and I have to say it worked.

Pedro went off to have a word with the lady carving the ham, and she came over to me with a plate. "Please try this ham señor. It is Iberico ham, the finest ham in Spain. It comes from black pigs which eat nothing but acorns."

It was fabulous, the only ham I have ever tasted which was creamy, chewy and cheesy. An explosion of taste in my mouth. I was still chewing when two other ladies came up to me. One lady was brandishing a platter of smoked salmon towards me and the other had a bowl of prawns.

Pedro explained. "Jim, the ladies would like you to try these prawns." These were the famous Garrucha red prawns, rare and expensive, so how could I refuse such an offer?

"Pedro, these prawns are fantastic!" I raved. "But I told Carrie I would be back for dinner around eight o'clock. It's nearly eight now, and if I eat any more here I won't be able to eat what she's cooked for me."

"Just try this home-made sausage before you go." Pedro offered me a platter of delicious-looking chorizo, the Spanish sausage made from smoked pork and paprika. It would have been terribly rude to refuse. Then another lady came round with some chicken liver pate on toast which she wanted my opinion on. This was at least an hour before their feast was to start, but it was clear to me that if I was a friend of Fran and Pedro, I should be treated like a special guest. Word seemed to have got around that this Scottish fellow was to have first dibs on any goodies going. This a typical example of Andalucian hospitality.

Easter Sunday was now upon us, and we had enjoyed the Good Friday pageant around the church in Turre. But we wanted to see the major pageant on Easter Sunday, when Christ is said to have arisen from the dead. We discovered that around noon we should simply walk up the hill to Bédar village's town hall square, where the pageant was to be held.

We got up to the square ten minutes before kick-off and the place was buzzing. The local brass band was tuning up, and a large crowd had gathered. Our mayor is always present at major events, and he was there with other dignitaries to witness the Easter pageant.

We could clearly see the brand new Virgin, a huge statue covered in fresh flowers atop a platform with handles on the sides, being held aloft by a bunch of strapping lads. Although this was Easter Sunday, and a serious occasion, one of the lads was sporting a yellow t-shirt with some writing in large letters. Next to him was an hombre in a black suit and a black hat. There were other statues, four in total, one obviously of Christ.

We met up with some friends and we all stood around while speeches were made in Spanish followed by the brass band playing serious music. Being no good at religion, I regretfully can't tell you what all the goings-on were about. The statues were paraded back and forth across the village square as the Easter story was related to us in Spanish. As a grand finale, all the statues were walked to the edge of the square, then all of a sudden the lads started running with the statues towards the band. The Virgin Mary wobbled worryingly, and some helpers rushed to get her upright again.

"I bet that's why they needed a new Virgin."

"What do you mean?" asked Carrie.

"I mean the last one probably got smashed. I don't mean she got drunk and lost her virginity. The pallbearers probably lost control while they were running."

Someone out there will know what it was all about.

After the celebrations, we all piled into a local bar where they do great tapas. The first time I went there, I asked for a glass of red wine and was shown a selection of bottles to choose from. I took the barman's recommendation and I was asked for a euro for the glass of wine. Watch out though, it's a good few cents extra if you want a tapa along with it.

There used be an agricultural store a few kilometres downhill from our village. We had seen the gradual development of this building - first a side extension, then a rectangular wall built around the perimeter. Then the Spanish owner built a grand arched entrance to welcome the ploughs and tractors. One day a lorry load of kitchen equipment was delivered. Then some Roman columns were erected onto the perimeter wall, followed by huge timber boards decorated with battlements. Letters were then affixed above the grand entrance, announcing to the world the title of the building 'Colloseo Romano' - Roman Collosseum.

We'd called in at Rome while on a cruise a few years earlier. In amongst the modern buildings, manic traffic and graffiti, we could just about make out the famous landmarks. The Trevi Fountain is tucked into a triangular square (if you know what I mean) outside a Benetton shop. And the remains of the Roman Collosseum were at a busy intersection. I remember it well, and I remember it as being a circular building. This was presumably designed to prevent the pesky Christians from finding any corners in which to cower from the lions.

The main difference from the original with our local Roman Collosseum was its shape. As I said, the original was definitely circular. This one was rectangular. There were other subtle differences - our local Collosseum had searchlights, a surround-sound PA system with a sound booth, and a tapas bar with a topless gay Mexican cocktail waiter. No lions, though.

The Collosseum is no more. It's still a bar/restaurant though. They've changed the name but kept the Roman battlements. The building is very close to the foot of the Filabres mountain range. It's now called 'La Cumbre' - the summit.

Every Spring for the past few years, there has been a fabulous music festival in Mojacar called Las Tunas. Universities in Spain have their own troop of entertainers, who dress in traditional costumers, play guitars and mandolins, and sing cheery songs in wonderful harmony. The custom started in Spain and Portugal in medieval days when students would use their musical talents to entertain people in exchange for a coin and a bowl of soup. They would also play their music under the windows of girls they wanted to court.

These days there's a student exchange scheme, and hundreds of these groups descend on Mojacar each year. They walk through the streets playing their instruments and singing to the passers-by, then at night there's a big concert at the big artisan centre building in Mojacar Pueblo.

An old friend of my wife's was over for a week's holiday. Maria is of Italian extraction, so I thought that she might enjoy hearing the mandolins, although I doubted that she'd hear the Italian classic 'O Sole Mio' played on them.

When we arrived in Mojacar late on the Saturday afternoon, we found some groups of students playing their instruments, singing and dancing in the street. It was all great fun and we decided to go to the concert after dinner at a nearby restaurant.

We arrived at the artisan centre just after 9pm, and the large auditorium was crammed, mainly with Spanish people. It was standing room only until we were lucky enough to spot people leaving. We could see around a dozen girls in traditional costume on the stage. Some were playing instruments and singing; others were doing things with flags, almost like cheerleaders. These were the flags of their university, and they were tossing them into the air then catching them and waving them about in complicated patterns while performing a dance. The choreography was brilliant. There were troops from all over Spain, and each troop was given around fifteen minutes for its spot.

Next on was a group of older men. We guessed they were university professors, as several were well up in years. They put up their university's flag on the stage, sorted out the microphones, then played and sang some beautiful songs. The mandolin playing was superb, and our friend Maria loved it. We reckoned the older gents wouldn't be dancing, but boy were we wrong! One by one, they would put down their instrument and do a wee dance. What looked to be the oldest one was the best dancer, bending his body in a way that I

79

couldn't do even when I was a young man. He got a great cheer from the audience.

The next act was a group of girls in what looked like district nurses' uniforms. They were terrific dancers and the things they did with flags – well, it shouldn't be allowed.

The last act we saw was a group of eighteen male students who stood in a row on the stage playing their guitars and mandolins. For their first song they swayed along to a lively sing-along waltz; I can best describe it as a Spanish version of the Tom Jones' song 'Delilah'. Then one of the singers came forward to do a solo, and we certainly weren't expecting to hear 'Spanish Eyes', but it went down a treat with the audience. By this time it was nearing midnight and my companions were getting tired, so we left the party while it was still going strong.

Goodness knows how many troops of performers we missed that night. Next year we'll make sure we get there early for a decent seat.

- - - - - - - - - - - -

One Saturday morning, I got a call from my bass player friend Robin.

"Jim, are you free on Monday during the day? I've been asked to sort out a band for a funeral."

"A band? What kind of funeral needs a band?"

"It's to be a jazz funeral."

The husband of a local lady had sadly dropped dead on the golf course a few weeks after getting the all-clear at a medical check-up. Apparently he had loved jazz, and wanted a jazz band at his funeral. He hadn't planned to have his funeral quite so early, though.

"Can you do it, Jim?" Robin asked.

"Yes, of course. But we need to decide on what tunes to play. I could meet you tomorrow and sort out a list."

"Perfect. I'm bringing a sax player. I've been told that the poor fellow who died absolutely loved the sax."

I'd played some funerals back in Scotland, including a humanist funeral which I landed through the Musicians' Union. The widow was looking for a pianist to play sedate music such as "songs from the shows", but not to include anything from 'Jesus Christ Superstar'. I played stuff like 'Over the Rainbow' and selections from Rodgers & Hammerstein musicals, plus a little Chopin just to keep the event respectful.

However, I had one naughty but risky trick up my sleeve. As the curtains closed over the coffin, I played the rather jolly 'So Long, Farewell' from 'The Sound of Music' - the song which the Trapp children sing on their way up the big double stairway to bed. The coffin headed for the fiery furnace to the sound of laughter, followed by goodbye kisses blown to the coffin by the congregation. I was relieved to see that the widow's tears were tears of laughter, and it earned me a lovely big hug. She wrote me a very moving letter afterwards which I still treasure, and I'm just glad that my electric piano helped her through a difficult day.

Anyway, I'd never played a jazz funeral. I'd often played with Robin at the Cellar Club jams in Garrucha, but we hadn't played any gospel music or hymns. By Monday, we had sorted out some tunes and keys. The funeral wasn't to be an overly religious affair, but I wanted to try and emulate a touch of the atmosphere of a New Orleans funeral by including some great old gospel tunes. I hadn't met or heard the sax player, but Robin reckoned he would be fine.

We arrived at the tanatorio (funeral parlour) and set up. There are lots of these in our area, and as I mentioned previously, they don't do the actual cremations there, just the funeral service.

As the congregation arrived, we warmed up with a slow New Orleans type blues, which was entirely appropriate for the occasion. We played some gospel tunes as the congregation settled down ready for the funeral service. I got the feeling that some people were not keen on a jazz band being there, but we had to make the best of it.

During the service, we were called upon to play 'The Lord's My Shepherd'. The minister who took the service addressed the congregation.

"Let us pray," he bowed his head solemnly, "that the pianist will play this hymn in the traditional manner."

There was a burst of laughter from the congregation, then the sax player produced a dirty great honk. The minister turned around and looked pointedly at him before commenting. "Perhaps it would be best if the pianist could play this hymn on his own."

Point taken. Then the minister turned around and addressed me like a teacher chiding a pupil.

"Do you promise to be on your best behaviour during this hymn?" He asked, in mock sternness. I cowed my head and pretended to be intimidated by him. This drew several laughs from the congregation, and the hymn proceeded in a relaxed atmosphere.

The minister had asked us to play a gospel tune near the end of the service. We played 'Down By The Riverside' and I saw some feet tapping and more than a few smiles.

At the end of the service, it was time for the coffin to be taken back out to the hearse. Before then, the widow was given the chance to say her last goodbyes to the coffin. The congregation stood, and I started to play that grand old hymn 'Just A Closer Walk With Thee' slowly on the piano. The widow stood over her husband's coffin. As she bent down to kiss the coffin, I gave the guys the cue and we went into my slow rocking boogie version of the hymn. Just then, the widow looked up at me and gave me a look that I'll never forget. It was a sad smile that said "Oh, Thomas would have loved this."

We continued playing the hymn as the congregation left the funeral parlour. Then, as the coffin was placed into the hearse, we played an up-tempo version of 'When The Saints Go Marching In' - a bit like the New Orleans funeral bands (albeit with a sax player rather then the usual Satchmo-like trumpet). At this point, the congregation started to drift in again, and we continued playing and getting applause.

Later, the widow came back in to the funeral parlour. It seemed that the music had helped her through the service. She sat and enjoyed our wee band, then when it was time to pack up, she came up to me.

"Everyone is coming up to my house for the reception. They really enjoyed your music, Jim. Would you and your friends manage to come for a bite to eat and play around the pool?"

We couldn't and wouldn't have refused. So we took our gear down and drove up the mountain to the widow's house. Her husband had made a cracking job of designing the house around a large courtyard bedecked with shrubs and flowers, with a stunning swimming pool in the centre.

The three of us set up next to the pool and played jazz and boogie all afternoon. This was the first and only outing for this particular trio, but the tanatorio took Robin's phone number, and you never know - one year we might be called upon for another jazz funeral.

Lesley has now become a good friend, and supports my music whenever she can. She was happy for me to share this event in my book, and I hope it would have given her husband a wee smile to know that his funeral has now been committed to literature of sorts. I'm just sorry I never got to meet him. I'd have had a few jazz stories for him and I get the feeling that we'd have become friends.

CHAPTER 5 - MAY

My phone had been ringing with singers wanting to work with me. I met quite a few and some were pretty good. One or two were quite dreadful and one fellow couldn't have hit the right note if it had been attached to the side of a bus with flashing lights saying "Over here". One Spanish girl called me and told me she sang songs in English. I went to hear her and you could have fooled me.

Another female singer in her thirties contacted me and asked me to come down to a venue on the beach and hear her sing. I thought she had a good voice but her lisp was the deal-breaker. After I heard her sing 'Thith-terth are doing it for them-thelves' it wasn't easy for me to keep a straight face when I made the excuse that I was leaving Thpain thoon and going back to Thcotland for a while.

I tried out some songs with an Irish lady singer. When I found out that she was too dim to grasp the scale of doh, re, mi which all infants are taught, I made my apologies and baled out. She fired back an email telling me that I was being "Holier than though." I was flattered to receive such a magnificently illiterate insult.

But one day a Facebook message arrived from a Scottish lass called Jill who had worked with a blues band in Scotland. She had performed on BBC radio and done some interesting work. She'd followed her parents to Almería and had been singing solo to karaoke backing tracks, which she had found pretty soulless. She was looking for a band or at least a pianist to work with. The only downside for a Glasgow bloke like me was that she was from Edinburgh. But hey, nobody's perfect.

I reckoned it was well worth a meeting to see if we had any common ground, so I invited Jill to my studio one Wednesday and promised to set up my piano.

What arrived at my door I can only describe as a stunning wee hippie with a plastic rose in her hair and a nose stud. More importantly, she also had bookfuls of blues, classic rock and contemporary songs. We instantly hit it off, and we found that we had mutual tastes. I wanted to give up the safe dinner dance type repertoire I had been knocking out for the older ex-pats – most of them weren't really interested in hearing any music written after the sixties. I have a low boredom threshold and I've never been one to dwell for long on dull, safe territory in music.

Jill was certainly not interested in being dull or safe, and within five hours we had managed to run through nearly sixty songs. During this time I had established her ideal keys for the songs. I'd never worked with anyone who covered so much ground so quickly, and I found myself in a whirlwind of ideas – a Stevie Wonder medley; Prince's 'When Doves Fly' with a bit of Bach; a slow bluesy version of Adele's 'Rolling in the Deep'. As an arranger, I had always wanted to mash up snippets of classical music into pop classics. Jill wanted to do some comedy songs (something I love doing) and although she had a deep timbre not unlike Alison Moyet, it turned out she had been operatically trained as a soprano.

After five hours, my head was spinning with ideas. Though Jill was 18 years my junior, I was delighted to have the opportunity to work with this delightful lass, and it seemed that she wanted to work with this old boy. Thus was born a rather interesting new act. Best of all, she was really bright and had more than enough intelligence to understand the basic sol-fa scale -doh, re, mi etc. This makes learning new songs so much quicker.

After the summer we started work on building an act, and this is where musicians can really be creative. Jill mentioned that she had recently sung 'Romeo and Juliet' with a local rock band to some acclaim - this is the brilliant modern take on the old story which Mark Knopfler wrote and recorded while he was in Dire Straits. I arranged the song just for voice and piano and Jill worked on her interpretation.

The result was a version of the song quite unlike any other version around. As my piano was the only accompaniment, we could slow down when we needed to, have soft passages and loud crescendos, rise and fall to express the song in our own way. I decided to use Mark Knopfler's theme from 'Last Exit to Brooklyn' as a long introduction to the song, and Jill produced a wee bit of her operatic soprano voice just before the last note of the song.

Our intense preparation paid off. At our first ever gig at a beach bar, arranged by Harvey, the manager approached us immediately after our first set and asked us if we could perform every week. We ended that gig with some rock and roll, and the audience were fired up and raucous. An encore was demanded. I kicked off the intro to 'Romeo and Juliet' and by the second verse we had total silence from the audience. We got a standing ovation, one of many which Jill and I got for our music.

At one of our gigs at Los Angeles (a local restaurant, sadly not the US city) one of my friends, Wendy Tallis, took a video of the last few songs of our show. We finished up with some fifties rock and roll, which never fails to get a great response. It's always great to have shouts for an encore, and when this happened, Wendy took a video of our performance of 'Romeo & Juliet'. Although our audience had been dancing and talking noisly, they gave 'Romeo & Juliet' almost total silence.

Carrie and I had met Wendy while she and her partner were on holiday in our area. She and her partner Keith are from the Birmingham area. We meet them once or twice a year, and when we meet up it's like we saw them only last week. I always ask after their parrot Basil who I've met several times. He's rather elderly, almost 40 years old and bald as a coot (whatever a coot might be). Basil is an enthusiastic talker, and some of the words he's learnt are a little racy.

Before flying out for a recent holiday, Keith was driving Basil to his brother's house where the elderly parrot was to be looked after during the holiday. Keith had placed Basil in his cage on the back seat of his car. On the way to the house, Keith was cut up by another car when approaching roadworks. As he braked hard to avoid a collision, there was an almighty crash from behind the driver's seat followed by an eerie silence.

Keith stopped the car as soon as he could, then got out and opened the back door. There on the footwell between the driver's seat and the back seat was Basil's cage, upside down with no sign of the parrot. As

Keith lifted the cage from the footwell, he heard a movement. Then he noticed a very shaken parrot covered in bits of hay. As he emerged from the gloom, Keith heard Basil emit those unforgettable words.

"Fuckin' 'ell."

Keith told me he couldn't have put it better himself.

- - - - - - - - - - - -

We had been living in Bédar village for a few months. Friends were phoning from time to time, threatening to come and visit us. We had been cautious in case visitors didn't like our house, which was still a bit of a project. The access to our only spare bedroom was through our own bedroom on the first floor, which was maybe a bit too intimate for house guests. Our only other bedroom was on the top floor and had childrens' beds. But one day the builders had gone and the conversion work was finished; the back bedroom now had its own separate entrance.

One day we bit the bullet and agreed that a long-married couple could come and visit. But there's a well-known saying - "visitors are like fish – they can start to smell after a few days".

We've now had loads of friends and family come out to visit, and they've pretty much all been really enthusiastic about where we live. One couple are friends from the street where we lived in our old village in Scotland. Although Brian's wife Christine has to use a wheelchair, they love it here. They love the scenery, the food, the weather, the music and the people. In fact they both love it to such an extent that they plan to live here most of the year, despite the difficulties of Christine getting about in this hilly part of the country. Her electric wheelchair helps. She has retained her zest for life despite her huge mobility problem, and as far as I'm concerned she is a real hero and an inspiration to me. She simply goes with the flow and relishes every day, sings in a choir, plays piano and has a magnificently dirty laugh.

I still keep in touch with many of my old friends. Alistair was my oldest friend from my primary school days. He'd become a successful sales executive with a personality combining schoolboy humour and overt pomposity. Alistair loved toilet humour. When we were at school, we would visit our friends' homes, he would make a lengthy visit to their loo, wails of pain would be heard from within, then he'd emerge with a cry of "Ah, that's better !!". My schoolfriends loved his eccentric ways. My schoolfriends' parents thought he should be put into care.

Through the years, Alistair and I had kept in touch mainly through Christmas cards. Our shared sense of humour remained intact via e-mail. In his early twenties, Alistair met a sweet girl from a council scheme near Glasgow, a dingy and down-at-heel dump, and the only place these days in Scotland where you can buy 'apartments' for £5000 which include your own doorstep drug dealer. Her father was a pleasant but grizzly old bloke who smoked a rancid pipe and seldom moved from his crumbling armchair.

Alistair and Moira got married a couple of years before us. We had them round for dinner a few times, but never got a return invitation. Then Alistair moved on with his job to a town near London. They later moved to their final home which was located in the Chilterns in south east England.

My wife and I stayed firmly in Scotland, and it was only after we sold our main business that we had time on our hands to visit Alistair and Moira. We stayed with them for a few days at their home in the Chilterns. Carrie and I had never seen a Chiltern before, and we found the area very pleasant.

Shortly afterwards, Alistair and Moira asked if they could come and visit for just under a week, and we readily agreed to return the favour of accommodation, as we thought they would enjoy several days in the sun.

Their flight was late on the night of their arrival. It was after midnight when I met their car at the motorway junction for them to follow me up to our house for some food and a nightcap.

For the following day, some friends had booked a party of us for lunch at a cracking rural restaurant about an hour inland. We asked Alistair and Moira to join our party, and they jumped at the chance. I drove us all up, and we had a great meal. Alistair was his usual pompous self, and treated our friends as though he was chairing a business meeting. After lunch I asked Alistair and Moira if they wanted me to drive them further inland up to Velez Rubio and Velez Blanco, and they were grateful for the offer. They explored the castles and churches of these lovely old Spanish towns and took lots of photos.

The next day we had to go to the local market for food supplies, and we drove down in our car. Alistair and Moira were not interested in helping us lug around fruit and veg to feed them, and we met up with them when we'd finished getting our supplies. They had enjoyed the tapas at our house, so I suggested going to a local tapas bar which usually had a couple of dozen types of tapas on offer. They wanted to sit outside, and Alistair went into the bar to choose the tapas he fancied. When the tapas arrived, Moira sniffed the plates. It's the custom in our neck of the woods for bars to provide wee dishes of tapas plus a basket of bread. Everyone gets a fork, then simply dives in and grabs what they want with their forks.

Not Moira. "Are we supposed to just dip our forks in the dishes? Does no-one here worry about spreading germs?" she glowered.

"As far as I know, no-one has ever died from eating tapas, Moira. Not since the great tapas shortage of 1952."

"What happened then?"

"Wine was banned throughout Spain. The original idea of a tapa was a piece of bread to place on top of your wine glass to keep the flies off. There was no wine so there were no tapas. The people were starving, just like I am right now." Moira actually took me seriously.

Moira declined to have any tapas on health grounds, preferring to eat a banana she had bought for herself at the market.

The Cellar Club was still open then, and that night I drove them down to my gig with a lady vocalist called Carol. They enjoyed our show, but by the time Carol and I were on our second break, Alistair was clearly rather well-oiled. He collared Carol at the table and told her of a device he used to improve penetration during sex. Now Alistair was of a rotund shape and appearance which made the idea of him performing any kind of sex act totally repulsive. His remaining teeth were worn down to stumps, affecting his ability to speak clearly when sober and not exactly enhancing his sex talk. My lady vocalist found his slurred conversation crude and offensive. If her hunky husband had been at the table rather than at the bar chatting up other women, Alistair would have found himself out on the pavement with a bloody nose.

The next day Alistair and Moira went off on their own in their hired car. We had arranged to meet up that night with some friends at a flamenco club, and they wanted to come along. I drove them down to the playa, where my young Spanish amigos Fran and Pedro were playing Santana-type material at a beach bar. Even before we got out of the car, Moira heard some loud music and made her feelings known.

"Well, I hope we're not going in there. I couldn't stand that sort of noise."

"They're our friends, Moira, and that's where Carrie and I are going. Would you prefer to stay in the car?"

She grudgingly got out and we all sat down at outside tables, and I got some drinks while the two of them sat with faces like fizz as my friends performed to an enthusiastic audience of young and old fans.

"We didn't enjoy that music, Jim," said Alistair as we got back in the car. "We've been friends for a long time, and I know you'd prefer me to be honest with you."

Of course I would. How thoughtful of him.

Next stop was a Chinese restaurant for a banquet meal, which they both tucked into with gusto. Before the food came, Moira ordered a whisky. Here in Almería province, the bottle is often brought to the table for the waiter to pour. Rather than use an optic measure, the custom is for the waiter to turn the bottle upside down and count to six seconds while the spirit glugs out from its security stopper, unless the customer says "stop" sooner. Moira sat and watched as the waiter stood at the table and poured the whisky into a tall glass – he seemed to be waiting for Moira to say "stop" and just kept on pouring until the tall glass was half-full. By the time the spring rolls arrived, she had downed the entire contents of this potent aperitif and had started on the house wine.

Alistair piped up. "The food is good, but the house wine is not great." Slurping down another glass he declared "We've spent a lot of time in the Far East, and we didn't enjoy the food in China at all. But the wine over there was better than this stuff."

After the meal we all went on to the flamenco club. Our Spanish friend Juan José from the village had suggested the visit, as he'd been several times and had greatly enjoyed the authentic flamenco. This was a typical Spanish place, rustic and friendly. Anything goes in these clubs including smoking and staying open until the last person has left the building.

Flamenco is the folk music and dancing of Andalucía. Proper hardcore flamenco is performed by gypsies, not a tourist show. Andalucía is the home of flamenco, and there are lots of Peñas – flamenco clubs – all over this huge region (Andalucía is considerably bigger than the entire country of Scotland).

As we entered the flamenco club, we saw some Spanish and British friends and went through the ritual of kissing and hugging. We had never done this in Scotland, where the greeting is usually a nod or a grunt.

The bar staff sat our party at two big tables facing a large stage. The staff then decided that we weren't close enough to the action, so some waiters moved our tables forward, almost right on the stage. The Spanish don't like to stand outside the fire. More friends joined us, and we all greeted each other with hugs and kisses in the usual way. Andalucian time is rather different from British time, and the Andalucians have a relaxed view of punctuality. This performance was typically late, and wouldn't be expected to begin until a decent audience had formed.

By half past ten, the club had just about filled up. As we sat and chatted, I could hear this noise upstairs, like a 45rpm record of marching played at 78 rpm. The noise got closer and closer, and suddenly from the side of the stage a trio of nubile young ladies appeared in flamenco dresses in different colours but matching designs. Then a scrawny and hairy guitarist shambled onto the stage, immediately followed by a small hunched male singer and a tall slim young man whose job appeared to be clapping his hands furiously in time to the music.

The singer was authentic gypsy flamenco – he sat on a chair and slowly turned purple by straining his voice in an arabic wail. The guitarist was a very passable accompanist. The girl dancers were terrific. I thought their footwork was awesome, and their general performance top-notch.

After a couple of costume changes on the part of the young ladies, the chap who had been sitting at the back clapping his hands in time to the music came forward and proceeded to dance. And knocked seven bells out of anything that had happened previously. He was simply stunning - stamping, clapping and pirouetting with unbelievable passion. Sweat poured off him like a lawn sprinkler as he spun furiously around. We were encouraged by a Spanish friend from our village to shout "Olé" and I added a few "Bravos" for good measure. He finished the first half of the performance to thunderous applause and a standing ovation.

There was a real buzz of conversation at the interval as the audience discussed this stunning and masterful performance. I went over to Alistair and Moira to ask how they were enjoying the flamenco.

"It's dreadful," slurred Moira. "That singer will have a sore throat in the morning. I used to be a speech therapist so I know what I'm talking about."

"Did you enjoy the dancing then?"

"Listen, Jim, we've been all around the world and we've seen a lot of flamenco. This was a very poor production."

Had we been watching different performances? It was raw passionate stuff, very similar to a gypsy flamenco performance by the renowned Jaleo troupe, which we had seen a few years ago. It was a memorable performance, on a rainy February night in a theatre in Ayrshire run by my friend Bruce, but 464 of the 500 seats were sadly empty.

"Well, I'll admit it's not tourist flamenco," I retorted. "It's proper authentic gypsy flamenco, and Andalucía is the undisputed home of flamenco."

"Oh, we've been all over the world and seen culture," Moira sniffed. "And this was not good culture. Maybe it's the wine talking."

Alistair had earlier sat entranced by the nubile young dancers, and never took his eyes off them, so I assumed that he had enjoyed the show so far.

"Did you not enjoy the girl dancers? We all thought they were excellent."

"It was all very average."

"What about the male dancer? I thought he was very passionate and lifted the whole performance. And he did get a standing ovation."

"The production was poor, and there were no spotlights." Alistair retorted.

"It's a flamenco club, not a tourist show."

"….and it was too noisy." Alistair continued.

I agreed that it was noisy, but as I've already said, the Spanish love noise.

"I've a splitting headache," said Alistair, warming to his subject.

I fought back. "Everyone else seemed to enjoy it. As you saw from the response."

"Well, we've been all round the world, and this was the worst flamenco we've ever seen. We've been friends for a long time, and I know you'd prefer me to be honest with you".

Despite the audience's great enthusiasm for what they had witnessed, and the fact that we were in the town which reputedly had the highest proportion of gypsy flamenco performers in the world, it wasn't good enough for Alistair and Moira. They had seen flamenco all over the world. Everywhere in the world except the home of flamenco.

During the remainder of their stay, we treated Alistair and Moira with kid gloves, and let them decide what they wanted to do. We prepared breakfast for them every morning, and Moira never at any time lifted a finger to help. Alistair helped clear the table on two mornings, but Moira sat and droned on in a dull monotone while the rest of us did the work and waited on her. I'm absolutely sure that Her Majesty the Queen would have been more down to earth than Moira.

The pair had travelled around the world, and practically every conversation would include interminable boasts about some country or other they had visited.

"Oh, yes, we take at least three holidays a year. Not including this break, Jim. This is not so much a holiday as a visit to see old friends."

"Oh, yes, we enjoyed Corsica, but not as much as Santorini."

"We like Spain, but we really prefer Italy. We're very old friends, Jim, and we've always been honest with each other, so I know you'd want me to speak as I find."

"Oh, yes, we've spent a lot of time in France, and the houses there are much nicer than in Spain."

Moira regularly compared our house with Polly's house in France, and it was clear that Polly's house was bigger and nicer than ours. Eventually Carrie got sick of their boasts and attempts at one-upmanship, and she was counting the days to their flight home. A friend described Alistair and Moira as "When we's". For example "When we were in Kuala Lumpur....", "When we were in Tokyo...." etc etc. The type of people who try to impress you by constantly shoving their expensive foreign trips down your throat.

When they started telling us about their cruise holidays, I casually told them that we had spent our spare cash on building up a very successful property business and that we hoped to see a lot more of the world when we retired. That shut them up for a while.

Alistair revelled in the local tapas, and the mixed fried fish, and the local leg of lamb, and the wine at five euros a bottle (Moira wouldn't touch anything as cheap). He downed food of every variety with great enthusiasm, scrupulously attending to the needs of his vast waistline.

Right from the start, Moira had interrupted everyone's contribution to the conversation with her own thoughts, delivered in her dull monotone. Like Carrie and I, Alistair would let her have her own way and let her rudely interrupt. But in the last couple of days of their stay, I decided to live dangerously. Whenever Alistair asked me a question, I looked him straight in the eye while I answered him. Within a few seconds, Moira would attempt to butt in with her own self-important opinions. I simply continued to look Alistair in the eye, ignored her interruptions, and continued talking to him. He seemed to realise what I was doing, and after a few of these bouts, he started to ignore her too as she droned on. And on and on.

We could see that Moira was not pleased about not being allowed to control the conversation, and as she sat down to be served breakfast on the last day of their visit, she became quite aggressive towards Alistair and me. But by now there was quite a change in my old friend - he asserted himself and simply would not let her rant on or let her have her own way. We rather put Moira in her place, and she left in an atmosphere of hostility.

Moira won't be back. And it would certainly not be in Alistair's interests to return, as Carol's husband is still looking for him after his offensive conversation with his wife at the Cellar Club.

Alistair did manage to sneak me out a birthday card, signed in his usual illegible handwriting, so you never know, he might yet kill Moira off and seek refuge with friends. It won't be at our house, though - it's no match for Polly's.

- - - - - - - - - - - -

Now then. This is the wonderful thing about being a musician:-
It doesn't matter how young or old you are.
It doesn't matter if you're good-looking or pot-ugly.
It doesn't matter what colour or religion you are.
The only thing that matters is how good you are.
Musicians are just not interested in racism or ageism. The colour of your skin is as unimportant as your age, religion or physical appearance. I'll say it again - the only thing that matters is how good you are. This is usually very evident when watching concerts by any major entertainer. Check out Paul Simon's band on a 2011 New York concert DVD. You'll see old and young, black and white. Awesome musicians of all ages and all ethnic backgrounds.

A local musician encountered both racism and anti-semitism after working with a girl singer for a while. The duo approached a Jewish gent who loved their music and had vast experience in advertising and marketing. They wondered if they should ask him to help with their promotion. So the duo arranged a meeting along with their respective spouses to discuss whether or not to engage his services.

"Do what you like. He's only a Jew boy out for all he can get," was the comment by the singer's husband Roger.

The musician was taken aback at this openly anti-semitic statement and retorted "I've got Jewish blood in me." Total silence. No apology from Roger. Only a shrug. Carrie was clearly shocked.

A few days later, when they were rehearsing for a show, the singer told the musician "You know, my husband wasn't being racist when he said that."

So there you go. There are some things in life which you just can't make up.

The musician's wife was appalled at the ignorant racist remarks and advised him to give up the act there and then before matters got worse. But the musician persevered and the Jewish gent worked tirelessly but unprofitably to secure them some great gigs. When Roger started eyeballing and bullying the Jewish gent, the music act fell apart.

Racism has no place in music. Back in the mid-seventies, when I began to get really active on the music scene, Rangers was a Protestant football club and Celtic was a Catholic football club. Rangers didn't sign Catholic players and Celtic didn't sign Protestant players.

At that time I was the only Protestant in a dance trio. I played a double-manual organ, and I was outnumbered two to one by a Catholic singer and a Catholic drummer of God-given brilliance. The drummer, Tom, regularly played the Protestant enclave which was the Rangers Club. His talent was way more important to the entertainment manager than his religion.

The night when Celtic won the Scottish league cup for the ninth year in succession, our trio played the team's celebration dinner dance at Glasgow's Sherbrooke Hotel. It was the shortest gig I've ever played. After a few half-hearted dances, wee Jimmy Johnstone asked me to accompany him on 'The Wild Side of Life'. He sang hunched round the microphone and for some reason he had difficulty standing upright. Then Danny McGrain asked me to accompany him and the team singing 'You'll Never Walk Alone'. By this time, several of the team could hardly stand, let alone walk. They were celebrating big time, and deservedly so.

Forty five minutes into the gig, Jock Stein came up to us.

"That's it, lads. Wind it up now please."

"But we've only played one set." We all protested.

"You'll get paid in full. Play the last dance now, then pack up." That was obviously an order, not a request.

So there I was, the only non-Catholic in the room. Later that night I was told by one of the hotel waiters (an ardent Celtic fan) that I had just played at the most important gig in the history of the world. He enjoyed my playing and admired my organ. Snigger ye not - it was an Italian 'Farfisa' brand instrument !

The following year, Rangers won the league cup and our trio played the same gig in the same hotel. At both gigs, we had been judged purely on our music, not on our religion or any other factor. The only thing that mattered was how good we were.

And we played huge gigs for Catholic chapels, including a memorable one on a Sunday night attended by around 300 people in a vast chapel hall. There was a quiver of excitement when the priest arrived, and there was a rush to get him a drink. A fellow in the audience found a pint glass, another chap found an opened bottle of sherry. I know what you're thinking, but you're wrong - the pint glass was only filled halfway up.

It's a matter of great delight for me that Andalucia's capital, Seville, provides a summer school for the West Eastern Divan Youth Orchestra. The renowned Argentine-Israeli conductor Daniel Barenboim and the late Palestinian-American academic Edward Said founded the orchestra in 1999. It's made up of musicians from all over the Middle East. Including Israelis and Palestinians, all performing together in a spirit of camaraderie.

Since 2002, the Junta de Andalucía (Regional Government of Andalucia) together with a private foundation have provided a summer school for the orchestra over several weeks in Seville. As Barenboim says "The orchestra was conceived as a project against ignorance. A project about the fact that it is absolutely essential for people to get to know the other, to understand what the other thinks and feels, without necessarily agreeing with it." One of the orchestra's musicians has stated "The orchestra is a human laboratory that can express to the whole world how to cope with the other."

Racism, looks, ageism and ignorance have no place in performing music. The only thing that matters is how good you are.

During the summer break, students descend on Almería looking for work and experience, and often perform at local venues. In the centre of Vera town, there is an old convent which now serves as an art gallery and concert venue. It has a stage, a wonderful grand piano and a 3-second echo which is great for slow songs but not in the least bit great for fast songs.

Here in Spain, I'm blessed with many friends, most of whom I've made through music. I have a Jewish friend, Harvey, who's regarded as a treasure by the local musicians. He's a benevolent Santa Claus of a man (complete with white beard) who has helped and supported musicians in all sorts of genres from acoustic folk music to opera. Harvey has set up gigs for them and helped to promote their work, and I'm painfully aware that he doesn't do it for profit. Harvey does not in any way agree with Israel's treatment of the Palestinians, and he renounced his religion several years ago.

Harvey and his lovely wife Kathy have been a great help to many. They don't waste their days doing trivial stuff - they make themselves useful to society, even though both are way past retirement age.

Harvey phoned me one day.

"Jim, are you interested in coming with us to see a young American singer at the Convento? She's performing with her guitarist boyfriend and she plays piano too plus a bit of opera."

"Yes Harvey. Like David Bowie, I'm unable to resist Young Americans."

Young Martha was enchanting. A dark-haired pretty girl, she opened the set by singing a Mozart aria while accompanying herself on the venue's grand piano. Her pure voice needed no amplification and it soared above the piano and filled the old building. Later into the evening, she and the guitarist sang folksy duets, and it was a really good concert. They received a great reception from the audience.

When they had finished and were packing up, Harvey went over to them and complimented the couple on their performance. He discovered that they were on a student exchange scheme, and were staying nearby. Harvey found out that they had no form of transport to get around. From that moment on, he took the young performers under his wing. He drove them around in his car to all sorts of gigs, made sure they were fed and watered, and generally looked after them like a doting father.

Harvey introduced Martha to an international opera coach, Jeanne Henny MBE, who lives two villages up from us. Although Martha hadn't yet formulated a career, she was encouraged by Harvey and others to take up music professionally. Before the couple returned to America, Harvey organized a farewell dinner at his home, and that night I was honoured to accompany Martha on the piano.

After Martha's final public performance at an acoustic night, she announced to the audience that she had decided to take up singing as a career. This was greeted with huge applause by all who had come to adore Martha. She told us that her decision was largely due to Harvey, who along with others had helped her to secure her a place at a music college in Phildelphia. Harvey was delighted, and shed tears of happiness.

Later in the month, a troop of eight opera singer from Hungary descended on us. A local music patron accommodates the opera singers at his home. Every summer Jeanne brings over a group of singers to help develop their performance skills. This particular summer, a group of eight operatic singers had been invited over from Hungary, where Jeanne was awarded the country's highest award for services to Hungarian culture.

Harvey arranged a performance of Mozart's 'Don Giovanni' in the main square in the old town of Vera, and over 500 people turned up to hear the singers. Sadly, I was gigging that night and had to miss the performance.

In recognition of Harvey's services to the local music scene, Jeanne had arranged a musical evening at her home in his honour. I was delighted to be invited to perform, but in all honesty I did not feel in the same league as the classical musicians that evening. But I had promised to play the piano and I could hardly refuse. So I decided to play one my daft piano arrangements - the one which starts with the opening of Greig's piano concerto and morphs into a fast stride piano version of "Tiger Rag". Jeanne's grand piano bravely endured my pummelling!

An operatic concert had been arranged by Jeanne and Harvey for the following evening, but as so often in our area, it was anything but conventional. The venue chosen was a disused quarry, one of many in our area. We were advised to bring our own chairs and water. There were no facilities whatsoever, no toilets and no bar. Basically, you drove to the quarry, parked your car on the rough ground, and walked up to a plateau in front of a mine shaft making a stunning backdrop for the performance. However, there was a sheer drop at one side, and the only protection for the audience was some flimsy orange plastic fencing which would have struggled to prevent a toddler from falling off the edge.

There is no way that this event would have been permitted in the UK. In Spain, there's no compensation culture. There's no chappie with a measuring tape employed by the council to check that there are no gaps more than an inch high on the pavements. Basically, you are expected to take responsibility for your own actions, and to watch where you're going. If you get rat-arsed on a Saturday night, stagger around, trip on a raised paving slab and crack your head open, well it's your own stupid bloody fault for drinking irresponsibly and not watching where you were going.

The concept of the public being responsible for their own actions is still alive and well in Spain. On UK television I've seen programmes about heavyweight fake blonde slags getting pissed, going out on a frosty night sporting an overhanging bare midriff and seven-inch heels, and ending up in casualty with pneumonia and a broken leg. The more fake blonde slags get downed the better, in my opinion, because these preening, self-obsessed moronic creatures could then perhaps learn to speak English during their recovery. Omygod, yea, we must live in hoap, like, babe. LOL.

Back to the Concert At The Quarry.

The Hungarian opera troop comprised eight singers – two sopranos, a mezzo-soprano, an alto, two tenors, a baritone and a basso profundo who produced the lowest note I've ever heard coming from a human being. They were accompanied by an immensely talented classical pianist called Barry. He played an electric piano run off a generator which had been set up out of hearing.

The concert wasn't advertised and people heard about it by word of mouth. On the Monday night of the concert, I abandoned my car on a dirt-track near the old quarry and trudged up the track clutching an old fold-up chair and a bottle of water. When I got to the end of the track, I found at least a hundred and fifty people including several of my friends. They had all arranged their chairs in rows in typical concert fashion.

The sopranos were first to perform, and the highlight for me was when the most petite and beautiful of the sopranos sang Puccini's 'O Mio Babbino Caro' ('O My Beloved Father'). In this aria, Lauretta pleads with her father to give his blessing for her to marry the boy she loves. Musically and emotionally, Puccini lays it on thick. This young lass had the most gorgeous and penetrating eyes. She singled out my Dutch friend Henk to be the object of her pleas and got down on her knees in front of Henk to sing her pleading aria to his face. I don't believe there was a single man in the audience with dry eyes. Henk certainly didn't!

The singers were all wonderful, and it was a truly memorable evening. The audience yelled for an encore, and the singers performed

98

the magnificent Chorus of the Hebrew Slaves from Verdi's opera 'Nabucco'. By the middle section of the piece, the hairs on the back of my neck were standing to attention.

Harvey is heavily involved in promoting music locally. He's recently been involved in promoting a 5-day flamenco festival at the bullring in Vera, and helping two major operatic troops. He gives his services without seeking financial compensation.

In 1985, Harvey was on the fringes of Live Aid, and had experience of working to help in a natural disaster, so when several people lost their homes in recent flash floods in Almería, he was right on the scene along with the Red Cross. He worked with his local mayor to organize accommodation for elderly victims, and he drove them to their temporary homes. He and his wife Kathy helped at the local Red Cross branch, and they're still involved to this day. Harvey teaches English to Spanish pupils for the Red Cross at Vera, and he recently arranged a fund-raiser event for them. He has done all this on his own time and at his own expense.

I'll leave you to guess who was the subject of the comment "He's only a Jew boy out for all he can get" earlier in this chapter. Sadly, racism and anti-semitism still exist in the world of football. Thankfully, such crass pig-ignorance simply doesn't exist in the world of music.

Many of my friends are like Marmite - they tend not to be run-of-the-mill individuals, and they're sometimes the type of people you'll either love or hate. But my greatest friends are passionate, spiritual beings, the type who can be brought to tears by music, the type who will rail against life's injustices. The type who'll hug me and get hugged back in return. Harvey is in this category, and my one regret is that we met fairly late in life.

But no matter, we still have work to do in music, and we can hopefully do this in the next life. This is not bull, it's something I have total cause to believe, although not through my own experience. God knows I'm not religious. Although my wife was a church elder in Scotland, I have too much of a sense of humour to be able to keep a straight face when some creepy geezer in a grand cloak and a tea cosy hat gives a speech in a plummy voice. And the impenetrable lyrics of most hymns belong to a grandiose Victorian era with which I have absolutely no connection. But gospel music on the other hand – wow, I'd have loved to have been born a big black mama like Mahalia Jackson or Mavis Staples.

I've met many religious people who are spiritually vacuous, and who couldn't be moved by great music even if God tapped them on the shoulder and said "Listen to this, it's a gift from heaven".

Speaking of which, if I ever do enough good stuff to get to heaven, I'm convinced the piped music at reception will be the slow movement from Mozart's Clarinet Concerto. If this beautiful music doesn't convince you that there just might be a heaven, maybe you're already spiritually dead.

CHAPTER 6 - JUNE

It was June, and the fiesta season was upon us.

There are countless fiestas in Spain in honour of religious saints. But locally, some of the biggest fiestas are those to celebrate the Moors & Christians.

For 600 years, Spain was ruled by the moors. They settled in Spain in the year 711, built mosques, and their architectural influence is still very strong in Andalucia. The stunning palaces and gardens of the Alhambra, set on a plateau above Granada, were built by the moors. The Nazrid Palace is the one which you may have seen in photographs, and it is truly beautiful. The interior walls are of delicate filigree plasterwork, like fancy Artex only rather more intricate. Don't bother sending pictures to a local plasterer and asking for this stuff on your ceilings.

The Muslim people lived peacefully in Spain for these 600 years. They made an immeasurable contribution to its culture, from architecture to music (flamenco singing is not unlike Arabic wailing). Much of the food down here is Moroccan-influenced, and the irrigation techniques for agriculture are still used to this day. But the Spanish eventually decided that their indigenous people should run the country, and the moors were fought and gradually forced out of Spain.

They say any excuse for a fiesta, and the Spanish celebrate their liberation from Muslim rule, just as the Americans celebrate their Independence Day every year. All right, maybe not in quite the same way. The Moors & Christians fiesta takes place over three days. On the first day (Friday) there are mock battles on the beach and the Moors win. The following day, the Christians win. And on the third and last day they all get together for a celebration of their brotherhood. The climax of the fiesta is a fantastic parade of local adults and children through the streets of old Mojacar, lasting around two hours. Brits and other nationalities also participate.

You possibly wouldn't see Christians and Muslims knocking seven bells out of each other for fun in somewhere like Birmingham, then having a party afterwards, but you'll often see it in southern Spain. And if there aren't enough dark-skinned Moorish-looking participants for the mock battles, the lighter-looking ones simply black up. That's something else you possibly wouldn't see in Birmingham!

Mojacar is the main resort of our Levante area of Almería province. It's really two separate towns - the charming original hilltop Pueblo (or village) with its Moorish arches and alleyways, and the sprawling low-rise seaside resort of Mojacar Playa. The Moors & Christians fiesta takes place in both towns. The mock battles take place on the beach, and the big parade takes place in the old Pueblo.

There is strong evidence that Walt Disney was born in Mojacar Pueblo to a dirt-poor Spanish family. When he was a baby he was adopted by an affluent American family. Sadly, Mojacar town hall doesn't consider this legend to be worth mentioning anywhere. You won't even find a photo of Walt Disney in Mojacar, or any suggestion of his connection to the area. The Andalucians are not strong on promotional skills, which is the reason why most folk have never heard of Mojacar. There is almost zero promotion of the place or the possible Walt Disney connection in the UK. It's highly unlikely that the Loch Ness Monster ever existed, but it never stopped the Scots from attracting tourists and making money selling toy monsters, t-shirts and boat trips.

Mojacar Pueblo is a real one-off. A walk through the town starts at the highly decorative Moorish fuente. This is a drinking water fountain with a washing area where women can still wash their clothes in the pure waters. Visitors can then wander up to the main square, the Plaza Nueva. From there they can walk through ancient Moorish arches and up and down alleyways, and to the site of the old castle right at the top of the village where the entire coastline can be viewed. There are traditional cafes and restaurants and hang on a minute, I'm not writing a tourist guide.

The Moors & Christians fiesta usually starts on the second Friday in June and finishes on the Sunday. On the Saturday night there are market stalls and several bands performing in every available inch of the Pueblo. There's a real party atmosphere and never any trouble. The last time we went up on the Saturday night, we left at 2-30am and there were still busloads of people arriving for the fiesta. There were signs at the bars that last orders were at 5-45am, so there was no need for them to rush....

The heart of the Moors & Christians fiesta is the Plaza Nueva. Parking is scarce up there, and unless the one-armed accordion player is around, the main source of entertainment on quiet days is to sit in one of the tapas bars watching illegally-parked cars being towed away by the local police.

Sunday is the day of the big parade which starts at the Plaza Nueva, and this would be our second year of witnessing the spectacle. In the afternoon Carrie and I wandered up to see what was happening. In the square was a medieval market. An Arabic band performed with reedy pipes, crashing cymbals and a sexy belly dancer. There was a stall with birds of prey, stalls selling trinkets and ceramics, stalls selling Moroccan bread and Turkish-type cakes, and tea-tents with hookah pipes.

Some friends had managed to book a big table at a restaurant a short distance down the hill from the main square. The restaurant overlooked the steep road on which the parade was to travel down. We had a lovely afternoon with a large bunch of our new friends, and the restaurant kept bringing platters of cold and hot tapas right through the afternoon.

The starting time of the big parade was advertised as 7pm, by which time the sun had lost much of its intensity and the participants were just starting to lug themselves up the hill to the square. The brass bands were having a real struggle - you try lugging a tuba up a steep hill in full uniform while puffing a fag!

Just before 7-30pm, we heard the sound of a brass band warming up. Sitting on the terrace overlooking the steep, narrow main road, we enjoyed the sight of the elder ladies of the village sashaying down the hill dressed in traditional Spanish dresses of many colours, followed by the village brass band thumping out a pasodoble. The band was followed by several unco-operative horses, their riders dressed in finery and puffing Spanish woodbine. The horses had left behind copious evidence of their presence - piles of it.

Next in the procession were young lads dressed in long flowing robes, then girls in long flowing dresses. We watched them march slowly downhill, swinging around wildly to avoid the large piles of horse poo.

At this point in the proceedings, there seemed to be some kind of hold-up further back up the hill. The participants in the parade marched on the spot, trying to give the impression of movement while looking around desperately. Perhaps one of the groups was late in arriving, which was highly probable. I checked the time on my watch, and the parade marked time for fourteen minutes until the procession eventually moved forward. Then a large group of men in long flowing brown and gold robes in Moorish designs sashayed down the hill. The organisers hadn't thought to employ someone with a bucket and shovel, so it was perhaps just as well that the bottom hems of their robes were brown.

More brass bands came down the hill, playing more minor-key pasodobles. Maybe it was the same tune, as they're all in the same tempo and to my Scottish ears they all tended to sound much the same. I well remember the time when a pianist friend had played a medley of nine Scottish reels to his mother. After he had finished after around five minutes, she made the well-meaning comment "That was a nice tune, son."

One brass band was different from the rest. They came down the hill in short-sleeved shirts, dressed for business. They had the benefit of a truly wonderful kettle-drum player, a young lanky lad whose sole mission in life was to thump his kettle drum as loud and as fast as humanly possible. Sometimes you'll come across a musician who exudes an air of total confidence in their ability which sets them apart from run-of-the-mill performers. There's a real buzz when this happens. This band had the added advantage of a swarthy, bear-like cymbal player who crashed his cymbals together enthusiastically. Every time he crashed them, the fag in his mouth would glow much brighter.

The Moors & Christians parade continued down the hill. A Spanish brass band would be followed by scantily-clad Arabic dancers. An acted-out mock battle would be followed by a local Spanish girls' dancing troup, followed by a float with birds of prey. There were fire-eaters and acrobats. The costumes were dazzling and magnificent, and the marching bands were terrific.

The parade lasted about two hours and finished just as the sun was fading. This event happens every June in Mojacar and it's a wonderful afternoon not to be missed.

Sammy is always delighted whenever a musician calls at the house, and there is often a musical instrument case to explore. Obviously, he has to check first that it's not a new litter tray! Imagine you're a new guest to our home. Once you're seated he'll give you the full feline welcome to his home, usually in this order:

1/ Jump onto your lap then rub his tail and backside in your face.

2/ Test if your clothes are suitable for kneading purposes. If satisfactory, he'll rub his nose into your face while drawing blood from your upper front body with his front paws.

3/ Jump up onto the back of your chair to inspect your hair for tasty nits or lice.

4/ Jump back down onto your lap and wash whichever of the more private parts of his body require urgent attention. If Sammy is relaxed enough to do his ablutions in your lap, it means that you've been accepted into his household.

5/ If he has now made a genuine connection with you, he'll pass wind from one end or the other, then close his eyes and settle down on your lap to await getting his ears scratched.

There are many cats in our village, including Sammy's sister Tina. She is the same pitch-black colour as Sammy. Sometimes she will pop into the house to check up on her brother. She'll just walk in, head for the food bowl, and get stuck in. She might stay for a couple of hours or a couple of days, then we won't see her until it's time for her next inspection.

Carrie and I had to go to Scotland for a few days on business and we had no choice but to put Sammy into a cattery while we were away. Our local vet had recommended a nearby 'Cat Hotel' which offered five star accommodation, albeit at a price to make a Scotsman's eyes water. Anyway, by now it was clear that Sammy was a Very Important Cat and we had to make absolutely sure that he was in safe hands.

We couldn't have made a better decision. After I had bundled Sammy into his travel box, I drove him to 'Kit Kat Luxury Suites' a few kilometers from our home. The owners met me at the main road and I followed their car up to the hotel and into a secure basement garage. Next door to the garage was a huge basement area, divided into rooms in which the cats resided during their stay.

We had used a cattery in Scotland many years ago and our ageing cat Eunice and her cat basket were put into a basic cage with a shelf. It was clear that Sammy was going to be enjoying a much superior standard of comfort. The cat rooms were actually bigger than those in some pricey hotels I've stayed at! Each cat room had a large sofa with cushions and rugs, an adventure playground, a scratching board, a box to jump in and out of, and several cat toys. The owners were clearly nuts about cats.

I noticed that there were a couple of large flat-screen TVs outside the cat rooms. A Disney type cartoon movie was playing. There was a large sofa in a corner with newspapers on it.

"We come down here for our morning and afternoon coffee," the lady owner told me. "We bring the papers down then play with the cats."

"And you clearly enjoy the cartoons on the telly."

"Oh, the TVs are not for us. They're for the cats." She replied.

I did a double take. The TV screens were certainly pointing in the direction of the cat rooms.

"Sammy will sometimes watch a wildlife programme but he's never seen any cartoons."

"Oh, the cats here love animated films," She explained. "Particularly Tom and Jerry cartoons. And they will lounge on the sofas to watch Disney and Pixar films. Benjy over there is watching 'Happy Feet'". Sure enough, a ginger tom reclining on the sofa did seem to have his eyes glued to the screen.

"Has Sammy seen 'Madagascar'?"

"Not as far as I know. Wait a minute, you're asking me if my cat has seen 'Madagascar'?"

"I planned to put it on the DVD player this afternoon, but if he's already seen it, I'll put on a different film."

It's not often that I'm speechless!

Needless to say, Sammy greatly enjoyed his stay. When I came back to take him home, he was spreadeagled on the sofa watching 'For the Birds' and had to be chased round his room several times before I could catch him and shovel him back into his travel box to his howls of protest. He didn't seem to want to leave his luxury suite.

He complained like hell when we got home, so I put 'Toy Story' on

106

the DVD player and that calmed him down.

There are several bird cages in our village, usually on the residents' terraces. We have a Spanish neighbour with an elderly parrot which she takes out for walks. That's to say, she does the walking, and as we live in a very hilly village, the parrot wisely perches on her shoulder.

We also have a donkey in our village (burro in Spanish) which is owned by an elderly Spaniard called Juan Pedro. One day, we were sitting on our terrace having lunch, when down the steep main road staggered this donkey with huge panniers either side, followed by a clearly inebriated Juan Pedro shouting "Burro, burro" and desperately trying to keep his donkey on the road while desperately trying to keep himself on the road.

Back to the music. It's always fun meeting new musicians.

At a gig a while ago, I met a singer/guitarist who has now become a good friend. He comes over to Almería with his delightful wife twice a year. He's only two weeks younger than me but he still has a boyish mop-top of hair, which makes me sick. He's very fit with a six-pack, wide shoulders and muscular arms, which makes me sick. He's a good singer and a brilliant guitarist, which makes me sick. He's a charming bloke with an enthusiasm for music and life, an electronics genius who also gives lectures on astronomy, which makes me even sicker. He's got a long and involved Polish first name and an even longer and more involved Polish surname Budyanzanynofski or something, but he's happy for everyone to save a great deal of their precious time by simply calling him Bud Martin.

Bud is one of the most hard-working musicians I know. He has his own band in Somerset; not that he really needs a band. He writes his own backing tracks from scratch, starting with drums. He plays and records these onto his computer using an electronic drum kit. Then he adds all the instruments – bass line, rhythm guitar, lead guitar, piano etc then often finishes a track off with harmony backing vocals. Like me, he's not a fan of karaoke backing tracks with a full orchestra including a string section. Bud's tracks are stripped-back with basic instrumentation which means they sound sharp and natural in performance, just like a live band.

An opportunity to work together on a gig came up a few months after the jam session. I was booked to perform with a lady singer at a house party to celebrate a golden wedding party for a charming couple called Peter and Angela who have a beautiful villa near Vera. I found out from Angela that Bud was coming - he had transferred some of the happy couple's old 8mm home movies to DVD. A projectionist had been booked to show the home movie compilation during the evening.

I got to the house early in the evening and set up my PA and piano. The lady singer arrived much later and although I had emailed her the set list well in advance, she hadn't sorted out her lyrics for the gig in the correct running order. Her memory was such that she needed lyrics in front of her, even for songs she had sung for years. She was still sorting them out when the music was due to start, so Bud gladly stepped in. He had already set up his electric guitar and backing tracks. He basically called out the key to me (G if you're interested), counted 1,2,3,4 and we were off with a Beach Boys song. We'd never performed together before, but Bud kinda suspected that I'd be capable of playing along with him. I even managed to add my own harmonies to the track.

Bud acted as conductor, and gave me superb guidance. He was a godsend at the gig. I was able to follow him on one song after another for around 20 minutes until the singer was able to start doing what she was booked to do.

After less than half an hour's music, it was announced that the home movie was about to be shown, after which the buffet would be served. We provided a microphone for the bride so she could relate the silent movie scenes to the audience. A few minutes before the DVD started, Bud came up to me.

"Jim, I've had an idea. Could you play some music to accompany the home movie DVD?"

"You mean there's no soundtrack?"

"No, there's not. I knew you were coming, so I thought you could play piano during the movie. You know that old-time tack piano sound you can get."

"You mean the honky-tonk sound like in the silent movies?" I asked.

"That's the one! That would be brilliant. It will be just like the silent movies. I'll prompt you on what's coming up. The whole movie is less than an hour long."

So there I was, sitting at my piano with my mouth open and my eyes peeled, with three minutes' notice that I was about to become the pianist for a silent movie for the first time in my life - and for a movie I'd never seen. At least there were only around fifty people present, so if I fell on my backside my reputation might not be too badly damaged.

The movie started with a wedding scene, and Bud stood beside me and called in my ear.

"This is the wedding, Jim."

I played 'Here Comes the Bride' while the bride of 50 years ago told the audience about the wedding. I thought to myself – this isn't too difficult, Jim.

The scene on the projector screen changed and Bud whispered in my ear. "The bridegroom was in the navy and got a naval salute from his comrades at the wedding."

I couldn't remember the Royal Navy march, so I played the old boy scout song 'Riding Along on the Crest of the Wave'. There were some puzzled looks from the audience.

Bud again. "The bride used to be in a dance troop."

A group of girl dancers appeared on the screen, and once again I had to think on my feet to find an appropriate tune to accompany the dancing. Perhaps there was a better song out there for a dance troop vintage 1960 than Bruce Springsteen's 'Dancing in the Dark' but that's what my memory came up with. Fortunately, the dancing soon changed to the 'Can Can' and I was back on safe ground.

The scene of the home movie changed again. Bud called in my ear, "They moved to Kenya in Africa."

Lions appeared on the projector screen. I couldn't quite remember the theme from 'Out of Africa' as all John Barry's movie themes are rather slow and similar, but I did manage 'Born Free' followed by 'The Lion Sleeps Tonight.' Tigers then appeared and of course what else could I come up with but that old African favourite – 'Tiger Feet' by Mud.

The scene changed again to what looked like a building site. Bud obliged. "They were having a new house built, Jim."

Okay, perhaps 'This Ole House' wasn't the most appropriate song as a musical background for a brand new house being built, but at least it was about a house. You try sitting at a piano and coming up with appropriate tunes from your memory banks at a few seconds' notice!

Cut to a scene of the bridegroom. He was a Royal Navy captain, resplendent in full naval uniform, being piped onto a rather smart ship. I couldn't really get away with playing the boy scout song again, so I racked my brains and started playing the only other naval tune I could think of. Sadly, this was not 'Anchors Aweigh' or any other stately march. The only other tune with a naval connection I could think of was the Village People's 'In the Navy'.

By the time I hit the chorus, at least half the audience turned their heads towards the piano and there was a distinct murmur. I'm sure there was stifled laughter, stifled because the buffet had yet to be served - some folk had come rather a long way and clearly didn't want to risk being chucked out of the party for making fun of their hosts while their stomachs were rumbling.

After quite a few more panic attacks on my part, the hour-long home movie finally came to a finish and the golden wedding bride announced "Would anyone like to see the movie again?" I'm sure she could hear my groans, and a few seconds later the projectionist started packing up.

The lady singer and I performed for another half hour or so until she announced that she was too hot and wanted a dip in the pool. Bud took over and we fired song after song while the dancing went on for another hour or so. I had played piano for well over three hours and the lady singer had done little more than an hour. She had arrived unprepared, hadn't helped in any way with the setting up or taking down of the sound equipment, and had performed rather less than Bud. But to keep the peace, I split the fee with her and that was the last time we ever worked together.

But they say "as one door closes" – this was the start of some great fun with my new mate Bud, who is a true professional to work with. We only do a few gigs each year, but when we perform together we have a lot of fun.

- - - - - - - - - - - -

On 23rd June we all celebrated the Night of San Juan by going down to the big party in Garrucha. San Juan is known to English-speaking people as St. John the Baptist, and in honour of this revered saint, hundreds of people go down to the beach and at midnight they baptise themselves to cleanse their bodies of evil spirits. Ok, most only get their feet wet, but several go all the way.

It's a magical night all about fire and water. There are bonfires along the beach, and when they die down, people jump over them. It's said that if you jump over a bonfire 3 times on the Night of San Juan, your problems will be burned away.

The event continues with a huge firework display, then a big showband entertains the crowd until the early hours while the bars dispense inexpensive drinks and tapas.

At the end of June we went to see a concert by a cracking choir consisting mainly of Brits. It was conducted by a brilliant choir-mistress. There is no way that a choir conductor can play piano and conduct at the same time - the result, sadly, is musical sloppiness. A choir requires a separate conductor and accompanist to sound tight and professional. Brendan had got me the job of playing piano for the choir the previous year. It involved reading some pieces of classical music, something I hadn't had to do since leaving school. My rustiness at sight-reading music made the work rather difficult for me. I had to practice for hours every day, only to find when I got to the choir rehearsals that it was bloody difficult for me to play the same pieces on the piano with a 30-strong choir in my right ear.

Eventually I sort of cracked it. The show was a great success, and I made several friends within the choir.

Thankfully, the choir had booked a different pianist for their summer show. Carrie and I went with friends to see the show at an auditorium about half an hour inland. It was a warm afternoon, and as the sun belted through the car windows, the air-con belted out refreshing cool air. When the show started, it was apparent to me that this time they had hired a proper pianist, a guy who looked relaxed and smiled broadly (unlike me) as he played all the right notes (unlike me) in the right order (unlike me).

It was an entertaining and professional show which included serious pieces of music and songs from the musicals. At the end of the show, the choir manager came up to the microphone to make an announcement.

"Ladies and gentlemen, thankyou for coming and we wish you a safe journey home. If you're not in a rush to get back, the Spanish people who run the hall have arranged for a fifteen-minute film to be shown. It's in English with Spanish sub-titles."

He walked off the stage, and we looked at each other. What was the film about? Carrie went over and asked him.

"Sorry, I've no idea. I was only told that it's a fifteen-minute film."

We decided that as it was half past four in the afternoon, and way too early to go for dinner, it was worth waiting behind to see this film. The setting up was certainly rather entertaining. Three Spanish señorinas and one Spanish hombre brought in a huge projector and screen, plus a DVD player and a black metal stand. The screen was erected, then the black metal stand was put in place. It was clear to all that the projector was too big and cumbersome to sit properly on this stand. Eventually, someone stood and held the projector in place on the stand to ensure it didn't fall off.

Meanwhile, one of the girls went up to a loudspeaker with a cable, and looked at it quizzically. The cable ran from the DVD player, but it was the wrong connection for the speaker. It was clear this was going to be a silent English-language film with Spanish subtitles.

By now it was nearly half an hour since the choir's show had finished. Several other people had also stayed behind in the hope of seeing this film, and there was still no sign of anything happening. The Spanish people who were organising the film would argue among themselves, then go away and come back again for more arguing. It was clear that they had not done any forward planning. They couldn't even find a power cable which was long enough to get the projector working.

Eventually, someone had the brilliant idea of moving the projector and screen closer to the power supply, and we were off. An out-of focus image appeared on the screen of a block of high-rise flats, then fuzzy pictures of a teenage schoolboy who clearly lived in one of the flats. There were Spanish subtitles to accompany this silent film, but they were too fuzzy to read properly.

Once the projector operator found the focus control, things improved greatly. It was clear that the schoolboy's name was Kyle, and he suffered from an embarrassing problem. Bed-wetting, to be precise. The film began by showing Kyle suffering taunts at school from other schoolchildren. Presumably they had rather more reliable bladders than Kyle.

The next scene showed him in a local shop in Ashburton, where he indulged in a spot of stealthy shoplifting. He was chased down the road by the shopkeeper. It wasn't clear what he had stolen until he got home and the shopkeeper arrived at his door to report the theft to Kyle's mother.

What followed was a conversation (silent, obviously) between Kyle and his mother, who opened up her son's coat to find the stolen item - a pack of nappies, obviously related to the bed-wetting. With this, the fifteen-minute film ended and the credits came up, followed by murmurs from the small remaining audience as they muttered "What the hell was that all about?" - "Was this what we waited all this time to see?"

We walked back to the car in the sunshine, giggling all the way and trying to figure out why the Spanish thought the Brits would have been at all interested in the film. Maybe they believed that people who go to choir concerts have children who suffer from bed-wetting. Maybe they just thought they were trying to be kind to us by showing an English-language film to English-speaking people. No matter, we had all been treated to a silent British public information film with Spanish sub-titles on teenage bed-wetting. It was just one of those days in Almería when stuff happens which you simply can't make up.

I'm still scratching my head.

It was nearing the end of June and I was doing a solo piano gig at a charming restaurant in Antas. The restaurant was run by a rather posh eccentric English lady called Lottie. She was (and I'm sure still is) rather rotund and jovial. She's now moved back to England.

I had played a few gigs for Lottie, and she liked the piano. Her ex-husband had been a pianist and she had followed his performances around Europe. Not everyone 'got' Lottie, but I did, and we rubbed along on well.

I'd had a good night, played lots of requests for the customers. After I'd finished playing and got my equipment packed up and into the car, I went over to the bar to collect my fee. After she passed it over, Lottie took an envelope out from under the bar.

"Jim, are you and your wife busy tomorrow night?" she asked.

"No, I don't have a gig. Why do you ask?"

"Would you like to take your wife to see the stones?" Lottie replied.

"Stones? What kind of stones?" I wondered if there was something in the area similar to Stonehenge.

"The Rolling Stones, you daft bugger! They're on at the stadium at El Ejido tomorrow night." She took the tickets out of the envelope and handed them over to me.

"Well, would you like the tickets?" asked Lottie with a big warm smile.

"Well, yessssss. Please. Crikey. Are you sure? The Stones! Bloody hell. Don't you want to go yourself?"

"I was going to go with my son, but he's had to go abroad for a few weeks, and I really don't want to go on my own." She explained. "You and your wife go. It's not really my cup of tea. I was only going to keep my son company."

"Don't you want to give them to friends, Lottie?"

"You're my friend, Jim. You always play out of your skin for me and my customers, and I've heard your boogie version of 'Honky-Tonk Women'. There's no-one I'd rather give the tickets to than you."

"Wow." I was really touched.

I offered her money. I offered to give her back my fee for playing the piano but she wasn't having it. I left the restaurant with the tickets, stunned and elated. I'd never seen the Stones and I'd never been to a stadium gig in my life.

I was offered the chance to see Rod Stewart at Glasgow's Hampden Park stadium one June a few years back, but a friend went and got pleurisy after getting soaked to the skin. Outdoor shows were always chancy in Glasgow. When we went to see Tony Bennett in George Square at the Glasgow Jazz festival one June, we could hardly see him for the rain. We had great difficulty hearing him too, due to the patter of rain on the audience's umbrellas.

Like all babyboomers, I had lived most of my life with the Stones and the Beatles. I well remember when 'Paint It Black' came out. It was 1966 and I was below deck with some friends in a Clyde steamer at the Riverboat Shuffle disco. There was an announcement that they were going to play the new Rolling Stones single, and the place was jumping to that jungle beat. The record went down so well that basically it was played about every second song. The Stones made great records for dancing. Their songs were a huge influence on me and more than a few others.

The Stones gig was at El Ejido, a big town a fair bit past Almería city. The town is the production centre for the fruit and vegetables grown in the thousands of polythene greenhouses in southern Almería province.

The next afternoon, Carrie and I ambled down in the old Mercedes. The sun shimmered on the sea as we passed Almería city, and the sun shimmered on the polythene greenhouses when we were in the vicinity of El Ejido.

We arrived early and parked the car remarkably near the stadium.

As we walked towards the stadium, we could see several stretch limos arriving and a helicopter landing. We went to the turnstile, handed over our tickets, and in return we received two vouchers for complimentary cups of gazpacho. Only in Spain! We had to finish our gazpacho before we were allowed in to the stadium. What struck me as we entered was the number of young people who had come to see the old rockers. The kids were laughing and happy, and they all had group photos taken whenever they arrived. I took photos for several of the groups, and there was a really good-natured atmosphere in the stadium.

The Stones were due on at 10-30pm, when it would be cooler. Before then, there were a couple of decent Spanish bands and an unremittingly loud Australian group called Jet who screamed and thumped away for a solid hour. There was absolutely no light and shade in their act. I nearly dropped off. Mind you, I saw the disgraced Gary Glitter many years ago and although he was loud, I slept though most of his show because of the sheer boredom of the music. I also slept through most of the first and second halves of 'Cats' as I was bored witless by the lack of any story and all that hammy prancing about. I seem to have a low boredom threshold and I tend to nod off unless I'm decently entertained.

Sorry, I digress.

Came the hour and we could sense the anticipation in the stadium. At one end of the stadium a set had been built which looked like the frontage of a hotel, plus walkways either side of the stage for Mick Jagger to run on plus a bridge device to take the band into the audience.

The lights dimmed, there was no long introduction, just the first chords of 'Start Me Up' then lights up and there's the Stones on stage. A huge cheer from the audience as Jagger strutted his stuff and pumped out the song. Keith Richards and Ron Wood were not exactly strutting. They were both hunched over their guitars, and didn't move much all night.

I don't know how many miles Mick Jagger ran that night, but it must have been a lot. The audience were ecstatic, as he was on top form. We were seated at the opposite end of the stage, so it was just as well there were huge TV screens above the stage, or we wouldn't have known who was performing. But the band did come out to the audience in their bridge device to do their more intimate songs. Now we could see them more clearly, although thankfully they weren't close enough for us to see their wrinkles.

It was a wonderful, memorable evening in the warmth of an Andalucian summer's night, seeing some of my boyhood heroes live on stage. The following week I brought Lottie a big bouquet of flowers for donating the tickets. It was the least I could do.

As a contrast to this huge stadium gig, I was also at the World's Smallest Gig.

We have a friend called Emma whom we met when she was the live-in girlfriend of Juan José, my local Spanish friend. She's a very attractive fun-loving lady in her fifties, with good teeth and auburn hair. Emma is to be seen at local bars when music is on and she's always the first to get up and dance.

Juan José had invited us to an end-of-season party at the local flamenco show. What we didn't know was that he insisted on paying for us. Juan José wouldn't take a centimo for the night's entertainment. The generosity of the Spanish people down here never ceases to touch me.

At the end of the evening, Emma told us that she was remaining friends with Juan José, but that she had moved back to the village where she owned a house. It was a bit off the beaten track, about half-an hour inland and nowhere near any large towns. She invited Carrie and me to come to her village one Friday night to hear a singer at her local bar.

So a date was arranged, and Carrie and I set off one Friday night with our new friend Matt and his Spanish girlfriend Gloria to find Abanilla village. Emma had told us not to drive right into the village as there was no parking available due to the narrow streets. She asked us to phone her when we were at the car park on the outskirts of the village, and she walk down to meet us and take us to the bar. So we duly parked up as instructed, and phoned Emma. Minutes later she came sashaying along the road to meet us.

We all walked up to the village, past the small village square, until we came to a house with wrought iron bars padlocked around the front door.

"Maybe I should tell you all. This is not an official bar," said Emma with a wicked wink.

She rang the doorbell. The door opened and a large chap appeared at the door to check us out.

"It's ok, Mike, these are my friends," said Emma.

Mike went back inside then returned with the key to a large padlock. He unlocked the wrought-iron grilles and we all went inside. Then Mike locked us in by securing the grilles. I asked Emma what was happening.

"They don't have a licence, so they have to be careful if the local police come around."

It turned out that Emma had pre-paid some euros as a 'float' to the bar, which covered us for our drinks. We were shown into the house, past a bedroom on the left and another bedroom on the right, and into the kitchen where a few folk had gathered. Beyond the kitchen was another room about 14 feet long by 8 feet wide. It had once served as a spare bedroom, but had since been promoted to being the local bar, in the absence of any other bar in the village.

As we entered the small room, we could see the drinks bar just beyond the door. At the other end of the room was a rather curvaceous karaoke singer called Kate with a huge PA system and a radio microphone. She was the partner of Mike who was running the bar.

I was given a beer and sat down on the only free seat with my right ear within a few inches of a large floor-mounted cooling fan. The room was so narrow that I had to sit with my feet tucked under my chair, so that people could walk past me. Not that there was space for a lot of people - I counted fourteen of us in total, and the room was crammed at that.

Kate the karaoke singer tested her microphone then put on a karaoke backing track and launched into an ear-splitting rendition of 'Simply the Best'.

My friend Matt was sitting next to me and immediately put his hands over his ears. From reading his lips, I reckon it was "Jesus Christ!" that he shouted, but I couldn't hear a thing for the deafening sound coming from the 500-watt PA system.

We were treated to a selection of songs from the past, delivered with great gusto at high volume in this small room. On 'Hi Ho Silver Lining', Kate took her radio mike out to her audience to invite some of us to join in the chorus.

At the end of her gig, she chatted to her audience and enquired if any of us required any baby lambs. As it happened, a local farmer had 89 lambs ready for slaughter, and we were told they'd be great for the barbecue. The Stones never offered us this at their gig. I declined the baby lambs, but perked up my ears when I heard that wild boar were also available.

Wild boar are plentiful in our area. One Sunday I was driving Carrie up to Lubrin market when she told me to watch out for the dog walking up the road verge. I slowed down, and when the beast turned round to look at us, the tusks were the giveaway that it was definitely not a dog.

I nearly ran over a huge hairy male boar one night, driving home from a gig. The beast was making its way back up the hill from the reservoir, had just worked its way onto the road at the same time as my car rounded a bend. I caught the huge image out of the corner of my eye, swiftly swerved at the same time as the boar backtracked, and we

117

miraculously avoided contact.

Then one Saturday night, Carrie and I were driving through the campo road to see a band at a local bar, when I saw a shadow out of the right corner of my eye. I slammed on the brakes just in time for a mother and her five little piglets to cross the road. They took their time, and once her babies were safely across, the mother grunted (in appreciation of my patience, obviously) then went to join her offspring.

Carrie shook her head and muttered something about Almería being different from Glasgow on a Saturday night.

CHAPTER 7 - JULY

Life in Spain is so different from our previous life in Scotland. We had lived in a rain belt near the Clyde Valley, and it seemed that most days of the year the roads and pavements were damp or wet. We'd wake up to a carpet of grey around us. I've always thought of grey as Scotland's national colour. You'll see entire council estates of grey houses with a horrible grey roughcast finish, necessary to prevent the rain from gradually destroying the bricks. And so many of the people were grey, lifeless characters, hardened by the gloomy weather. It's not hard to see why there are so many anti-social problems in Scotland, and I speak from experience as my wife and I rent out property in the Glasgow area.

On the other hand, the Scots are generally a kind people. Maybe it's because we have to dig deep into our pockets to disprove the notion that we're a mean race. And Scots have a pithy sense of humour (wishful thinking for your author).

Unlike our mornings in Scotland, we waken up most days in Almería to glorious sunshine. The province is said to have between 300 and 320 days of sunshine per year, depending on who you want to believe. We do get proper rain, and like any true Scot, I know what proper rain looks like. We live in a hilly village and although we're in

119

the driest climate in Europe, when it does rain here, it can cascade like a waterfall down our road.

It's a fairly steep climb up to the village's main street, and it can take a bit of time to get to the shops and bars, depending on who you meet on the way. People will give you the time of day here. They'll stand and chat until thirst takes over, which it swiftly does on a hot summer's day.

The size of Bédar's population is virtually identical to our old village in Scotland. When we left Scotland there was one pub restaurant and one tiny grocery shop in an extension of a villager's house. Our village in Spain, on the other hand, has five bar/restaurants, a supermarket like an Aladdin's cave, a tobacconist shop, a bank, a chemist, a hairdresser, a bakery and a small fish shop. There's also our small Wednesday market.

The bar/restaurants often have music acts at weekends. On summer nights I'll often sit at a table outside a bar with friends until very late, just chilling and listening to a band.

Walking back down to the house after a night out in the village is magical. Children will be out playing happily in the lanes. Some old men may be sitting on the church steps discussing politics in very loud voices, some ladies might be sitting near the statue to the miners, just chatting and taking in the amazing view of the coastline at night. All is peaceful, and the troubles of the world can be forgotten until the morning.

In a nearby town there's a supermarket as unlike a smart, colour-coded Tesco as you're likely to find anywhere on the planet. It sells everything from Indonesian sauces to rocking chairs – and from comedy beach shorts to pig's willies. The meat counter has excellent pork, but I always seem to turn up when the butcher is either outside the front door having a sly fag or hiding in the back shop, I suspect doing unspeakable things to dead sheep!

The tills at this shop are often manned by three mature senoras who are collectively known as the 'Sisters Glum'. These three totally disinterested women are often incapable of uttering a cheery "hola" to their customers as they attempt to scan their purchases before shrugging then slowly punching the numbers into the till. They have done you a favour turning up for work, so why would you expect them to be pleased to get your business?

The shopper in front of you in this supermarket is fairly likely to be a Spanish lady with mahogany cuprinol hair and a purse bulging with small change which will be emptied onto the counter over a period of several minutes. During this time the till operator will be holding conversations with someone about to enter the store while arguing with another member of staff over the price of a jar of olives, then shouting across the aisle for change from the nearest Sister Glum.

And woe betide any holidaymaker who tries to work out the price of any item in the freezer. The crazy system used by lesser supermarkets of having price tags next to the products in the freezer has been rejected in favour of the far superior method of having dozens of price tags all together at the end of the freezer isle. The shopper gets to enjoy an entertaining half hour attempting to link one of the dozens of price tags with the item for sale in the freezer. On the upside, the deli counter is run by a cheery and attractive girl who wears a Victorian style outfit, rather similar to what you'd expect a grocer's assistant to have worn around the time of the Boer War.

Supermarkets have all but killed local shops in the UK but they don't rule here in Spain. The folk around here use their town's weekly market to buy everything from fresh fruit and veg to underwear, from olive oil to shoes, from beer glasses to dried fish. The major supermarkets (apart from Lidl) are never overcrowded, and even on Christmas Eve they're not queued out.

The main supermarket in Spain is Mercadona. This supermarket chain spends absolutely nothing on advertising and uses social media like Facebook to promote its goods. There are no huge hoardings directing traffic to their stores, so their supermarkets can be tricky for new visitors to find. There are no 2-for-1 offers, so the colossal waste caused by these offers does not exist. They have long dispensed with unnecessary packaging. Their prices are kept low and the quality is kept high. Mercadona made over 500 million euros profit in 2012. Compare that with the bombardment of advertising by UK supermarkets.

Shopping in general is not a leisure pursuit around here. People spend much more time outdoors and socializing with friends. The weather helps.

Truth be told, when we go to the Friday market in Turre, we often spend more in the tapas bars than we do at the vegetable stalls. Everything here is sold by the kilo, from tomatoes to garlic. The markets have to close by 2pm, and we sometimes go late to the market when some of the stallholders do 'euro bags' of their

121

remaining stock - maybe a kilo or more of red peppers or half a kilo of garlic for a euro.

Most of the vegetables we buy here are sourced from the major growing area further south near Almería city, less than an hour down the motorway. For those buying Spanish tomatoes in the UK, chances are they'll have come from down there. Vegetables are grown in our area too, but in nothing like the same quantity as in the south of the province. As for fruit, the fields are groaning with cultivated olive trees and orange trees, and figs grow wild all over the place.

I believe that it's built into the Spanish constitution that any person can go onto unfenced land and pick two pieces of fruit. The Spanish will never let you go hungry, as evidenced by the quantities of food they serve up at the restaurants, especially the rural ones. However, getting money out of the Spanish can be quite another thing entirely. I think they may use the same pocket designers as the Scots....

- - - - - - - - - - - -

It was a warm and peaceful Saturday morning. I was deep in dreams of Kylie and me on our regular weekend visit to the Ann Summers shop in East Kilbride when the phone rang unreasonably early. At 9-25am to be precise. I groaned loudly and got up grudgingly, expecting some emergency in the UK which needed our urgent attention. It was Danny, a local sax player, asking if I could play a jazz gig on the playa the following afternoon. Being the new 'kid' in town, I happily agreed.

"It's a last minute booking. Another band had to pull out," explained Danny. "Our drummer has had to go to the UK, but he gave me a phone number for another drummer called Alec. He can do the gig. Only thing is, he doesn't have a car, so he needs a lift. He lives in Los Gallardos, and it's on your way to the gig. Could you pick him up, Jim?"

"Okay, but I'll have my piano and amps, so I don't know if the drums will fit in my car."

"Oh, don't worry, we'll use my PA system, so all you need is your piano. Alec says he doesn't have a big kit. I'm sure it'll fit in fine. Anyway, he's a fellow countryman of yours, so you'll have something in common."

So I phoned Alec and arranged to collect him and his drum kit on my way down to the playa.

"It's only a small kit. I don't use big tom-toms," Alec explained. "Let me tell you, son, ma faither was the first drummer in Scotland to use a hi-hat cymbal. It was back in the thirties, before these London pricks knew anything about hi-hats. I'm a chip off the old block. I've played all over Scotland, mainly with accordion bands, like. Barn dances, that sort of thing. But I can play in any style. In the seventies I was regarded as the best drummer in Clackmannanshire, no question. I moved to Spain two years ago for my legs. I just don't have transport."

So, the following afternoon I picked Alec up - not from his house, but from the pavement outside. As I drove up, Alec looked to be in his later years. He seemed a rather shrunken figure - stick thin, just over five foot high and with a pronounced stoop. His straggly white hair looked like it hadn't been near a barber for months. It partly hid a leathery face with only a few yellowed lower teeth remaining. He sported a luminescent yellow and black check sports jacket. He greeted me with an "Aye, aye, Jimmy". His attempt at a smile was rather frightening, and set me back on my heels. I offered my own greeting with as much nonchalance as I could muster.

Alec had laid out his collection of drums on the pavement. It was a colourful sight. The snare was light blue, one tom-tom was black, the bass drum was a yucky fluorescent red and the cymbals were grey rather than the usual gold colour. We piled them into my car, which now resembled a Chinese pound shop. Oh well, I thought, at least he's experienced.

"You'll no' be disappointed, son," he reassured me in the car. "I've played all over the UK. I'm the man for the job, aye. I played all through the fifties, sixties and seventies, and just got fed up with it. I can play anythin', but I dinnae like playin' jazz."

"Oh, dear!" I mouthed. I told him it was a jazz gig.

He turned to me, and I turned my head away quickly to avoid being gassed by his rampant halitosis, enhanced by alcohol fumes. "Oh, dinnae worry, son, it'll be fine. Aye, aye. I've played all over the UK. Listen, ma faither was the first drummer in Scotland to use a hi-hat. It was back in the thirties."

I reminded him that he had already told me all this on the phone, to which he sniffed and grunted.

"You'll no' be disappointed, laddie," he continued. "I've played drums since just after the war. Started when I was twelve and had my first band in 1946 when I was in my teens. All the women were hot for me then." I did a quick tally and worked out that Alec was a fair bit over eighty. Oh great.

I made polite conversation on the way to the gig.

"What brought you here, Alec?" I asked.

No reply. I repeated myself, louder this time.

"What brought you to Spain, Alec?"

"The pain's no' bad today, son," he replied. "I get it in my legs mainly, but it's no' too bad today. Let me tell ye, it was a lot worse in Scotland, with the cold an' rain. Aye."

We got to the gig, unloaded the car, and Alec started to set up his drum kit. He set up his drum stool at a rather low height. It's vital that a drummer sits level to play the drums. According to musicians who play real musical instruments, it's easy to tell when a drummer is sitting level - he'll drool out of both sides of his mouth...

Some time later Alec was ready to play - a small, wizened bloke the wrong side of 80, his backside on a stool barely above ground level, hidden behind a myriad collection of tatty multi-coloured drums and ancient cymbals. I'd no idea how he would manage to reach them all.

The rest of the band appeared and we did a sound check. They all introduced themselves. Danny was on sax, and there was a bass player and a guitarist, plus Alec on drums and me on piano.

We got ready to play the first number. I was asked to play the intro to a bossa nova tune called 'Blue Bossa', a short repetitive tune so terminally dull that it wouldn't make a TV show about sewing. I counted the band in, and the music started, but for the first couple of minutes there were no drums. Then halfway through the second chorus, there came a cacophony of sound from the wizened old figure behind the drums, much like the sound of a Transit van unloading a discarded kitchen into a skip.

We all looked at each other, clearly surprised that Alec's modest height and great age belied his ability to hit the cymbals full-on. His technique was to raise his arm high in the air and whack a cymbal, then catch another drum on the way down. Killing two birds with one drumstick, I suppose. Alec certainly gave value for money in terms of the number of drums he hit - it was just a pity he didn't hit many in time with the band. He might have had a lighter touch if he had been wearing his hearing aid, which he'd forgotten to bring.

The next tune was the old Duke Ellington classic 'Satin Doll'. Once again, I was asked to set the tempo and play the intro. The music started without drums, and it was only after the second verse that Alec joined in. He played at the same volume throughout, blissfully unaware of the musicians' solos. Unfortunately, he didn't play at the same tempo throughout, and had a tendency to 'race' - to speed up the tempo. Occasionally I had to thump my hand on top of the piano to show him the tempo the rest of us were playing at.

The tune eventually ground to a halt ten minutes later, after some long solos. I approached Alec as tactfully as I could.

"Alec, don't you want to start the drums with the band?"

"What'd you say, son?"

"I said don't you want to start playing the drums when the band starts?"

"Eh?"

"It's the usual thing for drummers to do."

"I don't hear too well, Tim, and I need to wait until I get the beat." He looked rather puzzled. "There's no point in me starting the drums if I don't know the beat."

I couldn't argue with that. "Don't worry," I said "The next tune is a bossa nova".

"What's that?"

"A bossa nova," I said again, louder.

"What's that?" Alec repeated.

"Like the first tune," I explained

"What was that?"

"It was called 'Blue Bossa'. The clue's in the name. It was a bossa nova." I explained again. Alec couldn't remember, so I played him a snatch on my piano.

"Oh, that. I thought it was a sort of rumba. It was definitely a latin beat. Was it a Roy Orbison song?" I could see that there was no point in me taking this conversation any further, and I was aware of a dreadful sinking feeling. I only wished I was on Roy Orbison's Blue Bayou rather than have to struggle through the rest of the gig.

Alec's drumming continued on the same skip-loading basis until the break, when he managed to cadge a glass or two of wine from the audience. The second set was a lot better than the first, only in the sense that Alec was rather subdued by the alcohol. That allowed the other musicians to be heard.

An hour or so later, the gig eventually shuddered to a halt. Alec went back to the audience to cadge more wine. By now he was too pissed to be of much use, so the rest of the band helped dismantle his kit and shovel it back into my car. As I drove him back to his flat, he nodded off to sleep and snored loudly in much more regular time than he could play the sodding drums.

Alec went back to the UK permanently a few months later. Perhaps he still plays his drums. Hopefully at care homes for the deaf.

The job of a drummer is to set and keep the beat and enhance the music. If you ever get a chance to see a video of the Buddy Rich Band, you'll see what I mean. The late Buddy Rich was arguably the best drummer the world has ever produced. His persona was the basis for "Animal" on the Muppet Show.

Buddy Rich was a perfectionist, and perhaps not your ideal dinner guest. He was not loved by his fellow musicians and he famously dissed Dusty Springfield after working on the same bill as her. When asked for his opinion of the then 10-year old Little Jimmy Osmond, he said "I'd like to stand on his face". After a long and great career, he died in 1989.

Legend has it that a former saxophone player from his band phoned his widow a few days after he had died and asked to speak to Buddy.

"I'm sorry, Buddy passed away on Thursday." she told him.

"Ok. Thanks for that."

The sax player phoned back a few minutes later and asked to speak to Buddy.

"I told you. Buddy is dead."

"Oh, thanks for that."

He phoned again a few minutes later and asked to speak to Buddy.

"Look, I've already told you twice that Buddy is dead. What's your problem?"

"I've no problem," he replied "I just enjoy hearing you say that he's dead."

Ok, maybe Buddy Rich wasn't the best loved musician, but at least he could keep time.

There was a drummer down in Almería with the opposite problem to Alec. Chuck was a laid-back hippie with a goatee beard and ponytail who hailed from Florida. I once asked him how he had ended up in the Almería area. He was such a laid-back character and took such pedantic care over the details that I very quickly lost all interest in his story. So I'm afraid I can't tell you how he got here. It's possible he was deported for being too dull.

I played with him at a jazz gig down on the playa one Saturday afternoon. At jazz gigs, the musicians all get a chance to "do a solo". For some reason, this was a six-piece band - five musicians plus a generously-proportioned lady singer. The singer would sing a song, then every instrument would do a solo on the song. Then the singer would return to sing the song again and the whole thing would eventually grind to a halt. If the song took two minutes to sing, this meant that it was followed by ten minutes of jazz solos plus another two minutes of the reprise of the song. Terminally dull doesn't even begin to describe it. It's a sad fact that much of the live jazz you hear consists mainly of opportunities for self-indulgence on the part of the musicians, with no thought for the audience being bored out of their skulls with interminable and meandering solos.

At this particular gig, time stood still while the guitarist, bass, drummer etc all took solos. But there was this amazing trumpet player on the gig, a young Spanish lad called José. He couldn't speak English and my Spanish didn't yet extend much beyond "Hola". But through the medium of music, we managed to communicate with absolutely no problem. When José played a solo, I could hear that he liked to start quietly and build up to a climax, so I egged him on by giving him percussive chords and cranking up my piano's volume. He loved this, and his playing just soared.

Meanwhile, Chuck was blissfully unaware of any change in the dynamics of the music. He diddled about with the brushes. These make a much quieter sound than wooden drumsticks. He stayed safely out of the way of any excitement.

He was asked to do a drum solo in one number. The band had all stopped and were waiting for his solo, while Chuck simply carried on keeping time on the drums and looked at us quizzically. So the bass player yelled "Drum solo" and Chuck obliged by hitting his cymbals for a few seconds then looking at the bass player, waiting for the band to start up again.

During the second set, I asked if I could play a boogie, as an antidote to the usual repertoire of 'Summertime', 'Fly me to the Moon', 'Blue Bossa' etc. Unfortunately, boogie was not considered part of the jazz repertoire, and the bass player asked if I had the chords. When I explained that it was simply a fast 12-bar blues, I was allowed to commence boogieing.

Chuck asked me "What do you want me to do? I've never played a boogie before."

I said "Use your sticks and follow me."

"I prefer using my brushes. Sticks might be too loud."

"Just follow me, Chuck. Let's do a bit of damage."

The audience had been lulled into a sort of trance, and they hadn't been expecting anything as lively as a boogie. When I started playing, they looked around at one another as if to say "What's going on?" Then someone in the audience started clapping in time to the music. Then most of the audience started clapping in time to the music, and I heard some whoops. The place had come alive thanks to what Jools Holland calls "The Power of the Boogie".

I signalled to José to play a chorus or two, and he just soared, so I powered along and called "Arriba" for him to go higher. When he couldn't play any higher he bowed out and got a huge cheer at the end of his solo.

The only problem was that Chuck hadn't come alive. In fact, he'd started slowing down and dragged my boogie slower and slower with him. Eventually, at the end of one chorus I signalled for the band to stop playing, then I re-started the boogie at the original tempo. I figured two more choruses would do it, as the drummer wouldn't get a chance to slow down too much within that time. Job done, and we got enthusiastic appreciation from the audience for our performance - much to the astonishment of the rest of the band.

The singer announced the next song – 'Summertime'. Normal service had been resumed and the audience settled back down again.

Chuck the Drummer. Oh yes, I was sorely tempted that day.

Our new cat Sammy, when he wasn't nagging, eating or racing towards his bowl, still seemed a bit dull and restrained, as if he was pining for something. He'd had the 'operation' so he couldn't be pining for female company. Carrie thought perhaps he needed some toys, so we visited a local shop and bought a nice soft basket and a few cat toys.

That night we presented the toys to Sammy. He wasn't at all impressed with the blue tinkling ball, he seemed scared of the hard green ball, and he dismissed the toy white mouse as a total con, looking up at me as if to say "You must be joking, pal". The only pastime which really floated his boat was disembowelling plastic supermarket bags, and our lounge floor was often covered in debris from his attacks. Sammy would hide behind a table, go into the panther position, yell "brooop", leap up in the air and launch his attack on an innocent plastic carrier bag.

Then Carrie's sisters came for a week's holiday. Her eldest sister is a cat person, and in the 1980s she kept a tabby at her home in Glasgow. She loved her tabby, despite the fact that it hated every other human being on earth with a passion. I once went over to pat the creature, but it went into the attack position then hissed and spat at me. It did the same when we visited the house with our then-young boys. It would just sit in a corner and hiss at us, mouthing "Sod off back where you came from" in cat-speak. In feline terms, it was the devil incarnate - an ugly, evil, foul-tempered, hissing, cantankerous, vicious, loathsome, anti-social feral beast. Carrie's sister named it Cindy.

In her luggage, her sister had packed a bouncy cat ball, with the clear intention of having some fun with Sammy. The only problem was, Sammy didn't know how to play. It was clear that his previous owner had never bought him a ball.

On the second day of their visit, Carrie's sisters kicked the ball about the lounge floor, while Sammy sat and watched the ball, clearly unimpressed and wondering what this was all about. Then Carrie got up and bounced the ball on the floor to see how high it would bounce. As it bounced several feet in the air, there came a loud cry and a scrabbling of paws, as Sammy jumped into the air and whacked his paws down onto the ball, like Peter Schmeichel deflecting a ball away from the goal-mouth.

From that point on, Sammy took up football seriously. He would catch the ball and wrestle it to the floor. When he missed the ball, he would scurry after it, skidding around on the laminate flooring and crashing into the furniture, oblivious to everything except his quarry. He would try to get up speed to scurry after the ball, scrabbling his paws fifteen to the dozen on the shiny laminate flooring, while growling and manically displaying his teeth.

Now that Sammy knew how to play, he made up his own games involving (among other pursuits) kicking bottle tops, tearing up newspapers, skiting pens along the floor, or hiding in a box then jumping out. But his favourite game was ambushing Carrie as she came into the lounge by jumping on her feet then scrabbling away from her as fast as he could, shouting "rrrooop" in the process.

Sammy was turning out to be a real character, and bright as a button. He once sat on the floor and watched an entire David Attenborough programme, mainly about tigers, from start to finish. This is something my lady wife has never been able to do - she finds

Mr Attenborough's voice so melliflous and restful that she has usually nodded off after ten minutes or so.

One day, Sammy was in the kitchen having his five o'clock snack before dinner (this followed his breakfast, his elevenses, his lunch and his mid-afternoon snack). After he had finished his nosh, he stood on the kitchen floor, declared "Rrroop", jumped two feet in the air then galloped the forty feet or so from the kitchen onto the sofa at the front window. He took a 30-second break then launched himself back off the sofa back into the kitchen where, clearly depleted by his efforts, he wailed for more food. When more food was not forthcoming, he rolled over on his back and produced a pathetic little wail.

Sammy became increasingly playful, and eventually made good friends with the white toy mouse. He would toss it in the air at regular intervals, just for something to do. He seemed to be a really intelligent cat. He picked up on our conversations around the house, and certain words seemed to attract his attention. He figured out what 'chicken' meant fairly quickly, and he could hear the fridge door being opened from upstairs.

One night when it was time for a nightcap, Carrie was sitting in the lounge watching TV with Sammy sound asleep on her lap, and I was in the kitchen removing the last vestiges of chutney from a cooking pot. I went into the lounge to offer Carrie a gin and tonic. I had got as far as "Do you want....." when Sammy looked up and howled "AAAWWWWWWW". He could now understand a bit too much for my liking. It was impossible for either of us to say "Do you want?" within earshot of Sammy without getting an immediate response. He knew it usually involved something nice to eat.

One of his favourite tricks is to visit the downstairs toilet which is up some steps behind our kitchen. He sometimes pops in there for a sly drink from the loo, because it obviously tastes better than the filtered water in his bowl. We'll be working away in the kitchen, then suddenly we'll hear this scrabbling of paws. Sammy will come belting out of the toilet down the stairs and rush past us with a triumphant "Brrrrrrrrroooooooop". He'll then pick up speed as he reaches the lounge, then a second or two later we'll hear the thud as he skids on the laminate flooring into the TV cabinet. We'll hear a muffled feline curse, then he'll nonchalantly lick his sore bits. He never seems to remember that laminate flooring is not the best surface for braking.

From the subject of cats to the subject of cars. It seems that if you want to perform as a musician around here, you should drive an old Peugeot. I don't conform to this principle, but just about every other performer has an ancient Peugeot. They're invariably white, to reflect the sun's rays from the equipment inside, and in various states of decrepitude. You can recognise a musician's Peugeot by the dents around the boot area, where the driver's aim of chucking an amplifier into the boot in a dark car park after a gig has not always been totally accurate.

Miguel Alfonzo had an ancient Peugeot in the worst state of disrepair of them all. The poor vehicle had door trims missing, never saw a car wash from one year to the next, and only ever had the one wheel trim. Architects could have used the dust-encrusted rear window to draft out projects. You always knew when Miguel was around. The creak from the suspension and the whine from the brakes gave it away.

The Mojacar area is still a target for hippies, and Miguel was the hippies' hippie. Spanish by birth, he spent his early years in Southern California, and came out to Almería in the late seventies to chill out and play his music around our Levante area. Miguel was tall and swarthy with a drooping moustache and matted greying hair tied at the back in a ponytail. He was charming and exotic and full of Californian bull. He was never without a hand-rolled cigarette of some herbal substance, and he always exuded a rather exotic aroma. You only had to walk up to Miguel and sniff him to feel relaxed.

Miguel's game plan at gigs was to get someone to set up his PA system, then he'd pick a harmonica, grab a guitar, a chair and a glass of red wine. After around ten minutes of tuning up and testing his sound, he'd start his gig.

"Good afternoon friends, buenos tardes amigos. Thankyou so much for making the effort to come here today. Please, chill out, have a drink or two, have a smoke or three if that's your bag, just rest your bones and enjoy the music." Miguel was just getting warmed to his hippie-speak. "We are truly blessed to be in this wonderful place on this glorious afternoon. We have the sun, we have our friends, we have the music, we can be at peace with the world. There are so many troubles in the world, but God has brought us all together today to chill out to the music. Bless you all, thankyou for coming."

The Messiah himself couldn't have put it better. Personally, I'm no good at talking hippie. God knows I've tried, but I just can't bring myself to call the plumber "dude" or call my wife "babe".

Miguel would start strumming some chords on his guitar for a minute or so to set the mood, before starting a slow, doleful song. One of his favourites to start his act was 'Everybody's Talking', Fred Neill's song from the 'Midnight Cowboy' movie. I've always found this song unspeakably boring, and when played at half the original speed it's inclined to send me into a coma. Miguel's version included a long meandering harmonica solo based on just two notes. Even Bob Dylan could have done better. From start to eventual finish the song lasted around seven minutes. There would be a smattering of polite applause for this non-event.

Then he would take a break before launching into a doleful hippie classic like Neil Young's 'Old Man', or a slow blues like 'Stormy Monday'. He never opened his lungs, never stretched himself at all, he just crooned away in a cracked but mellow voice.

I had first met Miguel at a Sunday night jam session in a bar at a one-bar village up the mountain. I was told that the bar was at the end of a dirt track, and that the best way to find it was to come to the village a little while after the start time and listen for the sound of music. So on the Sunday night of the jam, I put my piano in the boot of my old Mercedes, picked up some friends and headed up the mountain.

After half an hour of twisting road thousands of feet up, the road dropped down and landed us at El Pilar village. As instructed, I stopped the car, turned the engine off, and stood to listen out for the music. Two minutes later my friends and I were unloading the car at the end of the dirt track.

The bar seemed tiny as we walked through, with room for maybe a dozen souls in the actual bar, but only four or five drinkers. We walked past a back room which opened onto a huge terrace. There were around a dozen tables on one side of the terrace, buzzing with folk who'd come for the jam, and no less than eleven performers across on the raised performance area. The only lighting I could see was from the odd music stand lamp and an ancient standard lamp. I started to set up my piano in the half-light and not for the first time cursed the fact that I had an instrument with a black body and black buttons for the sound settings - a sick joke by the manufacturers of keyboard instruments.

A fellow with a guitar and a music stand with the words and chords to songs was standing at the microphone singing Bob Marley's

'Waiting in Vain'. This song has only two chords repeated throughout. It's surely one of the most turgid reggae songs ever written (and by God are there ever a few turgid reggae songs....). It was even more turgid when performed just with a plunky guitar rather than that driving reggae percussion. To add to the awfulness, the singer delivered the words in a cod-Jamaican Essex accent.

This was followed by a faster but just as deadly song - 'A Horse With No Name'. This is a dull, monotonous, self-indulgent and lyrically pointless drug song from the sixties ('horse' is slang for heroin and the song was banned by radio stations in the know). The verse comprises 65 words sung to only two notes (boring or what?), including the classic line "The heat was hot". I rest my case! But this Neil Young rip-off is a perfect vehicle for true amateur jamming. In addition to having only two notes in the verse, there are only really two chords in the entire song. At the jams, these two chords are continuously repeated for around eight minutes. Dead easy for the guitar players. Coma-inducing for the audience. 'Three Blind Mice' has a much wider melodic range and more chords, it makes much more sense lyrically and is a sophisticated song in comparison. That's probably why we never hear it at the jams!

I got my piano set up, but I was struggling to settle on a half-decent song to start jamming on. Then out of the blue, Miguel set up a great lick on his guitar and launched into 'Willie and the Hand Jive', a great old song from the late fifties. All the guys jammed along, I kicked in the Bo Diddley lick on my piano, and all of a sudden the place came alive with the audience clapping along to the beat. Some ladies even remembered how to do the hand jive. For the one and only time in my experience, Miguel got loud and enthusiastic applause from the audience.

It never ever happened again. I asked him several times to sing 'Willie' at other jams, but he always declined, saying he didn't like performing the song. Hell, if I could have sung and played and got an audience reaction like that, I'd have sung it on every gig. But that was way too much effort for Miguel.

Offers of gigs were coming in nicely for me. A tasty gig came up, playing piano every Saturday afternoon at a classy restaurant in Villaricos. I was booked to play background music and the piano was placed out in front of the conservatory so that the diners inside and outside could all hear me. I played requests, and during my break one afternoon I went to a large table of around a dozen people. There was a birthday cake on the table, so I asked whose birthday it was, then asked the oversized and sweaty birthday boy if he would like a request.

"Do you know 'You'll Never Walk Alone?'" he asked.

"Yes I know it, but it's a song about death. Don't you want me to play something more cheery for your birthday?"

"No, I'd really like you to play 'You'll Never Walk Alone.'"

After my break I went back to the piano, played 'Happy Birthday To You', then started off the song request slowly and quietly. When I got to 'Walk On, Walk On', the birthday table started singing and waving their arms about. Then other diners joined in the singing. I went along with it and cranked up the piano volume. By the time of the reprise of 'Walk On, Walk On', the whole restaurant was singing and waving their arms about. I pummelled the piano keys into a big finish and got a huge cheer.

I later apologized to the restaurant owner for straying from my duties as a provider of background music. But he told me if his customers were happy and enjoying themselves, it was fine by him and there was absolutely no need for me to apologise.

Another day I had a request from an Irish lady for the Jim Reeves classic 'He'll Have To Go'. Jim Reeves' rich mesmerising voice is still heard all over the world to this day, and he's still the best-selling Western singer in Nigeria and Kenya. Muslims play his music after dawn prayers. His records still sell extremely well in countries as diverse as Tasmania, Thailand, India, Norway and South Africa, so it was no surprise to me that an Irish lady wanted me to play one of Jim Reeves' songs.

At the table across from the piano were a Dutch gent and his family, clearly having a good time. The Dutch gent's car was parked outside and when the sun came round, he went out to his car and brought out his tiny Yorkshire terrier. He stood outside the restaurant holding his dog and giving it some water from a bowl. Then he started singing to the wee mite, making up new words to the Jim Reeves song for his serenade.

Instead of 'Put your sweet lips a little closer to the phone' the Dutchman sang 'Put your sweet lips a little closer to the bowl. Take a big sip of water, it's nice and cold.' He sang in a deep Dutch timbre and gave a whole new take on the song. He continued 'If you're thirsty, this will make you feel so good. Little doggy, you're so fluffy and so nice….' He carried on in this vein for the entire song, and I accompanied him with enthusiasm until we finished our performance to applause and cheers from the diners. The dog looked puzzled throughout, and a lot more interested in getting a drink than being serenaded by his master.

If I'm NOT the only musician in history to have played 'He'll Have To Go' on the piano to lyrics about a Yorkshire terrier and its water bowl, then I'm a Dutchman.

Later in the season, I had to cut this lovely Saturday afternoon restaurant gig to once every two weeks. Due to other commitments I couldn't manage to play every week, so I arranged for a suitable act to alternate with me. I got the boss's approval for my Californian hippie amigo Miguel Alfonzo to perform every second week, playing from two to five every alternate Saturday afternoon. I thought his laid-back style was ideal for the restaurant, just sitting and singing background music in a shady corner.

After only a few weeks, Miguel was fired from the gig. He phoned me to pass on the news.

"Hey Jim, the boss told me not to come back."

"Why? Did he not like your music?"

"Oh yea, man. He told me he thought it was ideal for his restaurant."

"So why would he fire you?" I asked.

"Well, Jim" Miguel drawled. "At my last gig I took my second break at a quarter after four, and some people at a table asked me to join them for a glass of wine. It would have been rude to refuse, so I just sat at their table and had some wine. The boss was at another table and he came over after half an hour and told me he was paying me to work till five."

"So why didn't you work till five?" I asked.

"I told him I had finished singing and was now acting as ambassador for his restaurant."

"What?" I couldn't believe what Miguel was telling me.

"The place was quiet, and these folks had invited me to have some wine and talk about my music, so I gave them my time."

"You mean you abandoned the gig at a quarter past four?"

"Hey, that's a bit strong, man."

"Did the boss ask you to act as ambassador for his restaurant?"

"Well, no, I guess."

"Then that's why you were fired, Miguel. Listen, I play till five and usually a bit longer if customers are still around and enjoying my music. But you're telling me you didn't play any music at all after a quarter past four?"

"I guess so, but there was no point, man. There were only a couple of dozen or so people still in the restaurant."

"And the boss was at one of the tables?"

"Yea."

Miguel never really understood why he was fired for finishing his gig three quarters of an hour early.

Later, the boss told me that he paid his waiters to be ambassadors for his restaurant, and he paid Miguel to perform music for three hours. I couldn't argue with that. But Miguel truly thought he was doing the right thing by finishing three quarters of an hour early and supping wine with the customers until the end of his gig.

As for myself, I prefer to give full value for money on a gig, but I couldn't argue with such dedication to laid-back hippieness. Miguel has now returned to California where I'm absolutely sure he's way, way down the list of potential heart attack victims.

CHAPTER 8 - AUGUST

Summer in Almería is fiesta time. It's easy to find a fiesta somewhere every weekend.

Bédar has its own Andalucian fiesta in early August. It's a new fiesta which only started in 2011, and this year the fiesta paid tribute to the area's Moorish influences. The name Almería (with the emphasis on the "í") comes from the Arabic name Al-Mariy-yat (the Watchtower). Almería is a province in Andalucia, and the name Andalucia comes from the ancient Moorish name Al-Andalus.

Fiestas are always announced with firecrackers. These are terrifyingly loud fireworks which resonate down our valley like blasts from a cannon. If you're in the middle of a siesta, too bad - it's time to get up, amigo! You certainly won't sleep through this, and in any event the village dogs will have started barking in terror. I've never met anyone who can give me a logical explanation why the Spanish insist on making this unnecessary racket. It's basically a disturbance of the peace with no pleasurable features except perhaps for the fellow who has the sadistic pleasure of lighting the firecrackers and scaring every animal and beast shi...I mean witless.

Most fiestas are connected with patron saints, but the Andalucian fiesta is different. As far as I know, there are no Muslim patron saints.

On the Friday night of the fiesta, a bar had been set up at the town hall square for drinks and tapas. A stage had been set up at the town hall square, and I joined a bunch of locals to listen to some rock bands.

On the Saturday night, as my wife was away on a long trip to the UK, I went up with my friends Christine and Brian to Bar El Cortijo in the village. The bar is run by the delightful Gonzales family.

We had pre-ordered their special dish of roast shoulder of lamb the previous night, and we decided to forego a starter - wisely, as it turned out. A bowl of rustic bread and alioli (a sort of home-made garlic mayonnaise and very light) was brought to our table and we all set to work on it.

Ten minutes later an enormous oval-shaped glass dish was placed on our table with one of the largest joints of lamb we'd ever seen. A large plate of patatas á lo pobre then arrived - potatoes cooked in the oven with olive oil, onions, garlic and red peppers. This was followed by a massive mound of cauliflower cheese. This was clearly going to be way too much food for the three of us. Fortunately our village friends Sid and Jackie spotted us and helped us munch our way through the delicious but colossal meal. We were given a doggy bag of the remaining meat and bones.

Fully replenished, we slowly made our way up to the town hall square, where a lighting rig had been set up and a childrens' dance troop was boogieing away to a Europop song.

Some time later, the children's dance troop was followed by a Moroccan group playing a variety of weird instruments - strange-looking brass instruments including one which looked a bit like a clarinet but sounded like something a snake charmer would play. The most interesting instrument was a hurdy-gurdy. This was a box which sat on the performer's lap while he turned a handle while playing a tune with the piano-like keys. The sound which emanated from it was rather similar to a small organ. Arabic wailing was accompanied by belly dancing from a very fit and lithe young woman.

After the Moroccan group, a standard Spanish Europop troop took to the stage. There were ten of them, including a couple of girl singers and a very decent brass section. I'm afraid I can only take about an hour's worth of this music before I start screaming inwardly – it's very simple and predictable stuff which all sounds much the same to me.

It was well after midnight when I walked back down to the house. The air was warm, children were still out playing, and as it was a special evening, candles were lit along the verges of the main street. I took a wee detour to the town hall square as there is a beautiful mural of Bédar on the main wall which I can never pass without admiring. It was softly illuminated by the lights on the wall. The tiled mural was created by Trina, a hugely talented Canadian lady who lives locally and runs a weekly workshop near the centre of our village.

Long after I got home, the band were still going strong and they provided accompaniment for my toilet visit at 4-30am. Working in a fiesta band is a young person's job!

By contrast, the next village along the mountain from Bédar has only a couple of dozen inhabitants, but Serena has its own summer fiesta. As my missus was in the UK visiting family, I was kindly offered a lift to the fiesta by some neighbours. It's the village with a scary road similar to the one on which my wife was singing 'She'll be Coming Round the Mountain' in chapter two. It's a very scenic road to Serena and an easy walk which Carrie and I have done many times. We usually meet someone we know who, like us, is out for a walk.

As you enter Serena village, there's a charming old fuente (drinking water fountain) on the right. Then there's some agricultural land before you come to the village itself with a few houses on either side of the road. There's also the ruin of a mosque, probably from around the 15th century. There are old houses along a narrow main road, with gaily coloured bouganvilleas arching over their walls. It's the kind of sleepy hamlet where you'd expect to find a dog lying in the middle of the road. True to form, we've often had to drive around a sleeping dog with only three legs. Perhaps it lost a leg by refusing to budge for a car…

The Serena fiesta was well under way when we arrived just after two o'clock in the afternoon. At the end of the village there's a small paved area where cars can turn, just outside a little shrine, and that's where the fiesta was being held. There are companies who come to the local towns and set up an enormous paella pan over a fire - the enormity of the pan depends on the size of your fiesta - and the fire was under way when we arrived. The villagers were all at a long trestle table, and one of the local bars had set up a temporary bar to dispense cold beer and wine. Like all Andalucian afternoons in August, it was a hot one, and we were glad to be sitting in the shade of a huge fig tree.

When the paella was ready, we all joined the queue and were served a plastic plate of paella with a chunk of bread. Paella was originally a poor man's food from Valencia, made with free local produce like rabbit, beans and almonds. We never expect seafood paella at the fiestas, and sometimes you'd be lucky to get a bit of chicken. I once went to a party at which a local Spanish hombre had kindly provided a big pan of paella for eighteen people. He made it with one rabbit and a bag of almonds - and a lot of rice. I was not lucky enough on that occasion to get a piece of meat, just a piece of bone and a few almonds with the rice. Poor man's food, but very tasty just the same.

At the Serena fiesta I was lucky enough to be served a couple of chunks of chicken with my rice. There were several dozen people enjoying the day, mostly from neighbouring villages, and the paella was enough to feed an army. Second helpings were available.

After the food, we had some music. Estoban and I had brought our guitars, and we played for some Spanish ladies who wanted to sing. To my shame, I probably know a lot more Spanish music than Spanish words, but I reckon I can be most useful to my community through my music. Everyone just chilled and sipped cooling drinks at the long table.

Then disaster struck - the bar had run out of wine. This was no problem - some villagers simply popped into their nearby homes and brought out bottles of cava and chilled white wine, and normal service was resumed. There were no toilet facilities set up, so the villagers made their homes available to those in need.

What I love about this area is that there are no airs or graces; people all muck in and do their bit for the community. This was one of these afternoons which I didn't want to end. But the tables eventually had to be moved, as a stage was being set up for the band providing the music for the evening's dancing. We had a lovely afternoon, and as far as I know, no-one at all drove off the mountain road on the way back to Bédar.

You'll have figured long before now that I just adore the way of life down here. Almería is a province of Andalucia, and the Andalucians are particularly laid-back. Some say lazy, but maybe that's going a bit far - they love life, and want to have time for their family and friends. A chap I know makes his living setting up internet web sites for businesses, mainly to British ex-pats. He used to struggle to get through to the Andalucians. It goes like this:

"Your business should have a web site, and I can set one up for you," he would say.

"Why do we need a web site?" would come the reply.

"You would get more customers and more business."

"But we have enough customers and enough business to get by."

"You'd make more money."

"We don't need any more money. We would have to work harder to get it, and we wouldn't have as much time to spend with our family and friends."

Who can say they're wrong?

Living in Almería is in many ways like going back in time 40 years for us Brits. Nearly all the shops and supermarkets close on Sundays. In the UK, shopping has become a leisure pursuit. For want of something better to do, my wife and I are guilty of having visited crowded retail parks around Glasgow on a Sunday afternoon. People shamble aimlessly around the shops, mainly to bring a bit of warmth and colour into their lives. When the retail park shops closed around 5pm, we would trudge along to do an hour or two's shopping in Asda or Tesco.

Some supermarkets in Scotland are open all night. Down here they're not. Sunday shopping in the UK is now a leisure pursuit. In our area, Sunday is a day for spending with the family, and going out to enjoy yourself. It's certainly not for shopping.

Things are genuinely different here in Almería. Spanish families put on their Sunday best and go out for a long and leisurely lunch. This will be a noisy and lively affair, and they spend the afternoon sharing dishes and wine. After lunch, they go on the "paseo" - a leisurely walk along the promenade or the nicest part of town in their Sunday best.

At fiesta time the families will make some food dishes and have a huge picnic in the centre of town. Ready meals are scarce here – pizzas, lasagne and possibly cannelloni are about all the ready meals you'll find in supermarkets. And don't ever expect to order soup in a restaurant and be served some ghastly gunge out of a packet or tin. It just won't happen.

Talking of food, in our kitchen we had the 'Mystery of the Broken Eggs' to deal with.

We used to leave our eggs in a rack on the kitchen worktop, and some days we'd feed Sammy then go out and return to find a broken eggshell on the kitchen floor. I would get censured by my other half for not tidying up after breakfast.

Then one day I had forgotten my passport and walked from the car back into the house to find Sammy tucking in to an egg on the kitchen floor. He had a guilty look on his face and he belted past me and ran upstairs. He had obviously worked out how to prise an egg out of the rack and push it towards the edge of the worktop so that it would land on the floor and he could then lick it up. Since then we've kept our eggs firmly locked away!

Sammy prefers my wife's lap in winter, particularly at breakfast tme. Carrie wears this incredibly soft and fluffy dressing down which presumably reminds Sammy of his mother. He's first to get fed in the mornings. After he's finished, he'll howl indignantly at Carrie to finish her breakfast so that he can jump onto her lap and knead her dressing gown with his claws. Within seconds he'll be purring his head off.

In summer, Sammy prefers my company and in the afternoons his preferred sleep spot is my lounge chair. On the afternoons when Carrie goes to yoga, I'll usually be upstairs in the office attending to emails and dealing with our rental property business.

"AAAAAAOOOOOOOOOOO"

"AAAAAAAAOOOOOOOOOOO"

This heart-rending howl comes from downstairs. It's Sammy's coyote impression. He's woken up and is panicking as he can't find anyone in the house.

"Up here, Sammy," I'll shout. There will be a bit of muted feline cursing then he'll come bounding up the stairs and into the office. He'll then jump onto the desk and settle down on the computer's mouse mat. I always have to shift him to the edge of the desk so I can use the computer again. I bought a second cat bed for him, and it's on the floor of the office, but Sammy much prefers to be close to me, lying on the desk. He sees himself as an important member of the family, not a mere cat to be relegated to a basket.

Carrie and I love going to events aimed at the Spanish. They're a lot more fun than the Brit karaoke night we attended years ago. Would I ever again want to spend all night listening to loud drunks singing out of tune? No thankyou. It was beyond grim.

But you never know what to expect at Spanish events. Like the time some Spanish friends invited us to see a Mexican mariachi band advertised to play a free concert in the Artisan Centre in Mojacar.

The concert was advertised to start at 9pm, so we got to the hall ten minutes early and found some empty seats about halfway down the hall. We were among the first to arrive. Over the next half hour or so, Spanish ladies arrived with their knitting, older gents arrived in groups, seemingly shouting insults at each other, plus a few young couples with children. The older ladies took out their knitting and got stuck in, gossiping away while stray dogs ran in and out of the hall. In Spain, there are always dogs.

Come twenty past nine, the concert still hadn't started, and an announcement came over the tannoy that one of the trumpeters had lost his trumpet. This caused some amusement among the audience. Trumpets are an essential part of mariachi music. Herb Alpert's Tijuana Brass were a great bunch of musicians who had umpteen hit records years ago like 'The Lonely Bull' and 'Spanish Flea', all mariachi-influenced. A typical authentic mariachi band will have two trumpets, a violin, a couple of guitars and a bass guitar, and the guitarists sing sweet Hispanic songs. It's a folksy type of music which oozes a kind of dishevelled energy. On this particular night, it was even more dishevelled than usual.

There was still no sign of any band by twenty to ten. Carrie and I were discussing restaurants with our friends and enjoying the chilled-out atmosphere. No-one was complaining, as it gave them more time to talk to friends or get on with their knitting.

The dogs continued to run around the hall, and they were having fun chasing each other up and down the aisles, barking loudly and generally having a great time. A cat popped its head through the door but was swiftly chased off the premises by the dogs in a rabble of barking. Forty-five minutes after the concert was due to start, an announcement came over the tannoy that the trumpet player had found his trumpet, and that the concert could now start. Deafening cheers.

It was only about a quarter of an hour later that the curtains opened to reveal a group of musicians in wonderfully colourful Mexican costumes and matching sombrero hats. The band started, and it was clear that although it was now ten o'clock at night, they had never bothered to do a sound check. They'd clearly spent more time on their stage outfits than their sound. Apart from one of the singers, all we could hear was the bass guitar and a muffled trumpet. We couldn't hear any sound from the violin or the rhythm guitars.

After another twenty minutes or so, the sound eventually got balanced out and we could hear the whole band. The Spanish ladies knew the songs, and sang along in the choruses. The only song Carrie and I recognised was 'Cielito Lindo' and we joined in the chorus "Ay, ay, ay, ay" to the clear delight of the ladies around us swaying happily in time to the music. It was just another eventful night in Almería province.

A few months previously, I had been given an opportunity to learn some new latin music. Harvey had called me to say he had met an American mezzo-soprano who was brought up in Argentina and had sung all around the world, including Carnegie Hall and the Lincoln Center in New York. He told me that she wanted to take a break from opera and wanted to perform latin songs and American songbook standards around Andalucia. Harvey thought I could help her and we arranged for him to bring the mezzo to my studio.

Carlita is a stunning lady, always immaculately dressed with long black hair and a winning smile. We tried a couple of American standards, one was 'They Can't Take That Away From Me'. Personally, I don't think this crossover thing works. I think opera singers should stick to singing the arias and pieces which their voices are trained for, and that pop singers like Michael Bolton should stick to singing pop songs and not attempt anything operatic. Especially not Massenet's 'Werther'in French thankyou, Michael.

So when Carlita attempted to sing the Gershwin song, it wasn't for me. On the other hand, I knew some Spanish songs such as 'El Relicario' and it looked clear to me that I could find some meeting ground with Carlita. Then I had an idea.

I had learned quite a few latino songs from listening to Nana Mouskouri of all people. Ms Mouskouri is a Greek singer who was hugely successful in the sixties and seventies. She had her own television series and an amazing backing group called the Athenians who could play bouzoukis in unbelievable tempos like 11 beats and 13 beats to the bar. The only dance I would ever do is a waltz, and that's got 3 beats, so imagine trying to dance to 13 beats to the bar. It would be immense fun to play it for ballroom dancers though....

Ms Mouskouri speaks several languages and she used to sing a beautiful song called 'Cucurrucucú Paloma' which I loved. It's a Mexican Huapango song, but you probably knew that already!

Carlita yelled with excitement. "You know that song, Jim? I was brought up with that song in Argentina. I LOVE it!! You've just told me you're from Glasow, so how on earth do you know it?"

I explained, and we set about finding a key. Harvey was sitting on the sofa wondering what was coming. I gave it my most sensitive shot, not to overpower the singer, and by the end of the beautiful song, Harvey had tears in his eyes. Carlita and I seemed to have something here.

We ended our session with the Habanera from Carmen, which everyone knows, and even without the music I seemed to have made a passable attempt at an accompaniment. I don't suppose either Carlita or Harvey thought that their visit would result in much, but by the end of the morning, we were all excited at the prospect of the match between Scotland and Argentina. Argentina would win, of course.

So now I had to learn lots of Spanish and South American tunes and a bit more opera. It actually surprised me that I knew several of the songs Carlita wanted to sing, as there were English translations of some of them. 'Quisas, Quisas' was recorded in English by Doris Day as 'Perhaps, Perhaps' and there were other easy ones like that. The hard work was learning coplas, boleros and zarzuelas. These are authentic, traditional songs which the older Spanish people know. Sheet music doesn't exist for most of them, and anyway I will always make sure I play a song in the key which is best for the singer. If the key is too low, the singer won't be able to project the notes properly as low notes use a lot of breath and can be almost inaudible. If the key is too high, the singer will have to scream to hit the top notes, or miss them altogether (as happens so often in karaoke sessions).

From our first meeting back in April, Carlita and I had worked solidly. I had transcribed the song structures and chords, and Carlita had learned the lyrics off by heart - being a concert artist, she doesn't like bringing lyric sheets on stage with her. We had made a demo CD which Carlita had taken round some town halls, and also to the administrative centre in Almería city. To cut a long story short, we were offered a mini-tour of towns in the Almanzora valley, six gigs from early to late August. We were also offered an interesting concert. Carlita phoned one morning.

"Jim, how do you fancy doing a gig in a prison further up the coast?"

"Look, I'm not exactly Johnny Cash, and you're definitely not June Carter."

"No, they want us to perform at a book launch. It's a new book about prisoners."

I thought about it a moment and figured, what the hell. I came here to say YES to everything and I'd had the time of my life so far, so why would I want to say no to performing in a prison. It would probably be in an open prison, of course. I reckoned there was no way the gig would be in a maximum-security prison.

"It's in a maximum-security prison," explained Carlita.

Oh well, in for a penny… We were to play at the prison in the afternoon, then go to a conference centre at night to repeat the book launch cum concert at a lawyers' convention. So, two lots of crooks in one day. Nice!

We loaded up my old Mercedes with my piano, microphones and stands, plus my big PA system and speaker stands, as we were sure there would be no PA system at the prison. We arrived at the prison a couple of hours before the event was to start, just to make sure we had plenty of time to set up and do a sound check. Just as well, as it happened....

Carlita got out of the car and went into the prison reception to arrange for the car to enter the prison to unload the music gear. This involved the prison guards opening an enormous up-and-over door. Imagine something ten times the size of an up-and-over garage door. I drove the car into a parking bay and the enormous door thundered shut behind me. My car was searched and I had to surrender my passport. Once the prison officers were satisfied, they opened an identical door on the inside.

I drove my car out of the bay into the courtyard, where more prison officers were waiting with a huge trolley, like a cage on wheels. We emptied the music gear from the car into the cage. A prison officer then told me I had to drive my car out again immediately and into the public car park, so I went through the same procedure to get out again. I was given my passport back as I went out. Just as well, as I needed it to get back in.

Getting back in to the prison by foot took much longer. There were several checkpoints and I had to surrender my passport at the final one. Eventually I reached the inner courtyard and met up again with Carlita and the prison officers. We followed them along several corridors with tiled murals on the walls, past a courtyard garden area with beautiful shrubs and flowers, along another corridor and past a kitchen until we arrived at - the theatre! We certainly weren't expecting to find a 200-seat theatre complete with PA system on the stage, a control booth at the back of the stage, and lighting rigs.

To cut a long story short, it took us nearly two hours to get into the prison and set up. Some prisoners were there to help, and they seemed very pleasant chaps.

Finally, the audience was allowed in, and a long table was set up in front of the stage for the book launch. Those involved with the book sat at the table and there were speeches in Spanish which lasted around an hour. Meanwhile, Carlita and I got changed for our concert out back in the dressing room.

Our audience was a mixture of civilians, prison officers and prisoners. Our short concert of Spanish songs was really well received, and when we played our last song, there were cries for more. We didn't want to start a prison riot, so we performed for another fifteen minutes or so before they would let us off the stage.

It took nearly as long to get back out again…and the evening concert for the lawyers wasn't nearly as much fun.

My tour of the Almanzora valley with Carlita was an adventure in itself. The first town we played was at El Chuco, and we had been told by a town hall official that we'd be performing at the swimming pool just outside of town. When we arrived at the swimming pool, we were told that the plans had changed and that we were to make our way to the town square.

"What's the access like?" Carlita asked an official.

"Difficult," came the reply.

I gulped. Thankfully I had taken our small Opel Corsa as I knew the difficulties of getting around small Spanish towns and villages. The old towns were built when donkeys were the only means of transport, and even small cars can sometimes have problems turning the corners. In El Chuco, we found no sign anywhere indicating where the town centre might be, and I had to do a bit of fancy reversing. As time was moving on, Carlita phoned a town hall official and was given directions to the town square.

We found the street up to the town hall square. It was so narrow that we had to fold in the car's wing mirrors. Even at that, it was tight. One corner required a 7-point turn to get round it. The street up to the square had been steep up to this point, but nothing like as steep as what we saw in front of us. The heavily-laden car groaned and suddenly I could see smoke coming from the engine bay. We were only a few yards from the square, so with the help of a town hall official, we unloaded the car. The official was well used to the challenging hill, so he drove my car up to the square and parked it outside the town hall.

The next challenge was the stage - a narrow affair, about 5 feet off the ground and without any safety rails to stop a body from falling off. Our concert was to start at 10 o'clock and by now it was getting dark. The only means of seeing anything on stage were a couple of street lights, which were nowhere near the stage. How was I to see my music? One of the officials went into his house and came back with a standard lamp with a light on the top and another on the side of the stand. The top bulb didn't work but the side one did, so that was the only stage lighting.

Our concert was well attended, and we kicked off with a lively song with a long piano intro which allowed Carlita to walk down the steps from the town hall then up the steps to the stage. Our second song was a ballad, and was enlivened by young Spanish children doing wheelies around the stage on their bikes. A few songs later, an elderly couple arrived late then started arguing loudly with each other during the lovely ballad 'La Paloma'. The church clock joined in every quarter of an hour, not a real clock but a scratchy old recording of a rather bright and cheery clock.

At six minutes past eleven, the church clock struck eleven, preceded of course by lead-in chimes. Many clocks around here repeat the time a minute or so later, in case residents were in the loo or out of range when the first lot of chimes were sounded. This clock was one of this type. Carlita and I had managed to start our rendition of 'I Dreamed A Dream' from Les Miserables just before the first set of chimes, and the second set of deafening chimes arrived just as we got to the end of the song. My final soft piano chords were drowned out by the blasted bells. The audience didn't seem to mind. They were obviously well used to living with them.

After the show, the people from the town hall took Carlita and me to a local restaurant and plied us with food and drink. We sat at a long table with the organizers of the concert and the town's mayor (we met the local mayor at every location we played). First of all, drinks orders were taken. Then plates of ham, cheese, freshly roasted almonds, bread and alioli were brought to the table. Then fabulous 'raciones' - like tapas only in much larger portions. These included large prawns, chunks of fried fish in lemon, garlic mushrooms, lamb chops, and the softest pork fillet I've ever had in my life, with a sweet honey sauce. Starters and 'raciones' are tradionally shared in Andalucia, and the food just kept coming. The Spanish venues always look after their musicians, and at every town and village except one we were treated to some amazing food after our concert.

The one town we didn't stay for food was a very late concert well over 100 kilometres away. To get there, I drove 80 kilometres along decent main roads and came off at a big town to take the long road up a mountain and down the other side. When we arrived at the town the 'lady from the town hall' opened the side door to the theatre and let us in to unload our gear. She then locked the door again so that we could set up and have a run-through of some of our songs without being disturbed. The special evening had begun for the guests with a meal at a nearby restaurant before going on to the concert, so we were due to start quite late - eleven o'clock to be exact. We were going to be late home that night.

Carlita and I set up, ran through some songs then went backstage to change, ready for the concert.

We came back to the stage at ten to eleven, then went backstage again as we like to present ourselves to our audience from the wings in the time-honoured way. Just before eleven we could hear knocking on the main doors of the theatre, so we went to investigate. People were trying to get in, but the lady from the town hall hadn't yet returned to open the theatre. Carlita shouted to the audience through the glass, then tried to phone the organizer. But the town was in a valley and telephone reception was very poor, so she couldn't make contact. So here we were now, ten past eleven at night in a theatre in the middle of nowhere, trying to do a concert with an audience battering on the door to get in. People were simply giving up and leaving to go back to their homes.

By 11-20pm I was thinking that we might just do the concert anyway and crank up the volume so our small remaining audience outside could hear us. I was just setting the volume when the lady from the town hall arrived to let the audience in. By the time all eighteen of them got seated it was half past eleven. Carlita and I agreed that we should do a much shorter show. More people turned up and we ended up playing to around forty. We even got a standing ovation at the end. We packed up around one in the morning and drove home. I hit the sack around 4am.

But the latest gig I've ever played down here with Carlita was a Spanish celebration around a swimming pool at a huge rural hostal. There were a dozen large round tables for ten, set ready for the meal. The audience arrived for dinner at 10pm, and Carlita and I were invited to join them. As usual, there were several different starters, first cold ham, cheese and salad then hot starters like croquettes, pinchos (skewers of meat) and aubergines in honey. Our main courses arrived at six minutes past midnight. The food was lovely, but it was quite impossible to see what on earth we were eating as there was only one candle on the centre of each large round table.

After dinner there were long, rambling speeches then a reasonable flamenco singer and guitarist hit the stage at 1-30am. A Cuban rapper cum singer was on next, and Carlita and I finally got onto the stage at twenty past two in the morning. We had planned to do twenty minutes, but we were so well received that the audience demanded more and we had to do several encores. Just the thing you want at three in the morning! The entire Spanish audience had stayed to the bitter end - something you won't catch most ex-pats doing.

Anyway, I haven't come down here to sleep. I came here to get my teeth into music after 29 years of having to treat it as an occasional hobby.

I cut my professional musical teeth in Glasgow in the early seventies. Jazz has always been popular in Glasgow, and the city hosts an annual International Jazz Festival, at which I had played the occasional gig. In fact, I had managed to play occasional jazz gigs around Glasgow for nearly 40 years without ever having played a blues gig. Blues is the absolute basis for jazz, yet apart from trad jazz musicians, the jazz guys around Glasgow had little or no interest in the blues. It was regarded as basic and unsophisticated. It is said that jazz is played with the brain, but blues is played with the heart. Playing around Glasgow, I never had an opportunity to find out if this was true.

A few months after we had moved to Almería, I was approached by an English bar owner in Almanzora to play at his one-day blues festival. Paul loved blues piano and wanted me to open his festival at three in the afternoon by playing solo piano. I agreed to play, but I didn't have high hopes of a big turn-out or getting much money for the gig. However, I'd never played a blues gig before in my life, so I applied my theory of saying "YES" to everything and agreed to perform.

As I was booked to start the blues festival, I thought the best thing to do would be to play music from the start of the blues - old trad jazz numbers like 'St Louis Blues', 'Basin Street Blues' and even some ragtime which was the precursor of the blues. So three o'clock in the afternoon came and I sat down at the piano and proceeded to play my first-ever blues set.

Fortunately, the audience loved the old tunes - they hadn't been expecting this sort of stuff. I decided to play my rocking slow boogie version of the old gospel song 'Just A Closer Walk With Thee', which has been performed by countless jazz performers from Kid Ory to Chris Barber. By the time I got to the second verse, the entire audience was whooping and clapping along in time to the rocking hymn. I had never received anything like this sort of response playing jazz in Glasgow.

I was in the middle of my set when a Spanish hombre came up to me and asked if he could play harmonica with me. I nodded my head and he took his harmonica out of his pocket and we proceeded to jam. I finished up with a really fast old tune 'Tiger Rag' and gave it a big finish. I was totally stunned by the applause. This was my first ever blues gig and I had just received the best reception of my life.

But things were about to get even better. When I went to take down my piano and go home, a couple of guys came up to me and asked me if I could leave it on the stage as they would love me to play piano for them on some Chicago blues songs later in the day. Then a huge guy with an even huger voice asked me if I knew some Muddy Waters songs and could we do a duet later? A visiting guitarist asked me to jam with him on some Gary Moore numbers. And a one-man blues guy along the lines of Seasick Steve pleaded with me to accompany him on his swamp blues songs and he just wouldn't go away. How could I ignore such attention?

To cut a long story short, I started playing piano at three in the afternoon. I took quite a few breaks for drinks and food, but basically I was still playing my piano when it was approaching midnight. Talk about a baptism of fire!

I've always enjoyed latin music, and in the sixties I enjoyed seeing Los Paraguayos on the telly with their seemingly colourful outfits, odd-shaped guitars and the Paraguyan harp. But I was never a fan of the tame Edmundo Ros-style ballroom dancing.

I've had a hatred of ballroom dancing ever since I played a regular Saturday night gig at a dinner dance in Scotland back in the seventies. Every few weeks a local couple would come and take over the dance floor, diving about so quickly and dangerously that the other dancers had no choice but to give up and get off the dance floor. Ballroom dancers are exhibitionists in my book.

My hatred of ballroom dancers reached its peak in 1982 when my band played a gig for a dancing club in Glasgow. This time we had not just one ballroom-dancing couple. We had a roomful of exhibitionists.

Several came up to the stage and fired orders at us about the dances we were to play and the exact number of beats per minute they required. Thankfully, our drummer had recently played on a cruise and had experience of the tempos we were to play at. However, we were a dinner dance trio and were mindful that the guests would be dancing after a 3-course meal, so we didn't think they'd want anything too taxing with all that nosh inside them. We'd normally play at an easy bounce tempo so that the dancers weren't tripping over each other. But this lot wanted us to play at "competition tempo". So instead of an easy bounce, we had to play at 200 beats per minute, which is pretty frantic. The ideal tempo for jiggling around the dance floor is thought to be around 120 beats per minute, so at 200 beats per minute the dancers are flying around.

As it happens, we didn't have to play much that night as the dancers were awarding each other prizes and making long and pompous speeches. We played less than an hour, but by heck we earned our money playing at the furious tempos demanded by the ballroom dancers.

We got our revenge during the last waltz medley when we kicked off with an instrumental version of 'Edelweiss'. The three of us made chicken noises at the top of our voices while the ballroom dancers whirled around and scowled at us in disgust. It's the last song Rodgers & Hammerstein ever wrote, and after years of writing totally unsuitable songs, they finally came up with the ideal one for chicken noises.

The ballroom dancers' gig was the exact opposite of a gig my band did a few months later. It was for a ski club near the Campsie Hills beyond Glasgow. About half the audience had some kind of bandage. Those whose legs were free of bandages often had an arm in plaster. Not too many were fit to dance, so my band had an easy time. Since that gig, I've never had a desire to go skiing....

I don't wish to boast, but I was once fleetingly a member of the pop scene in Scotland. I've stood on a stage with a 'beat group' and been screamed at by an audience of girls. Ok, it was a good few years ago, they were schoolgirls and the stage was only a few inches high, but we seemed to tower above our audience. I was still at secondary school, and my mates and I had a beat group. None of us could sing very well, so when the Beatles, the Stones and the like became popular, we all sang the songs in unison. A sort of Mike Sammes Singers version of rock music, but it made sense to us at the time.

One Saturday night, we got to play at a dance at Cathcart South church hall, on the south side of Glasgow. Our group usually went out for 10 shillings - 50p in today's money, which worked out at 10p each for a 2-hour gig. Our band comprised Ivor who had a bass guitar with a hopelessly twisted neck, Graham on a charity-shop drum kit, Ricky on a fake Fender 6-string lead guitar with the bottom 2 strings missing, and my rough-as-get-out Egmont acoustic guitar with a 2/6d pick-up screwed into the sound hole and the wires dangling down. For reasons which escape me, we were augmented on this occasion by the creepy church organist. He had a foul-smelling checked sports jacket and even smellier trousers, and battered out strange ecumenical chords on an ancient upright piano which was way beyond holy salvation.

Our PA equipment for the microphones consisted of an enormous wartime valve radio, thrown out by someone's aunt and rescued by me. The casing had been removed and the innards exposed so that we could knock up a microphone input by connecting bits of wire to the chassis. We had two World War Two microphones between us, bought with our pocket money from the government surplus store on Glasgow's Stockwell Street. As for microphone stands, they were a distant dream. But we had the luxury of a borrowed Vox AC30 amp for the guitars. This produced an undreamt-of 30 watts of output.

Our parents had driven us all to the hall and dropped us off at the church. We set up our equipment in the Victorian church hall with a small stage at one end. This was a big event for the youth of Cathcart, and by the time the gig began, the hall was half-full of teenagers. We started with some of our old Shadows repertoire. 'Apache' went down well, but our rendition of 'Foot Tapper' would have breached Trading Standards regulations. 'Dance On' went unheeded.

Then we all sang some Beatles songs. To sing, we had to bend down into the solitary microphone which was sellotaped to the top of a garden hoe jammed between our two amplifiers. We got some applause from the boys but total disinterest from the girls. Today, some would view our act as having been groundbreaking pre-punk minimalism, but the teenyboppers were not impressed - they simply ignored us and chatted amongst themselves. At one point, a tall lad with open-sore acne was desperate enough to dance in the vicinity of a podgy girl in Buddy Holly specs, but no-one else was impressed enough to dance to our beat group.

When we ran out of material, we took a break. As I recall, we weren't exactly bombarded with requests for autographs during the interval.

The second half of our gig began, and this time the creepy bloke at the piano had given up by popular demand, and stood in front of us holding a microphone right up to the mouths of our singers. This made an enormous difference, as our audience were now able to actually hear what we were singing. We started into a re-run of our Beatles repertoire, and to our astonishment some girls started screaming to exactly the same songs they had ignored in our first set. Within seconds every last girl in the hall was screaming at us, pushing their way past the lads to the front of the stage. We all exchanged looks which said "this is fab - we should be good for a grope tonight".

Half an hour later, we played our last song to deafening screams, then shouted goodnight to our audience, assuming that the female adulation would continue until we all had a girl on each arm. But the screaming stopped as suddenly as it had started. It was as if someone had flicked off a light switch. The lads and lasses simply turned away from the stage and collected their coats from the cloakroom. The girls filed out of the church hall in almost complete silence. Maybe not that surprising as their throats must have been knackered.

We packed up our gear in the forlorn hope that some girls would be waiting for us outside, but of course they'd all gone home. Anyway, our hopes of a 'lumber' were doomed from the start - most of us had to wait for our parents to collect us and our equipment and drive us home.

I was fifteen and I've never been screamed at since.

CHAPTER 9 - SEPTEMBER

I find tribute acts rather depressing. There are whole swathes of copyists out there without any original ideas of their own, pretending to be Rod Stewart or Cliff Richard etc etc. We're lucky in our area that copyist acts are fairly few because there are some really talented youngsters on today's scene. These youngsters can play their own instruments really well and get good audiences with original ideas and they often perform songs of their own.

I make two exceptions to my dislike of tribute acts – Elvis and Abba.

Abba's music is simply not going away, and I'm proud to say that I do a boogie version of 'Waterloo'. I will put my hand up and say that if it's good enough for Meryl Streep in the 'Mamma Mia' movie, then it's more than good enough for me.

I have to confess that I was, for one night only, part of a tribute to Abba at the Tall Oaks hotel in the Lake District, which we used to frequent. I was the blonde Agnetha in a novelty tribute act for the evening. I was not so much a tribute as a caricature. A lady friend who introduced me to my wife all these years ago had lost a lot of weight. She happened to be discarding some clothes and a rather generous-sized cream coloured cat suit was going spare. This was about the same time as my petite sister-in-law went to a car boot sale and bought a bra on my behalf.

If the expression 54DD means anything, you'll realise that I was a proper woman that night. My re-imagining of the wondrous Swedish dolly bird was made complete with the addition of a bad eye, a fag hanging out of my mouth, a pronounced stoop and an occasional spit on the floor. My friend Brendan was the redhead Anna-Frid and his ginger beard neatly complimented my fag-touting blonde with her enormous bosoms. Our lady partners playing Benny and Bjorn were not much better. I'll spare you the details but our Glasgow pub-singer version of 'Haww, Take A Chance on Me, pal' was rather different from the original.

As for Elvis, well the Steve Wright Show on Radio 2 is keeping his memory alive. He's still out there dispensing advice on oil filters for Morris Minors and suitable varieties of beetroot for allotments. He's still indispensable!

There is a delicious act further up the coast - the Everleery Brothers. They include a tribute to the Everly Brothers in their act, so no surprise there. Except that the reason the Everly Brothers became a legendary act was due to their beautiful soaring 2-part harmonies. The Everly Brothers were famously a duo, however our local Everleery Brothers are a trio. When I first saw them they had dispensed totally with the harmonies, and two of them sang the melody, thus lending a completely new slant to the legendary duo's songs. Doing a tribute to the Everly Brothers without the beautiful harmonies is nothing if not original.

Last time I saw them, things had greatly improved – they had bought a clever voice box which plugs into the guitar, takes the chords from the guitar and produces appropriate harmonies from a single sung note. So rather than no harmonies at all, this device ensures that you can now enjoy the Everly Brothers' legendary 2-part harmonies in 3-part harmony. If there had been three Everly Brothers, it would have made sense and sounded more accurate. There are some things in life you just can't make up!

I once saw a Queen tribute act with the same vocal toy. You think you're going to see a 4-piece band like Queen. All you actually get is one bloke with a karaoke machine and a voice box prancing about in a yellow suit and a stick-on moustache. It is of course fairly cheap for the venues to book acts like that, but the public may eventually lose the will to drive to a gig if all they get at the other end is a bloke with a karaoke machine.

The problem with singing along to karaoke backing tracks is simply this - they will often be in a key too high or too low for the singer. If the key is too high for the singer's voice, there will either be some screaming involved to get to the high notes, or if the singer can't get high enough, the notes will fall painfully short of the target. If the key is too low, the singer can't project the notes properly. James Blunt sings high, Neil Diamond sings low, so if you are unlucky to encounter a professional act which uses backing discs of both singers, you can count on an interesting evening with some songs having inaudible low notes or painfully high notes.

The other problem with karaoke tracks is that rather than having a proper finish to the songs, the tracks often fade out exactly as they do on the original record. So at a live performance the audience are often left wondering where the music went and whether the hell to applaud or not.

Live bands often have the same problem when they play in the key of the original record. Real musicians play the songs in keys suitable for the singer. Pianists can play in any key, but you can't expect a contralto like Alison Moyet to be able to sing a song in Jessie J's high range.

For me, the funniest thing ever is to watch is a singer performing 'All Right Now in the style of Free' (this is the actual name of the karaoke track which the performers can buy). In the middle of the record there is a guitar solo which lasts nearly two minutes, so it's great fun to figure out what the singer is planning to do during this extremely long break in the lyrics. It will often involve the performer doing some embarrassing dancing or possibly shouting "Oh Yea", "Whoo", "Come on", "Let's rock" or similar hackneyed phrases to the audience.

"Whoo" is my personal favourite as it's:

A/ Easy for the performer to shout

B/ Nice and short

and

C/ Can be understood in any language.

By now I was starting to gig regularly with Jill, the blues singer from Edinburgh. We were asked to do our show at the fabulous La Envia golf resort halfway up a mountain near Almería city. The gig was on the evening of a major golf tournament and we were booked to play after the barbecue. That was about all the information we were given.

We normally travel in two cars, but to cut down travel expenses we had borrowed a diesel van which struggled up the side of the mountain. The car was loaded with Jill, her husband Simon plus me and the piano, synth, lighting rig and a full PA system with speakers and stands. We eventually arrived at the golf resort and found staff going about in very smart black jackets. They found a huge trolley and very kindly helped us unload our gear from our car and take it to the outdoor stage.

On the patio around the outdoor stage were a dozen or so big round tables with twelve people at each table, plus several other tables, so it was a sizeable crowd. Simon started setting up the lighting rig while Jill and I set up the instruments, the mixing desk and our microphones.

A lady came up to the stage.

"Are the Blues Brothers coming?"

"Sorry, I took the booking and there was no mention of the Blues Brothers," I replied.

The lady shrugged and went away. A few minutes later, a large Scottish chap came up and approached Jill.

"I've never seen a Blues Brother wearing a frock."

"What's all this about the Blues Brothers?" Jill asked the chap.

"They come every year to this tournament. It's a tribute act, like. We weren't told that they weren't coming this year, so everyone who booked for tonight is expecting the Blues Brothers."

Just then the manager came over and asked us if we were okay. I mentioned that the audience seemed to be looking for the Blues Brothers. He explained that we got the booking because the local Blues Brothers tribute act had given up working in Spain and gone back to the UK.

We groaned. Before he booked us, the manager had asked what kind of music we played and we told him everything from Adele ballads to Chuck Berry rock and roll. He seemed satisfied with that, and I didn't remember hin asking if we performed any Blues Brothers songs.

"We might be in trouble tonight," I whispered to Jill.

"We'll be fine, JB. We've got a far bigger range of material than the Blues Brothers."

For reasons best known to her, Jill calls me Jim Bob, or JB for short. I've no idea why. I was never in 'The Waltons'.

We finished setting our gear up and went to get changed into our stage clothes. When Jill came out to the stage, shimmering in a long flowing dress, a hair extension, and wearing the reddest lipstick in the shop, it was absolutely clear that she wasn't going to be mistaken for a Blues Brother.

We kicked off the gig. Nearly a hundred and fifty people were sitting at the tables waiting to see what kind of music we were going to offer. After the smattering of applause for our first song, it was clear that they didn't regard J & J Music as a satisfactory substitute for the Blues Brothers.

We did a few more really lively songs, but no-one got up to dance and we only got light applause. It looked like it was going to be a long night. Simon did his best to support us by grinning at us and cheering us on, but he was about the only one. Jill and I have an easy rapport, we have a lot of fun on stage and that night we joked with the audience, but there seemed to be a barrier which we just couldn't knock down.

I played an instrumental number, a good-going boogie, while Jill went backstage. I finished my solo and she came back out onto the stage.

"That's better. Can you see what I've done?" she asked the audience. "I was tripping over my long dress, so I went backstage and tucked it into my knickers. Can you see?"

Jill did a pirouette, the audience burst out laughing and the ice was well and truly broken.

"I bet the Blues Brothers never did that!" she continued to more laughter.

Job done brilliantly and we were off. Our next song was an old Motown number and a few people got up and danced. We went straight into our next number and more folk got up to dance. Eventually we gave them a break from dancing and Jill asked the audience if they'd like an Adele song.

We've found that Adele's music is enjoyed by all ages. The oldest fan I know in our area is well over eighty. We performed 'Someone Like You', just voice and piano as on the record. I found the original piano part rather monotonous, so I changed the arrangement to give the song more light and shade. I've also given the song a more definite finish rather than the half-hearted 'yeah' and muddy chords at the end of the record.

Jill maybe doesn't quite have the power of Adele, but she has a really wide vocal range. On our quiet songs, she really pulled the audience into the song and she usually achieved silence. We took the chance to perform 'Someone Like You', and by God it worked. The audience gradually quietened down when they heard what was happening, and by the middle of the song we had almost total silence. Jill got thunderous applause, and as always she gave due credit to the piano man. By the end of the first half, we had the audience well and truly on our side.

We took a break, and received several lovely compliments. When we kicked off the second set, most people got up to dance. With us being a Scottish act, there's one song which I knew would work for us. Jill wasn't so sure, as she thought it was too Scottish. But the Proclaimers' '500 Miles' does it every time. We'd never performed it in public before, but I wanted to give it a go.

I could see Jill was nervous, but when I kicked off the first staccato chords on the piano, there were gasps and a few yells, and the entire audience to a man got up to dance. Wow! I wasn't expecting that. I sing part of this song, and as I'm not a great singer, I make it rather more Scottish than the original - "I'll get back hame to yeeeeuw" if you get my meaning.

We finished the gig with some fifties' rock & roll, and it never fails. I did my Little Richard and Jerry Lee piano stuff, battering my Roland piano into submission. We had a ball, and the audience demanded a couple of encores. After an ovation from the audience, I gave Roland a wee kiss and put him back in his case.

Before we left for home, the manager got us some drinks and we sat at a table to collect our our fee. A Scottish lady came up to us, rather the worse for wear, and kissed Jill and I.

Jill apologised to her. "Aw, I'm sorry you didn't get the Blues Brothers tonight. I know we were second best."

"Whit are ye talkin' aboot, lass?" She slurred. "The Blues Brothers were guid, but by Christ ye were much better. Bluddy brilliant!"

We were booked there and then for the following year. Nice one, Jill.

The following week we had a rather novel experience. We were booked to play a Sixties' Night at a restaurant at the end of Vera Playa. I play a wee bit of guitar, but I'm not a natural player. I have to work at it.

The owner of the venue had heard me playing a few tunes on my electric guitar at a jam session, and had asked me if I could do a short set of tunes by The Shadows, who sold huge amounts of records in the sixties, with and without Cliff Richard. I loved the way Hank Marvin twanged the notes – he did this with the tremolo arm on his Fender Stratocaster. This device enabled him to hit a note then make it go a bit lower, then twang it back up. I love the twang so much that some years ago I bought a guitar which swings both ways – it has a tremolo arm which not only moves the note lower, it also moves it higher. It does this due to being fitted with a thing on the guitar's body called a Floyd Rose bridge.

I'm telling you this as a warning not to make the mistake I made and buy a guitar with one of these blasted devices fitted - unless of course you enjoy spending your days tuning electric guitars. Think of it as a balancing act. Without wishing to bore you with a detailed explanation, I'll just say that if the springs holding the bridge in place are not evenly balanced, your guitar will not stay in tune. This was the problem I was having at the Sixties' Night. As soon as I got my guitar in tune, it would slip out of tune. After fifteen minutes trying to tune it, I had to give up.

So, what to do? We had advertised that I'd be playing a set of Shadows tunes on my guitar, and I had made up some backing tracks to play along to. But there was no way my electric guitar was going to stay in tune long enough for me to play half a dozen or so Shadows hits.

In my act with Jill, I play a full 88-note stage piano with a bracket on top holding a 61-note synthesizer. The synth is amazing. It doesn't have as many notes as my piano, but it has a huge range of sampled sounds and allows me to get organ, accordion and string sounds to enhance the piano. I can write drum backing tracks on it too. It also has guitar sounds and crucially it has a lever which allows me to bend notes. So, after some discussion with me, Jill made an announcement to the audience.

"Eh, you may have noticed that Jim has been having problems with his guitar tonight. Sadly, he won't be able to play his Shadows set on the guitar." Groans from the audience. "But Jim isn't going to let you down. Heaven knows what this is going to sound like, but he's going to play the guitar sound on his synthesizer."

There were a few cheers and more than a few murmurs of surprise from the audience. Jill picked up her tambourine to provide some accompaniment, and I kicked off with the Shadows backing tracks which I had written for my set.

'Apache' went pretty well, and I have to say that my synth played a blinder. I played all the right notes (something I don't always do on the guitar) and used my synth's lever to twang away. No-one got up and danced, but they did give me some polite applause.

My next instrumental was 'Foot Tapper' and this time some people got up and danced. By the time I started 'FBI', the floor was filled with happy people just going with the flow and grooving along to my keyboard guitar sounds and Jill's tambourine. I even managed to kick a leg in the air, the way Hank Marvin and the Shadows guitarists used to do. Ok, maybe I didn't kick as high as they did, but you try kicking your leg in the air while playing a keyboard! I must have been stark staring bonkers, but in for a penny.....

The evening was a great success and I was delighted to instigate what I'm sure must be the only Shadows set not to feature a single guitar.

- - - - - - - - - - - -

It was ten o'clock on a Monday morning. Carrie and I were still asleep after a late one. We'd been out with a bunch of friends for a Chinese meal, and ended up at Tom and Julie's place. My battered old acoustic guitar had somehow found its way into the boot of the car before we left, so Tom and I knocked out some blues until the early hours.

So although the sun split the skies, as far as my brain was concerned it was a Stormy Monday. A paracetamol and sunglasses day.

I was having a rather nice dream about me and Keira Knightley on a desert island with only figs to eat and fig leaves to cover our bodies. We had just settled down for the night in a bamboo hut with a heart-shaped bed covered in dark red satin sheets strewn with rose petals. Keira was wearing a cream-coloured satin bra and panties which contrasted beautifully with the dark red sheets. On a table next to the bed was a bottle of champagne, and a large bowl of figs to keep us regular.

I was just about to move myself into position above Keira when the phone rang. I winced, then answered the call.

"Hola," I croaked.

"Is that Jim?"

"Yes it is. How can I help?" I croaked.

"Joe here from Ye Olde Pisse House on Mojacar Playa" (I've changed the name ever so slightly to protect the guilty). Joe sounded like he was on the set of Eastenders.

He continued. "Christ, you've got a deep voice, mate! You were recommended to me by one of my customers. I need a pianist to play a dinner dance the last Friday of this month. I've heard that you play dance music. Are you free?"

"I'm free." I must have sounded like Barry White mimicking John Inman.

He responded drily. "Can you sing as well as play the piano?"

"Sure, if you want an early night."

"Why, are you not a good singer?"

"Not compared to the singer I work with." Ok, I was being hard work, but it was only half past ten in the morning.

"Who's your singer?"

"Her name's Jill and she's got a great voice. We work as a duo and we do a lot of boogie and rock and roll."

"Oh, fantastic. That's just what I'm looking for. Can the lady come too, then?"

"Yes, if you want to pay for us both"

"Ok, no problem. The dinner dance starts at 8 o'clock."

This sounded a bit early to start dancing. In my befuddled state, I thought for a moment.

"Hello, are you still there?" Joe asked.

"What time will you be starting to serve dinner?" I enquired.

"8 o'clock"

"And you want the dance music to start at 8 o'clock?"

"Yes. Oh, I see what you mean. Can your lady do some quiet songs when they're eating, then start the dance music later on when they've finished eating?"

"Yes, no problem. That's what we normally do."

So Jill and I were duly booked for the dinner dance.

I made a note in my diary and rolled over in the vain hope of Keira and me picking up where we left off. No chance. The figs Keira had eaten had clearly taken effect, and strange noises were coming from the bathroom. I woke up again just as she was asking me to slide some tissues under the bottom of the bathroom door.

A week before the Friday gig, Joe 'phoned.

"Jim, you know this fund-raiser you're playing next Friday?"

"Sorry, Joe, I don't know anything about a fund-raiser. You've only booked us for a dinner dance."

"It's for an animal charity."

"Oh, we have our own animal charity."

163

"What's that?"

"Blind dogs for the guides."

Straight over his head. "No, the gig I booked you for next Friday is a fund-raiser."

"That's news to me."

"Maybe I forgot to tell you. Sorry, mate. It changed a couple of weeks ago. The dinner dance is still on, but it's now a fund-raiser for an animal charity."

"Do you still want us to play?"

"Oh, yes. We're sponsoring the event. And I've booked a great comedian to do an interval spot."

"We'll be happy to do the gig next Friday, Joe, and as it's for charity I'm sure we can do it for a lower fee than normal."

"Oh, you don't need to do that, mate. I'll make sure you get properly paid."

Robin, my double-bass playing friend, heard that the gig was a fund-raiser, and he kindly offered to come along and play bass with us.

Friday arrived and we got to Ye Olde Pisse House at 7pm to set up. Our respective spouses came along for the meal and to support the charity. Joe was nowhere to be seen.

The bar manager came over. "We just need you to play quiet background music from half past eight until ten o'clock, when the raffle starts, then do your dance music from about half past ten until half past eleven. Can you finish dead on half past eleven? The folk here don't like late nights."

I explained that Joe had specifically asked us to start at eight o'clock, not half past eight, and that's why we had arrived an hour early to set up.

"Maybe he forgot to tell you. The comedian's on at eight o'clock for half an hour, so you don't have to start playing until half past eight. Play whatever you want, I'm really not bothered what you do as long as the punters are happy."

Such dedication to duty.

Jill and I set up, then Robin arrived. We had time to spare, so the three of us went to the ice cream parlour next door for a coffee. People started arriving and we could hear some raised voices, then angry shouting. Seems that everyone had booked a table, and the charity organiser had given Joe the number of diners. Problem was, Joe had given the staff an entirely different number by the management and they hadn't set up enough tables. A lot of the folk who had bought

164

tickets had to have their meals outside on plastic chairs, thereby missing the entertainment. This was only the first problem of the night....

At 8-15pm, the bar manager came over to the coffee house looking for me.

"Jim, you were to start playing at 8 o'clock. What are you doing?

"But an hour ago you told me that you wanted us to start at half past eight."

"Did no-one tell you? That's all changed. The comedian's not well, and he's not here yet. Can you start playing now?"

"Ok, no problem, but I'm not psychic. Where's Joe anyway?"

"I've no idea. He hasn't turned up or phoned to say why he's not here, so we're trying to sort things out for ourselves. Joe was supposed to MC the event, but I've had to get someone else from the hospital charity to do that".

"I thought it was an animal charity."

"Who told you that?"

"Joe."

"Oh. He must have got things mixed up. It's much the same thing. Don't worry, mate, it's only a charity do."

Jill, Robin and I played soft ballads through the meal, and we got a good reception. A better reception than the food, which had to be divided up among a lot more folk than originally planned due to the cock-up over the numbers.

Ten o'clock arrived, and the comedian was annnounced. He was an absolutely enormous man of grey complexion, slumped at a table near the stage, clearly not in good health, and on crutches. Two heavies helped him to the side of the stage, but even though the stage was only about a foot high, there was no way they could lift his vast bulk onto it. So they put him on a chair in front of the stage. It was clear that the effort of getting there had taken its toll, and he sat slumped on the chair unable to raise his head, legs askew. He started telling jokes in a monotone voice, barely able to hold the microphone under his chin. For a man in such obvious poor health, I thought he was very brave in attempting to perform.

There was a black couple, well-known locally for their charity work, about ten feet or so from where the comedian was slumped, and bang in his line of sight. If the poor chap had managed to raise his head a bit to see them, maybe he wouldn't have started telling jokes about Pakistanis. The members of the audience were understandably

165

mortified, and no-one had the courage or inclination to laugh.

After nearly 10 minutes of racist jokes and stunned silence from the audience, the two heavies returned. They told the comedian to finish, and helped him off to a smattering of applause before he caused further embarrassment. Bernard Manning would have struggled to cause as much offence that night!

As the comedian disappeared round the corner, Jill and I thought, that's good, at last we can play our dance set now. Actually no, we couldn't, as we were then given a long detailed talk about the hospital charity, followed by another talk by a oldish chap who had survived a serious illness and had come to praise the charity's work. Quite right, and we didn't mind waiting the half hour or so for this information to be delivered. After the talks, we were told that the raffle was about to start.

It was now half past ten, and the dance element of the dinner dance had been completely missing up until this point. However, the raffle was about to start. It took nearly an hour - there were loads of items to raffle and every item was raffled off individually, including several bottles of nasty red wine given away free by some Chinese restaurants to customers who had paid their bills. We wouldn't even use this chemical concoction for cooking, as the red wine faded to orange after a few weeks in the cupboard.

Every blessed item, however worthless and humble, was raffled off individually. Some folk ended up with several items - I had bought some raffle tickets and I ended up with a bottle of Chinese liqueur (guess from where?), a tatty red scarf with a Chinese design, and a yellow plastic fruit bowl stamped "A Present from Beijing".

After the first fifteen minutes or so, the audience started to lose interest and talk among themselves. Some went outside for a smoke. Seeing the vast amount of stuff still to be raffled off, Jill and I strolled over to a nearby hotel, where we managed to catch the last ten minutes of an excellent parrot show, where we watched parrots riding bicycles and doing trapeze work and suchlike.

When we returned to Ye Olde Pisse House at 11pm, the raffle was still not finished and there was an atmosphere of boredom and desperation on the part of the audience.

One chap in a dinner jacket came up to me. "I thought you were going to play dance music? That's what was advertised and that's what we've paid for. My wife wanted to dance after the meal, not sit on her arse."

I responded. "We're desperate to kick off, but we can't. The boss was supposed to run the show, but he's nobody knows where he is and the charity are doing their best to run it themselves. As you can see, they're not exactly ripping through the raffle. I'm really sorry, we desperately want to get the dancing started, but we've been hanging about ready to begin for well over an hour and we can't do anything about it. After the raffle, there's going to be the auction, so it could be a while yet."

He shook his head, muttered something under his breath, and indicated to his wife to get her coat.

After the raffle had finished, the auction began. It should have been successful in raising money, as the goods on offer seemed of decent quality. But the audience were clearly bored and disappointed, so there was scant support for the auction. It was a tedious affair, with each item taking several minutes to reach its reserve price despite the auctioneer's best efforts.

By now it was after half past eleven and we still hadn't played a note of dance music. As the last item was being auctioned, Jill, Robin and I got ourselves set up on the stage, ready to start performing. We started our dance set within seconds of the auctioneer leaving the stage, but the remaining audience started leaving in droves as it was by now way past their bedtime. One couple sort of danced their way out of the door, and that was the only dancing that night. After two songs the place was deserted. We packed up and put this disaster down to experience.

Joe never did turn up that night. I never did get to meet him. We never did get paid. The venue closed down two weeks later, after Joe did a runner, owing back rent. The staff got the wages they were owed by selling off the entire drinks stock before they handed the keys back to the landlord.

It's now a charity shop....

We have a great support system down here in Almería, and there are some really worthwhile charities run by good people. The two most well-known are PAWS, a charity which takes in abandoned dogs and cats, and MACS, a charity which offers support to families struck down with cancer. The musicians around here provide wonderful support for various charities, providing sound equipment and giving of their time, usually without recompense for their expenses, and often having to buy their own drinks!

Brendan had arranged for me to play at a jam a few nights later at a bar called 'Sax Talk'. It was a small bar not far off the beach, run by a tall and elegant Canadian gent called Hutch. He was a really cool sax player, softly spoken and always immaculately dressed. He was always very friendly towards Carrie and me.

Hutch was also full of ideas for gigs and events. No idea was too big for him. He planned to have a Mojacar jazz festival, and bring over some jazz stars who, he told me, were his personal friends. Sadly, it never got off the ground.

One Thursday I got a call from Hutch asking if I could play a gig on the Saturday afternoon at a chiringuito (beach bar) on the playa. The owner of the chiringuito had asked him to provide a band, and he wanted me on keyboard. I accepted the gig, but on the condition that the set list must include tunes that I knew, as there was no time for rehearsals.

"Don't worry, Jim," Hutch reassured me. "We'll just improvise. I've played with quite a few of the major jazz stars, and that's what we usually do."

"What tunes do you want us to improvise on?"

"Oh, we'll sort it out at the gig. Bring your piano down and I'll set up a PA system, that's all we need. I've got a great young drummer coming, a Spanish lad called Raul, plus your mate Graeme on guitar and Phil on bass. I'll bring my clarinet as well as my sax. We'll be just fine."

"Don't you want to organise a set list?" I suggested.

"Listen, Jim, I've played all round the world with loads of major players. I've never worked with a set list."

I knew that I could probably follow Hutch, but there was just a hint of doubt in my mind. Although the money wasn't great, the beach bar was fabulous and they were feeding us after the gig. The Spanish venues always look after their performers.

As I arrived on the Saturday afternoon, Hutch was already setting up. I touched base with the other musicians and they all seemed nice guys.

The chiringuito was right on the beach, with several levels of wooden decking and with tables and chairs dotted around. The sun glinted on the sea and customers were arriving to chill out and listen to the music. It looked as if the gig was going to be fun.

"What are we starting with?" I asked Hutch.

"Whatever you want, Jim," came the reply.

"It's not my gig, Hutch. I don't know what the other guys can play."

"Just start jamming, man!"

It's the story of my life. I'm hired for someone else's gig then I'm expected to call the tune, as it were. The audience had already been waiting a while as Hutch had difficulty tuning up his sax and his clarinet. I was keen not to keep them waiting, so I decided to make a suggestion.

"Ok, guys, can I suggest we start with a 12-bar blues. Key of G."

"Not G, Jim," moaned Hutch. "I can't play in G".

I was a bit taken aback. "All right, key of C then, guys."

"Can you do a blues in A minor?" suggested Hutch.

"Ok, sure, A minor it is. We're all agreed, guys?" Heads nodded and I waited for the drummer to count us in. Nothing.

"Hutch, can you count us in. I don't know what tempo you want."

"Oh, just pick a tempo, Jim!"

The others looked to me for guidance, so I counted us in at a nice easy tempo so we could work our way into the music and find out how best to play together. After a couple of choruses, our pick-up band was starting to gel. Hutch, however, was playing a puzzling series of notes, not all related to the 12-bar blues or to the key of A minor. I put this down to opening nerves. Surely an international jazz saxophonist with friends in high places would be well able to play a tune on the instrument. It didn't sound to me like A minor was a good key for the saxophone.

We all managed to finish the blues in unison, and I waited for Hutch to tell us what the next tune was to be.

"All right, guys, let's do a jam in A minor," he announced.

"What chord progression do you want?" I asked him. This is pretty vital information, in order that the musicians are all playing off the same hymn sheet. If we were all to play different chords, it would sound like an open day at a music school.

"Oh, just jam in the chord of A minor."

"What, the same chord for the entire tune?"

"Oh, yes, it'll be fine Jim."

No, Hutch, it'll be boring, I thought.

"Hutch, can you get Raul to set the tempo and count us in?" I asked.

Hutch took me aside and whispered in my ear.

"He won't do that, Jim. He won't take the responsibility since he left rehab."

I set the tempo as a fastish funk number and left it up to Hutch to play whatever tune he had in his head. Only problem was, he didn't

169

actually have a tune in his head. He just riffed the odd note on his sax and looked expectantly at me.

I swiftly worked out the semblance of a tune. With only about ten seconds to compose it, I can't say it was exactly memorable. Hutch played around a bit with my 'tune', then the other guys improvised around it, but it was all pretty boring as there were no chord changes to provide any interest, just the chord of A minor. We got a smattering of applause.

"That was great, Jim." Hutch complimented me.

"What next, Hutch?" I asked

"Well, that went pretty well. Why don't we do another of the same."

"You mean another jam in A minor?"

"Yea man, let's do...... like, a reprise. Play the same tune and we'll all just jam along. Keep the tempo the same too. But I'll do something different this time, just watch."

Without a word of a lie, we started playing exactly the same 'tune' in exactly the same key of A minor. But this time, when Hutch stepped up to play a solo, he played both his sax and his clarinet at he same time, one in each hand. When I say played, he sort of honked staccato notes out of both instruments at once. You couldn't call it music, but the audience loved it and applauded Hutch enthusiastically. He gave good value and honked out the same notes for fully five minutes. As far as I was concerned, we were only filling in time, and I just wanted to get the funk out of it.

I wanted Hutch to play some sax standards, the classic tunes that every jazz sax player knows.

"Let's play 'Watermelon Man'," I suggested. Herbie Hancock's rocking tune is still very popular and I was sure it would lift the gig.

"I don't know if I can remember that one, Jim."

"I'll play it then, and you can improvise around the chords."

"I'll do my best, but I don't know it so you'll need to play it in A minor."

'Watermelon Man' is a staple of every jazz sax player. It's like 'Stranger on the Shore' to a clarinet player. It's normally played in G major. It's a fun tune. It's not a sad minor key sort of tune, although it sure was that day.

"Hutch, you must know 'Summertime'." I almost pleaded with him. "Every man and his dog plays it around here."

"Oh, sure. Everyone knows 'Summertime'." Hutch responded.

Well, nearly everyone. Hutch certainly knew the first 8 bars, but the rest was a mystery to him. He didn't even know 'Fly Me to the Moon'. During our break he explained the problem.

"Jim, here's the thing. All my sheet music is back in Canada, and I don't really play tunes as such around here." Now this was something different - a musician who could really only play in one key and who didn't really play tunes anyway. By now it didn't altogether surprise me.

As we were taking our break, a Spanish couple in the audience came over and asked if we could play 'La Bamba'. It's the simplest of songs, 3 chords repeated more or less throughout the verses and chorus of the song. The guys were up for it, particularly the by-now cheesed-off drummer Raul, who even offered to set the tempo. Hutch seemed a little non-committal, but I was sure he would be fine.

We concluded our first set with 'La Bamba', in A minor of course. Raul was delighted to be in familiar territory, and all the guys knew the song. Well, nearly all. Hutch could only play the first four bars of the verse, which he repeated ad nauseum for the next few minutes. When he ran out of ideas, he just over-blew random notes on his sax. The audience loved it, but there was no 'Ba Ba Bamba' chorus for them to sing along to.

After we finished, Hutch asked me if I knew 'The Shadow of your Smile'.

"Yes, it's a nice song. Delicate and lovely."

"Well put, Jim. I'd like to play that song. I seem to recall that it was written in A minor."

I smiled knowingly.

To be fair, the first part of the tune went really well. Hutch missed a few notes and played the odd wrong note, but on the whole you would have recognised the tune.

The problem started in the second part of the song, where the composer cunningly changes the key from the starting key of A minor to finish the song up in the relative major key of C. Hutch had clearly forgotten about this and searched in vain for the correct notes in A minor. Sadly, the second part of the delicate and lovely old song lacked all traces of delicacy and loveliness because the sax player was playing in an entirely different key from the rest of the band. Imagine, if you will, a love-starved buffalo suffering a strangulated hernia to the accompaniment of a pleasantly competent jazz quartet, and you'll get an inkling of what our version of 'The Shadow of your Smile' sounded like. It was 'orrible.

171

The gig ground to a halt with the same simple 12-bar blues we had started with, once again in the key of A minor. The audience loved it when Hutch once again blew two horns at once. I can't say he actually played two horns at once. He blew some random notes, that's all I'm saying.

But of all the musicians at that gig, Hutch was:

The one who didn't know any tunes

The one who honked a load of rubbish out of two instruments at once

The one who could only play in the key of A minor

The one who actually got us the gig (admittedly)

.....and he was the one who got all the adulation from the audience that day. The rest of us were merely his accompanists.

Am I the only pianist ever to have played an entire gig in the key of A minor?

CHAPTER 10 - OCTOBER

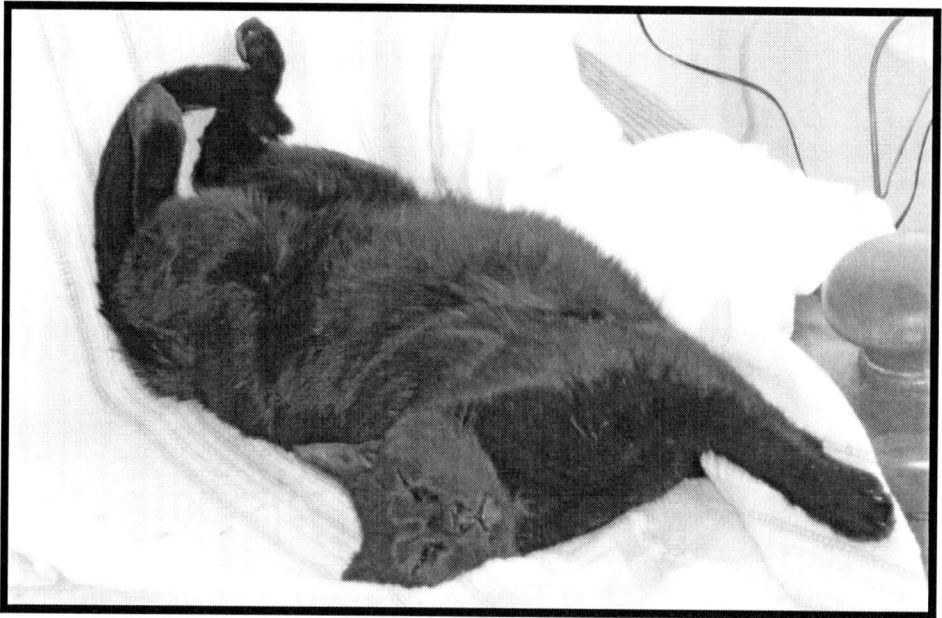

Our mental cat Sammy continues to oversee our home and tweak it to his satisfaction.

Sometimes, when we close up the house to go out for the night, Sammy decides to go out for a bit of nocturnal wandering.

A few hours later I'm driving the car up the lane to the house. The headlights shine on a large black cat sitting stock-still, slap-bang in the middle of the lane, lips back and teeth gleaming in the car's headlights, as if to say "Oi, what time do you call this?" If he could fold his arms in repressed anger, I'm sure he would. I usually have to stop the car to let Carrie out to shoo him away while I drive on and park the car.

There's that familiar "Waaaaaaaaaaaaaa", and we're hassled all the way up to the front door, where we're given strict instructions to get food on his plate without delay. While gulping down his nosh, Sammy occasionally raises his head from his bowl to voice further chastisement with his mouth full. Bad manners, I know, but do remember that we haven't been able to train him from the time he was a kitten.

When it's time for us to go to bed at night, Sammy is usually sprawled out on Carrie's lap. I try to get him to go into his basket.

"It's bedtime, Sammy."

"Wwwaaaaaaaaaaaaaaa." Catspeak for "Aw, not yet."

"Honestly, it's bedtime. We're all going to bed now."

"WWWWAAAAAAAAAAAAAAAA." Catspeak for "Bugger off and leave me alone."

Eventually I have to pick Sammy up and deposit him in his basket. A few curses later, he settles down, always in disgust and with his back to me. I gently place his soft woollen blanket over him with his nose poking out, and loud contented purring begins. This means I'm forgiven for disturbing him – daddy has tucked him in so all's well.

There's a great Garth Brooks song called 'Standing Outside the Fire'. It contains the line "Life is not tried, it is merely survived, when you're standing outside the fire". Ok, we've all heard better rhymes but the message is sound. In Scottish parlance it means "gie it laldy" (give it your best shot). If Sammy had a talent for songwriting, he couldn't have put it better himself. He's not the type of cat who's content to sit at the back and say nothing. To put it bluntly, he's very vocal. I'm absolutely convinced that he doesn't really think of himself as a cat. In his mind, he's the head of the household.

Sammy has a thing about telephones. When I'm on the phone, he likes to get in on the act. He sits on the floor and yells at me, then jumps up into my lap, climbs onto my shoulder and nuzzles the phone to join in the conversation. It reminds me of the time when I was a teenager and my mother would sometimes 'inadvertedly' monitor my calls and end up talking to my friends.

One morning, I'd left my mobile phone on charge upstairs in the bedroom. I had disrobed and was just about to get in the shower when I heard it ring. I wasn't in any position to answer it, so I hoped that Carrie would hear it from the lounge downstairs. After I had showered and dressed, she appeared, red-faced and laughing.

"Your cat has just told me to answer your phone."

"Sorry, what did you say?" I couldn't quite take this in.

"I was sitting watching the TV news and I heard your mobile phone ring upstairs. I assumed you would answer it, so I didn't get up. Sammy went flying up the stairs then he came flying down again. He skidded to a halt at the bottom of the stairs and was literally shouting at me, and you know how loud he can get. He just shouted and shouted at me to get up, then he followed me upstairs nagging me until I answered your phone. Then he sat on the floor and wouldn't shut up. I could hardly make out what the fellow on the end of the line was

174

saying. Sammy just kept howling at me"

"Were you standing up while you were on the phone?"

"Yes, I suppose."

"Ah! He likes it when I talk on the phone," I explained to Carrie. "But he hates it when I take the call standing up. He needs me to sit down so he can nuzzle the phone and purr. He likes to get involved in the phone call, so you have to answer the phone promptly and sit down to take the call."

"You're telling me I've to take orders from a cat?" said a face like fizz.

"You just did. He got you to answer my phone, didn't he? But next time just sit down to talk and you'll be fine."

I got a dirty look and turned to go upstairs to the office.

"Do you not want to know who the phone call was from?" Carrie asked.

I nodded and she explained. "It was from the telecom company. Why were they calling you? You told me you were going to call them."

"I did call them – five times between yesterday morning and this morning. I tried three different departments and none of them had anyone answering their phones, so I left a message asking them to call me back."

"You're telling me that we're dealing with a telephone company who don't answer their telephones?"

"I'm afraid so," I replied. "You couldn't make it up, could you? They never answer but if I leave a message they do always call me back. Eventually. It's always the same bloke who calls me back, so maybe he runs all the departments. That's technical progress for you."

Although our local vet confirmed that Sammy had definitely been neutered, I discovered that he has an erogenous zone. One night, we were sitting watching the TV. Sammy was on my lap purring loudly and I was stroking his back, when I noticed that his purring went into overdrive when I moved my hand around the area near his tail. I decided to investigate further, so I gently caressed the area between the end of his back and his tail. He arched his hind legs, stuck his bum up, narrowed his eyes, put his nose in the air and slowly moved it from side to side while purring like Eartha Kitt on heat. He was clearly in a trance-like ecstasy. Carrie thought it hilarious that I had the ability to turn on a doctored cat, but I could sense that she was rather envious. Occasionally Sammy would bare his teeth and threaten to bite my hand, as if to say "I really, really, really like what you're doing, but you're taking our relationship too far."

Although Sammy has access to the countryside around our house for his ablutions, on cold winter nights he prefers to use the litter tray which we keep in a corner of the downstairs loo round the corner from the kitchen. I'd put a label on the litter tray saying "For emergency use only" and Sammy sticks faithfully to the rules.

But even a humble litter tray can cause entertainment in our house. Imagine a particularly cold and windy night unsuitable for important cats to be out in, and we're in the kitchen cooking dinner. We hear a familiar scrabbling sound, then a "Yaaaaaaawwww" as he searches for a suitable spot, followed by a soft satisfying "Brrrrrrrp" as he settles down to business. A minute or so later a small black figure scurries past us with an almighty "Brrrroooooooop" then skids on the shiny laminate flooring and crash-lands somewhere in the lounge. This always signals a successful event in the bowel department, as if he's announcing "Ah, that's better!"

And Sammy fills up his digestive system with great enthusiasm. He enjoys the usual things like cat biscuits and milk but he won't have anything to do with budget cat food. He can't say "sausages" like a certain TV dog could, but he can certainly devour them as fast as many canines.

He also devours cooked ham, mince and potatoes, paella, chicken fajitas, crab sticks, mussels, marmite on toast, Stilton or any strong mature cheese but please don't insult him with tasteless mild cheddar. Oh, and pasta Bolognese, foie gras but only on Carr's water biscuits (so crunchy...) and potato crisps (sensationally crunchy). Then there's pistachio nuts, French toast, meatballs, sweetcorn, pork stuffed with prunes, chicken and date tagine and sticky ribs. He adores the fresh sausages from the Superclara shop in the village as they're virtually all meat. He once tried Richmond Irish pork sausages but they're only around 40% meat and the rest is filler, so he wouldn't touch them. He's not so keen on prawns unless we bring him a doggy bag from the Peking restaurant in Garrucha, preferably along with some of their very tasty beef in oyster sauce with the crunchy water chestnuts.

As for dessert... Though seldom available in our household, sticky toffee pudding is yummy and very acceptable. Proper home-made egg custard is great (he'll force down Bird's imitation custard if things are really desperate but only if I add real vanilla) but his favourite by far is Lidl's gorgeous Dulce de Leche ice cream with caramel sauce. And we've really no idea why Sammy is so keen on marzipan – we got a gift of some, and he sniffed around until I gave him a morcel. He's lapped it up ever since. He also loves Malva cake which Carrie makes from an easy recipe on the internet. Try it and don't tell me it's not utterly fabulous!

Sammy has a more sophisticated palate than certain humans I know. It always seems to be the women who're the fussy eaters or vegetarians. I've certainly never heard the phrase "My husband is a vegetarian."

Sammy's favourite live snacks are stick insects as they're easy to toss in the air for a while and super-crunchy. The toy you can eat!!

There are many cats in our village, including Sammy's sister Tina. I often walk up to the village post office via a rough stony path behind our house, and I always meet some beautiful cats just waiting for me to admire them and get their ears scratched.

There are also several bird cages on residents' terraces. We have a Spanish neighbour with an elderly parrot whom she takes out for walks. That is to say, she does the walking, and as we live in a very hilly village, the parrot wisely perches on her shoulder. I told you it was elderly!

We also have a donkey in the village (burro in Spanish) which is owned by an elderly Spaniard called Juan Pedro. One day, we were sitting on our terrace having lunch, when down the hill staggered this donkey with huge panniers either side, followed by a clearly inebriated Juan Pedro shouting "Burro, burro" and desperately trying to keep both his donkey and himself on the road. The pair zig-zagged their way all the way down the hill past our house, Juan Pedro constantly yelling at his donkey while staggering unsteadily.

- - - - - - - - - - - -

Some mornings, we hear the village band practising, which is rather lovely to hear from a safe distance. But the weirdest thing of all for my wife and me (as true Scots) is to hear the sound of the bagpipes in the distance from our terrace some days. There is a Scottish fellow in the village (Scottish Jim Number One), who sometimes plays the pipes on market days, and it is amazing to hear them in the distance, echoing down the valley.

The reason I emphasise 'in the distance' is that when I was in my last year at primary school, my class of around forty-five pupils had a wonderful teacher called John McFadyen. He was a highlander who told us that he played the bagpipes. That summer, just before I left the school, I was one of around thirty schoolmates at a school camp in the middle of nowhere, where no expense had been.... spent. We slept on beds salvaged from a sunken ship, and dined mainly on hard rolls and runny jam.

One morning Mr McFadyen announced that he was going to treat us to some tunes on the bagpipes, but that firstly he was going to walk about a mile out on the hills. My schoolfriends asked him why he needed to do that, and he just said "Oh, you'll find out why". We had left behind our comfortable homes and home-cooked food for this shithole, and we were thoroughly miserable.

When we heard the eerie sound of the pipes echoing in the distant hills, every one of these kids understood why our teacher had walked so far away. We all got chills hearing this eerie sound, and cheered Mr McFadyen when he returned. Here's the thing - if you've ever been in a room where the pipes are played, you'll realise that your ears are best kept at a safe distance.

And we'll sometimes hear our neighbour John the Banjo plunking away. We have a new neighbour who's from Devon who has played flamenco guitar since he was a teenager. Around 1970 he had a flamenco guitar hand-made for him by a renowned guitar maker in Cordoba. He plays his guitar most days. He's a lovely man, well-liked by all who've met him. We call him Flamenco Sid, and he is a cracking guitarist.

I had made several new friends at the Cellar Club, and my two most loyal supporters were Ross and Hazel. Like me, Ross is a Scot, but unlike yer Glaswegian author, he's from Edinburgh. He made a decent living as a surveyor from his base in Milton Keynes, and he also got bookings as a Sven-Goran Eriksson look-alike, through an entertainment agency. Hazel is tall and slim with an unmistakably Brummie accent, She's a dedicated fan of Barry Manilow, and way beyond responding to treatment.

My first impressions of Ross were of a very sincere and serious chap, and Hazel seemed a fun-loving lady who gave me wicked looks whenever I misbehaved. We became really good friends, and one of the lovely things about living here is that our friends became their friends, and vice versa.

We've had several adventures with Ross and Hazel. Our most memorable adventure was when I lost my passport.

I had been dispatched by our builder to a shop in nearby Antraix to pick up some building materials for an outside wall. Chip and pin hadn't yet reached Antraix and I knew that the shop would requird my passport to check my signature on my bank card. So I took my passport out of the car's glove box, and put it on my lap while I swapped over my sunglasses for my clear glasses. Then I promptly forgot about my passport as I got out of the car.

When I arrived at the till with my purchases, I didn't have my passport. So I went back to the car, looked on the floor, all around the driver's seat, and on the ground outside. I looked everywhere for about ten minutes but it was nowhere to be seen. The only thing I could reckon was that someone had seen it while I was in the shop, and picked it up.

This episode neatly balanced my efforts the previous month when I broke a leg off my glasses on the winow of the driver's door while getting into the car.

I reported my lost passport to the shop and they told me no-one had handed it in. I had to assume it was gone for good. According to information I found on the internet, I had to report my lost passport to the police in the town where I had lost the passport. I would then be given a document enabling me to get a replacement passport. Ross speaks much better Spanish than any of the rest of our crowd, so I got him to volunteer to help me report the loss and obtain the police document.

I drove the four of us along the country road up to Antraix, through acres and acres of orange groves. We were right out in the country, about halfway to Antraix town, when I rounded a corner and a police officer waved me down and signalled for me to drive into a track just off the road.

"Oh, great," said Carrie from the back seat. "You're out here with no passport. They'll throw the book at you."

Ross was in the front seat and could see what was happening. "It's a procession of some kind. They obviously want us off the road."

I remembered that Antraix had had a fiesta at the weekend, but although it was Monday morning, it appeared that the festivities were not over yet. Round the corner came a large contingent of Spanish folk in all their finery, followed by a red tractor pulling a trailer. Placed precariously on top of the trailer, and supported by the throng, was a wobbling tableau of the virgin Mary. We all stood and stared in disbelief.

"Be honest," I said. "There can't be many places in the world where you can go out on a Monday morning and see a tractor pulling the Virgin Mary."

Ross chipped in "Yes, but look what's behind her."

The Virgin Mary was followed by two industrial rotovators, each with a bamboo shed built around the driver's seat. They looked a bit like rickshaws. Behind them was a three-carriage road train, the kind you usually find at seaside resorts rather than inland Spanish towns, full of kids waving at us enthusiastically. Behind the road train were some decorated floats, classic cars and more tractors. We couldn't see the end of the procession, but we could see a float with Jesus on top, pulled slowly by a group of rather asthmatic smokers. I tried to figure out the religious significance of this float. An old Rikki Fulton sketch from BBC Scotland comes to mind, where a depressingly dour Church of Scotland minister reflects that "Life is like an ashtray - full of little doubts." For the uninitiated, a 'doubt' in tobacco parlance is a cigarette stub.

Ross has impeccable taste and smokes cigars. He took the opportunity to light up a cheroot, then he walked up the road a short distance to what looked like stables.

"Hey, Jim, have a look at this."

I walked over to where Ross was standing at the edge of the road. Down a short path were stables and four magnificent grey horses being groomed by several men, presumably getting ready for the festivities. One of the men signalled for us to come down and see the horses, so Ross went down and took a few photos on his mobile phone.

Eventually the end of the procession tailed into the distance, followed at a slow walking pace by a dozen or so cars and vans.

Hazel was astonished and looked at me. "Where do you think they're all going, Jim?"

The next town was several miles away, but I figured that perhaps they were all headed for a religious site closer to home.

Eventually we were able to drive on, and after a couple of miles we reached Antraix town. Hazel spotted a sign pointing to the 'Policia Local' (local police station) and the 'Ayuntamiento' (town hall) so I drove down a narrow one-way street and looked for a second sign to the police station. No sign appeared, so I continued driving down the hill. There were no more signs for the police station, so I found a road leading back uphill. At one point the road got so narrow that we had to stop and pull in the car's wing mirrors, and proceed with inches to spare on either side. I re-traced our steps and stopped the car near a second sign for the town hall. Ross and I got out of the car and went looking for the police station.

"It should be easy to spot," Ross explained. "The Spanish flag will be flying outside."

To cut a long story short, we found the police station at the other end of town, nowhere near the town hall. True to form, a huge Spanish flag was hoisted on a pole above the police station. The four of us walked in, to find an attractive courtyard setting with various doors to offices, none of which were locked. We knocked on each door, but no-one was home. I clocked the contents of the courtyard:

Two enormous police motorbikes, complete with Spanish flags on the handlebars.

Six boxes of photocopier paper.

A 3-seater green leather sofa.

A statue of the Pope (the Polish one, clearly still number 1 in the pope charts)

A standard lamp with a brown leather shade.

The biggest photocopier in Spain.

Two wingback chairs in maroon fabric.

An 8-feet long glass display cabinet containing a Christmas nativity scene. I noted that the elephants were not to scale with the lions, and that the three kings with sideburns riding the lions resembled the other king, Elvis. It looked like the spit-roast chicken stall in the middle of the nativity scene was being basted by one of the three identical Virgin Marys.

It was a hot day in early October, and either I had entered another dimension or I was in dire need of a beer.

We had been hanging around outside for about ten minutes, looking for any sign of life, when an ancient van chugged up the hill and parked outside. A rotund and swarthy hombre emerged from the van, grunting heavily and sweating profusely while smoking a cheap cigar and talking on his mobile phone. A badge on his shirt confirmed to us that he was a council worker. Eventually, he closed his phone, popped it into his shirt pocket and approached the four of us rather suspiciously.

Ross was our interpreter, and he asked the fellow if there were any police available. The reply was a series of grunts and random noises emanating from the left side of his mouth, while the cigar quivered on the right side of his mouth.

Ross had great difficulty in picking up what the fellow was muttering. "It sounds like he's saying that the local police are busy sewing cod."

We all shook our heads in bewilderment, and the council worker extracted his mobile phone from his sweat-stained shirt pocket then made a call.

"Wanmithyegawipeethanyopedro. Eecartaombrethspeetamanuel. Bally?" He muttered from the cigar-free side of his mouth.

It didn't make any sense to Ross either. The phone call finished, the council worker sweated some more, wished us Buenos Dias and coaxed his van back to life by swearing at it and spitting tobacco at the dashboard.

Five minutes later, a smart police car screeched to a halt outside the police station and two tall, cool-looking young dudes in sunglasses emerged and engaged in deep conversation with Ross. The jist of the thing was that they couldn't help as I had to go to my local police station to report the lost passport and obtain the form.

We gave up our efforts and went off to lunch.

So the next day, I wandered into our town hall to see our local policeman. He is a charming fellow from the village. He'd got married the previous month, and his wedding was a big occasion in the village. At a Spanish wedding, the bride and groom have to visit every house en route to the church. Practically the whole village had turned out to see Diego and his bride. Diego was still on honeymoon and unable to deal with thefts of oranges and the like.

An English-speaking lady at our town hall told me that I couldn't get the form I needed from our village policeman, and that I'd have to go to Vera, as the main police station for the area was there. It turned out that the main Vera police station was the only one with the computer facilities I needed to print out the form.

So a few days later we all set out for Vera police station. We were seen right away by a charming young police officer who told us we couldn't get the form that day as their computer system was down. "Maňana" he shrugged apologetically.

So yet another trip was planned for the next day. We made our way back to the police station and, hallelujah, the computer and printer were working again. Within minutes I had the document I needed to obtain my replacement passport. The police officer refused to accept payment, so I splashed out on celebratory beers at an outdoor bar in the town hall square.

We had some time left until lunch, so we decided to visit Vera's bull ring – it's allegedly one of the oldest in Spain, and the traditional stonework has been lovingly restored. We walked around and were approached by an elderly Spanish gent who insisted on showing us round. He showed us the vet's room, where the bulls are checked over before being sent to a certain death and cut up into steaks. He was especially proud to show us the operating theatre, a bright, spotless and sterile room where gored matadors had it all sewn up.

- - - - - - - - - - -

I really enjoy playing at jam sessions. I love the challenge of meeting a new performer and trying to get the piano to enhance their performance while not getting in the way. I would never ever attempt to play a song I don't know, as it's inevitable that I would simply get in the way of the performance.

I'll try to play in any style from opera to reggae. For me, there should be no limits on the music I perform. For me, there is only good music and bad music. As I said earlier, the only musical genre I just don't 'get' is rap. Okay, maybe I'm overly picky, but I just don't enjoy it when a large and notorious American gentleman bellows at me to someone else's backing track, effing and blinding about stealing money at gunpoint, smacking up his bitch, killing the police and machine-gunning his enemies.

On the other hand, I relish just about everything Bruce Springsteen does, as it is done with a true passion for the music. And like a growing number of music lovers, I am well aware that the criminally underrated Gerry Rafferty is unquestionably the greatest Scottish songwriter since Robert Burns.

Six kilometres up the hill from Bédar village, there's a bar/restaurant in a small hamlet. Bar La Montana is one of the highest-rated places for food in the province of Almería. The young couple who run the bar, Mat and Carol, came to the place with plenty of experience. Mat is a charming host and very knowledgeable about wine. His wife Carol is from Argentina and is a fabulous cook. Her lamb is sensational and I had the best sirloin steak of my life in the restaurant. Her desserts are amazing too. They do a lovely goat's milk cheese starter with cheese from the goat farm at the end of their track.

Anyway, my book is not a restaurant guide, and on a Sunday afternoon, music is the reason why people from miles around head for the bar. There are regular jam sessions, and when I'm not working on a paid gig, I'll get the old Mercedes out of the garage and head up the winding road to La Montana. It's a slow but glorious drive. The scenery changes by the minute until I'm two thousand feet up from sea level and there's a stunning vista to my right. The drive is even more stunning on the way back down, because then I can see right down over the mountain to the coastline.

One day as I arrived at the bar, I stopped the car next to the outdoor tables and chairs to unload my cumbersome stage piano. A Spanish hombre came over to embrace me and help me unload and said in his best English "You have big one, Jim". I shook my head modestly before I realised he was looking at my piano, and he helped me lug the big one to the usual spot reserved for my piano - right in front of a huge and spiky aloe vera bush. This keeps me alert and makes sure I never drop off during my performances.

Musicians and singers simply turn up out of the blue to perform, and large audiences will faithfully turn up to partake of the fantastic food and listen to the music. There are a few faithfuls like Ponytail John, a slim, greying bloke. As well as having a ponytail, he's a wizard at setting up his PA system and plugging in all the instruments and microphones. John is a brilliant chap and plays a very decent bass, solid as a rock.

Phil is a singer/guitarist who usually kicks off the proceedings with a few songs and some very neat guitar playing. I'll sit in on piano when I hear a song I know and like, and do what I can to enhance the music and not get in the way.

There's an American lady called Nadine who hails from the Appalachian mountains. She sings country songs with her guitarist partner Andy - he's our local tortoise repair man and a truly terrific flat-picker. They also go to the Travelling Acoustic nights - acoustic sessions held in different bars in local towns.

Kevin Borman and his wife Troy often entertain us with acapella songs, some of which are quite racy! Troy helps to organise acoustic music nights. I don't think my Roland piano would be allowed, so if I go to one of the acoustic sessions I simply bring my Spanish guitar and do my best.

Other local musos like Bruce often come and join in the proceedings. Bruce lives in the village and is a well-respected sax player who also plays a great tin whistle. Then there's Joe Evans, a very talented singer/guitarist who does some great boogie songs. I'm able to raise the bar and give my piano a bit of welly when Joe is performing at a jam.

Pete Thom is one of my very favourite performers in our area. He's a well-preserved Geordie singer/guitarist and a real entertainer. He's got quite a bit of stuff on youtube. Pete does a deliciously vulgar version of the old Steeleye Span song 'Gaudete' which always has the audience in stitches. Most of his songs are quite thoughtful, apart perhaps from his encore song 'Dead Skunk in the Middle of the Road'.

'Ponytail' John Wallis will play with Pete and sometimes our mutual friend Dennis Danzelman who lives near the bar will play a wonderful bit of guitar along with him. Pete will sing, play guitar and thump a bass drum with his foot, and throw a bit of great old skiffle into their set list. Kevin Borman plays drums and percussion with them. The quartet are called 'Pulse' and if you ever want a joyful toe-tapping fun night out, do catch their show. I love to join in with my piano on their inspired music-making at jams sessions.

My good friend Mike Carter-Jones sometimes comes to the jams when he's over from Wales - he's a tall bloke who writes lovely reflective songs, sings in a rich mellow voice, and plays a terrific bit of jazz guitar. He's had some of his songs played on BBC radio. He works with the Coventry Folk Circle, and sometimes writes songs with other people. We email our new songs to each other, but I have to say that the old master puts me to shame - his output of original songs is far, far greater than mine. Mike is also on youtube.

One of our most popular local singers is Tony Justice. He does a lot of Sinatra-type material and his voice is also great for blues. Everybody likes Tony, and he's now involved with his lovely wife Julie at Bar El Pinar in the village immediately below Bédar. The food there is scrumptious and in good weather it's a joy to sit around their pool and enjoy the great meals their chef Dean produces. We also get to hear music acts there at weekends.

Simon Sinclair is a talented singer and guitarist, and a French polisher to trade - he did a cracking restoration job for me on a lovely old oak dining set.

My friend Bill White sings with a choir and he's an absolute hoot on stage - a born comedian if ever I met one. I love comedy songs, and

185

Bill and I have been talking for some time about doing a double act. He's just as busy as I am with projects, so we might be in wheelchairs before we get around to it!

My Spanish friend Juan José will sometimes pop up when I'm able to play, and we'll get together for some lively Spanish songs. He sings and plays guitar and we all have a great time when Juan José performs 'La Bamba'.

My friend Bish who runs the launderette in Mojacar is a regular at the jams. He's one of the nicest blokes you could ever wish to meet. He's soft-voiced singer, plays a nice guitar and writes some cracking songs. His son Jake now lives among us and his voice is the opposite of his dad's - a big raw, bluesy sound, although he tones it down considerably when he sings along to his ukulele.

A lovely lady called Kay Frances came to one of the first jams and sang some Amy Winehouse songs with me and the guys. I'm delighted that this gave her the confidence to develop as a singer and entertainer.

We also have a charming country singer called Kris Kelly, a really sweet little lady with a big voice and a good guitar.

There are some extremely talented youngsters on the scene here. Danny Ogden is a young man in his early twenties who has worked his socks off to become a stunning guitarist. He has his own rock band "Adelante" and they perform to enthusiastic audiences.

Young Ashley Cathcart is a great singer and guitarist with some really original ideas. I've never before heard a man performing a rock version of "I Will Survive", but Ashley certainly does!

A chap in the audience at a jam session once confided something interesting to me. He commented that it seems that the lesser the talent, the longer a performer will hog the show. He's right – the musicians dread when someone with scant talent sings an interminable collection of dreary songs, then mucks up other singers' performances with painful attempts at singing harmony. Oh, it happens all right, and that's when I'll go and do something more interesting like chat to a goat.

The best performers at a jam session always do the right thing - sing three or four cracking songs then let someone else on. I've known several occasions when the audience have been bored out of their minds listening to pointless percussion-free reggae, biding their time until a decent performer knocks out a few brilliant songs then gives up the stage to the next act. Of all the music forms in the world, the one which needs percussion to work is reggae.

The audiences always wait to hear Terry Gildert. He's well worth the wait - a stocky folk singer and guitarist who does a great comedy version of 'Ghost Riders in the Sky' He's subtly changed it to 'Ghost Chickens in the Sky' and he gets the audience to join in, making chicken noises in the chorus. A truly joyful experience, and you know how I love chicken noises! Terry told me that he can get rather nervous when he's performing, and that he feels more relaxed when I play piano with him.

A while ago, Terry fancied coming down to one of my gigs with Jill at a beach bar on Mojacar Playa, and I invited him to perform some songs during our break. He sang four great songs and like a true pro left 'em wanting more. The audience adored him, and I was delighted when Terry told me that it really made his day.

There seems to be a dearth of pianists in our area, but there's another piano boogieman around here. He goes by the grand name of Dominic Dolittle and he has a great boogie left hand. He sings a lot better than me, but I hope that one day we can host a "Battle of the Boogiemen" and I'd love to throw in some vocal harmony.

Clive Robin Sarstedt lives locally. He had a huge hit in 1976 with 'My Resistance Is Low'. Clive is a great performer and works with Maurice Casenove from Madagascar. Maurice is also a great singer and guitarist and he can hold his vocal notes longer than anyone I know. Around 5pm on Sundays during summer, people mosey on down to Tito's beach bar on the playa to chill out and listen to the music. Clive's brother Richard had several big hit records in the sixties as 'Eden Kane' and his other brother Peter is of course renowned for his song "Where Do You Go To My Lovely" and other hits. Sometimes they meet up to sing and play their guitars at a local bar, and it's always a delight to see and hear these musical legends.

One of most interesting performers around here is a tall swarthy guy called Laurence Burton. He has a place down in Tabernas where he holds hippie weekends and film nights. Laurence is a member of the Blackfoot Indian Nation but was actually born in London. He has the look of an Indian chief about him, especially when he hollers a lullaby in his native American language.

Laurence plays wistful tunes on a tin whistle, but his forté is his double-bass recorder. This instrument is nothing like the ghastly things we all played in school - his recorder is almost the size of a didgeridoo and was made in the 18th century from pearwood. Laurence normally plays solo and gets amazing sounds from this huge instrument. But he sometimes persuades me to join in on piano on a tune he calls 'The

187

Train'. The premise of this piece is that the train leaves the station and picks up speed. I'm chugging along on the piano right behind Laurence. He'll give me a piano solo and this may include snippets of 'Scotland the Brave' or 'Viva España' or whatever is in my warped brain at the time. Then we'll slow down and take the train back into the station. It's a totally improvised piece and anything can happen!

Laurence's 'place' in Tabernas can't be described as a house. He lives pretty much like a native American, and sleeps in a large Moroccan tent called a Yurt. He holds outdoor movie shows some weekends and invites his friends down. I recently had the privilege of enjoying some great nosh with a bunch of really interesting people, then watching an old black & white movie under the stars. There is no running water, so I had the dubious honour of peeing into a trough of cat litter. My wife was in the UK at the time. I don't think it would have been her kind of thing!

Sometimes my great friend Tom Lee will turn up at the jams, and we'll give the audience some blues and rock crowd-pleasers. Tom and I usually go on near the end. As it's a Sunday jam, I'll open our set by playing some hymn-like chords on the piano, then Tom will sing a verse of 'Amazing Grace'. This will morph into a slow verse of 'Honky-Tonk Women', then I'll kick in my boogie piano and we're off. The audience invariably start clapping along to the boogie, and sometimes they'll sing the chorus with us. We finish the song and I always kick in a short reprise which ensures whoops and cheers at the end. It all makes perfect sense to Tom and me. He usually finishes with a Chuck Berry medley which goes on for nearly 10 minutes, with Tom calling for solos from the musicians as we go. He's a total pro and a real joy to work with.

A local Spanish chap, Mario, is usually there. Not to make music, but to drink to excess then dance. His dancing is not the type you'll see on 'Strictly' - the kindest thing I can say is that it's freeform. It's best to stay out of his way. Just another character we treasure.

I hope I'm forgiven if I've missed out any performers, but I've played with literally hundreds in my time in Almería. I'm proud that most of these people have become my friends.

Apart from my British and Spanish friends, I have a Dutch friend who is a great supporter of the local musicians. Like our mutual friend Harvey, Henk Ankersmid is a big man with a big heart, a true Gentle Man. He will often come to gigs with his big camera and take professional quality photos. Like most Dutch people, he speaks excellent English.

At many of my gigs, I use two foot pedals – one is my piano's sustain pedal and the other is for my synth's effects. When Henk discovered that I had to get on my knees to gaffer-tape both pedals to the floor at every gig to prevent them going walkabout, he worked out a way to make a wooden board which fits beautifully between the legs of my piano stand. It's totally brilliant. I can somehow work out how to make music, but making things out of wood is a total mystery to me. Henk's invaluable gift to me was the mark of a true caring friend – someone who sees you have a problem and quietly goes about solving it for you.

Bar La Montana is in an agricultural area not far from the olive oil processing plant in Lubrin. There are olive trees and farms dotted all around the area. One afternoon I was playing my piano at the jam for a Spanish blues singer when I spotted two very large turkeys waddling excitedly down the road towards the bar. They avoided cars along the way and showed no sign of slowing down. When they realized the seas were not parting for them, there was a noisy flurry of legs and wings, and the two turkeys settled down to listen to the music. A couple of months till Christmas, and they were being eyed up by quite a few people!

There's one lady I miss from the jams. Sue was the unofficial third owner of the bar, and she served the customers with enormous flair. She was the epitome of sexy sophistication, tallish with immaculate hair, slinky dress, knowing looks with wandering eyebrows. She would often climb the stairs to deliver meals to the diners on the upper terrace, then shimmy back down the banister with a sigh and a worldly grin.

Sue was a one-off, and she brought panache and class to the rural outpost. I think I may have been the first to call her Sassy Sue, and I wasn't half right. Nearly halfway through her sixties, she was still well able to turn a man's head.

"Hel-lo dahling" she would breathe before pulling my weak and feeble body towards her strong frame for two huge kisses and a bear hug. "Are you going to play my song for me today?" Sue's song was Mustang Sally, and no I don't have a sensible explanation.

We had a joyful Sunday jam on the day of her 65th birthday. The following day she was still celebrating and drove her car off the mountain and down a steep ravine. She was killed instantly. The following Sunday the same musicians who played at her birthday party

189

played at her wake. I really miss her.

There was something irresistible about the advert in the Sol Times.

'Scottish Ceilidh to help and advance the local community. Guid food.'

The advert asked for performers to help with the entertainment. It took me less than a minute to phone the organiser for more information. He confirmed that, yes, there was to be a ceilidh and it was to be held in a church in a local town to help the local community. He told me that the church provided food for local people in poverty, and for immigrants who came to Spain and were unable to claim state aid under EU regulations.

"It's to be held in our church, so there will be no alcohol served."

"A Scottish Ceilidh without alcohol? Are you sure?"

I didn't wait for an answer. I hadn't come to Spain to say "no" to interesting challenges, and this was the first time in my life that I had ever realised that the words "teetotal" and "Scottish" could be found in the same sentence. A teetotal Scottish ceilidh was something I couldn't not attend. I put my name down as a performer.

Came the night of the ceilidh, I went down a couple of hours before kick-off. I wanted to set up and find out what I could do to help the performers. I could only find two - a bagpipe player and a big, stocky old chap called Hamish. He wanted to sing a song about a Scotsman who was about to be hung on the gallows.

"It's McPherson's Lament," he told me. "I knew you were coming tonight and I was told that you're Scottish, so presumably you'll know it."

I didn't like his aggressive tone or the slightly threatening way he looked at me.

"Sorry, pal, I cut my teeth as a jazz pianist in Glasgow playing stuff like Ellington and Basie. I'm not strong on laments. I know - it's lamentable."

This went right past him.

"Now he tells me," he muttered through gritted teeth. "Look, I'll sing a bit of the song, and you follow me. I'll do all ten verses later, but we don't have to do all of them now."

I managed to pick up on the song fairly quickly, and it was going to be all right on the night. Lengthy old Scottish ballads were never of much interest to me. When I was at school I played some hoochter-choochter stuff with a couple of accordion piss-merchants but I've never been into that scene. I prefer to play reasonably cheery and sophisticated music and I prefer to play sober.

Then the piper came up to me with a list of tunes he planned to play for dancing, and asked me if I would play piano along with him on the tunes. Although I had lived in Scotland for over 50 years, I was never into the heedorum-hoderum music. I was more into 'Watermelon Man' than 'Miss McDairmid's Farewell to the 73rd Highlanders Regiment', 'Lament for the Earl of Antrim' or 'The Massacre of Auchtermuchty'. So when I failed to recognise any of the bagpipe classics on his list, the piper gave me a withering look, then asked me if I knew 'Scotland The Brave'.

He was relieved to find that I did, so he fired up his bagpipes. If you've never heard this done, it's a bit like a siren going off. It takes a fair amount of time, blowing air into the bag to get the foghorn-like drone started, then pressing down on the bag to provide enough air for the chanter, which needs a good few minutes to loosen up and get nearly in tune (and 'nearly in tune' is as good as the bagpipes get). There are quite a few notes which the bagpipes struggle to reach, and pipers have to alter tunes and adapt them to fit this primitive and extremely piercing instrument.

By seven o'clock, nearly seventy people were crammed into a low-ceilinged room not much bigger than our lounge. The evening started with the piper marching up and down between the tables. When I tell you that the piper didn't need a microphone, that doesn't even begin to describe the ear-splitting racket endured by the audience. Several people held their hands over their ears and others winced in genuine pain, while the hard-of-hearing swiftly turned off their hearing aids and applauded vigorously. I remembered why the pipes sound best from a mile away.

While the piper marched up and down, the deafened victims were served traditional Scottish food including Scotch broth, cock-a-leekie soup with prunes, and haggis with turnip and mash. No alcohol was served, of course, but 2-litre bottles of water had been placed on the tables as an accompaniment to the food. Oh goody.

Then a charming and rotund lady from Ayrshire came up to me and asked if she could sing a Burns song. I was delighted to let her sing, hoping it would be quieter than the piper. The song was all about calling the yowes to the knowes. Although non-Scottish readers might think this could be a song about cows, it's actually an unaccompanied song about sheep (yowes being ewes). It's certainly not a number I ever got to play in the jazz scene around Glasgow.

Next up was a huge sweaty bloke in a size 32 kilt. He treated the audience to a long and involved dirge about the massacre of Glencoe. This was fairly short and snappy compared to the ten verses of 'McPherson's Lament'. I played an introduction in the key of E flat as we had agreed earlier in the evening, but the huge sweaty bloke ignored this and started singing three keys higher, possibly due to his excitement at performing to an audience.

The next act was a couple who wanted to sing unaccompanied. They performed a couple of folk songs in a really entertaining way, but it wasn't exactly ceilidh dance music.

We were then treated to an unaccompanied song by a different lady - 'John Anderson My Jo' - a mercifully short Burns song about a wife reminiscing about the days when her dodderly old husband was young. The song was touching but not exactly cheery.

None of these songs were suitable for ceilidh dancing, of course, so when I kicked off with some cheery dance music, the audience were happy for such blessed relief. For the first time in nearly three hours, they were able to get up and dance to real ceilidh music - jigs and reels, featuring the sounds of my piano and synth accordion plus the odd song. And when I sang 'Donald Where's Your Troosers' they all sang along in this cheery song where absolutely no-one gets massacred or hung on the gallows. Result !

Later in the evening, after donations had been made and raffles drawn, the church leader got up to make a speech. He was an Englishman, and dressed rather less impressively than the Scottish performers. He told the audience that the funds raised to help and support the 'local community' (as advertised) were in fact going to locations in South America and Africa. I could clearly hear the audience murmuring to themselves that these locations were not exactly 'local'.

At this point most people just left, and the evening came to a premature end. But not before some rather muted singing of 'Auld Lang Syne'.

CHAPTER 11 - NOVEMBER

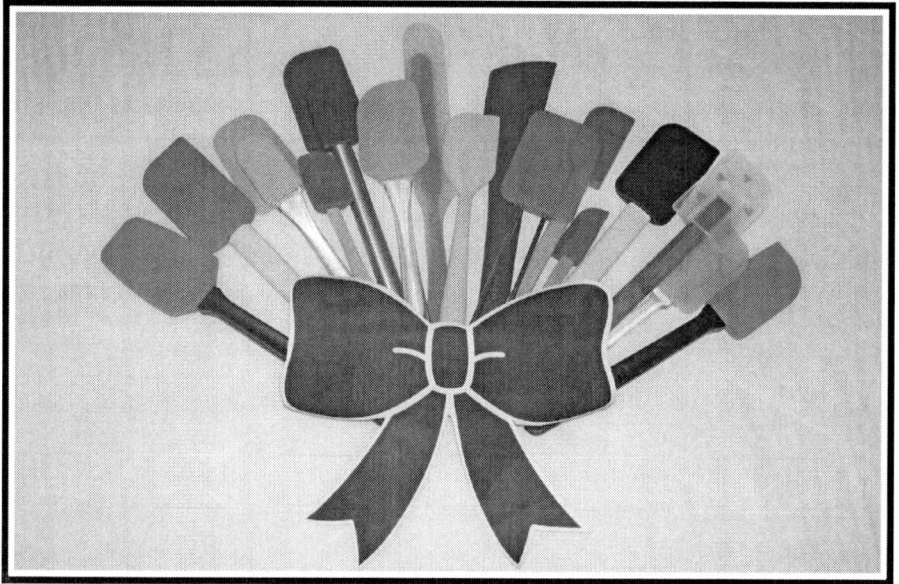

I have a great respect for Carl. Ok, he's not exactly God's gift to women, unless there's a woman out there who prefers her men bald, fat and pot-ugly. But he's a really good soul singer and a terrific sax player.

One day, he called round to check out music keys for a fund-raiser gig at which a bunch of us were playing. His wife came along, an unsmiling specimen of fading womanhood. She was clearly uncomfortable at being in a strange house with strange people she'd never met before. She refused all offers of tea or coffee, winced at the offer of wine, and sat bolt upright on the lounge settee inspecting our walls.

She sat even more upright when she heard Sammy wailing at the window to be let in.

"Is that a cat?" she hissed.

"He's called Sammy," I replied. "If you like cats, you'll get on with Sammy."

"I absolutely detest cats," came her reply. "Please don't let that animal anywhere near me."

"The thing is, dear, Sammy lives in our house, and he wants in." I put her straight.

Carrie was at the other end of our lounge and hadn't heard this conversation. She innocently opened the dining room window. Sammy came crashing in, missed his intended landing pad of a dining chair and collided with an innocent table lamp in the process. He emitted a curse "Rrrrrraaaaaaaaaaaa", scrabbled his feet on the shiny laminate flooring, picked up speed with a triumphant cry, and skidded into the kitchen for an urgent check on his food bowl. The kitchen has non-slip tiles, so Sammy never ever crashes into anything in there.

Carl's wife asked for a glass of water, so I fetched her one from the kitchen, then offered Carl a beer. He looked sheepishly at his wife, who closed her eyes, nodded her head very slightly and sighed to indicate that she would permit him a beer. I headed back into the kitchen, and had just opened the fridge door when I heard a loud scream.

The worst had happened. Sammy had finished his snack, bolted behind my back into the lounge, and jumped straight into the lap of our new lady visitor to inspect her for fluffy clothes suitable for kneading purposes. He certainly hadn't been expecting to be greeted with a deafening scream, and in terror he had jumped straight into the air from the lap of the poor woman, scratching her legs in the process and resulting in a second scream, even louder than the first. In true Tom & Jerry style, Sammy had transformed our lounge from a haven of civilised conversation into a hellhole of hysteria in five seconds flat.

Sammy bolted for the back door and yelled to be let out and well away from this screaming anti-social creature.

When Carl's wife's legs had been bandaged up and things had calmed down, Sammy wanted back in. It was decided that Carl and his wife should go upstairs to my studio to prevent any further disturbance, and that Sammy was to stay downstairs. Carl sat down on the sofa and his wife sat beside him. While Carl and I talked about musical stuff, his wife took a dark blue napkin from her handbag, unfolded it onto her lap and proceeded to set about biting her fingernails. She did so in almost Germanic efficiency, beginning at the pinkie of her left hand and proceeding in strict rotation through all her fingers. She would gnaw through one nail until she had a discarded piece of fingernail, then deposit it onto her blue napkin. She would then start on the next nail.

By the time Carl and I had got around to working out a suitable key for 'Sweet Home Chicago', his wife had reached her final destination - the pinkie of her right hand. By now there was a neat pile of discarded

194

nails on her napkin. Like a pan-pipe player going up and down the scale, she did the rounds of all her nails for a final check, then neatly folded up her napkin and put it back in her handbag. Then she sniffed loudly and asked Carl if we were finished doing our music. It was clearly time for Carl to leave.

As she made her way back downstairs in front of Carl and me, Sammy appeared and did his level best to trip the woman up by silently bolting upstairs and straight across her path as a punishment. He missed her feet by inches, causing her to throw her arms in the air and drop her handbag. Its contents spilled all over the stairs, including her keys and passport, a Ladyshave, several sachets of KFC ketchup, a pair of plain white cotton knickers, a packet of tissues, two AA batteries (no questions please), a packet of Bird's Instant Custard, plus of course a dark blue napkin full of nail clippings. It must have caused the poor woman great embarrassment to have to get down on the stairs and shovel all this stuff back. I looked on while she did this, as it's obviously not right and proper for a man to interfere with a woman and her handbag.

If there happen to be any other cat haters among my readers, may I assure you that I did not find this woman's visit deeply amusing and highly entertaining in any way. Please don't even begin to imagine for a moment that a gentleman like me would ever be so insensitive as to relate the incident in great detail to friends in need of a good belly laugh!

Although the woman didn't actually fall down the stairs, Sammy's feline subtlety in setting up such a destructive chain of events on behalf of a cat hater was of course wholly unacceptable. But quite brilliant. We could still hear the woman cursing and moaning as she staggered on her high heels down the path to her car with her feckless husband in tow struggling with his saxophone.

She never came back.

- - - - - - - - - - - -

I enjoy meeting new musicians, tuning into them and creating music. I've found a level of creativity similar to that which I had in my youth. I think that as human beings we have to create something to leave behind, and sometimes I'm frustrated that my songs are of a transitory nature and not solid objects. So I compensate by making chutney and jam.

Fig chutney is my favourite - figs grow in the wild down here, and they can be picked from the side of the road. Figs don't travel well as their skins are so delicate, and I still remember when Carrie and I went to see Sinatra at the Albert Hall in London in the eighties, we shopped in Harrods and our purchase that day amounted to two figs for £1 which included the all-important Harrod's carrier bag.

For me, there are few sensations in life as sensuous as manipulating a quality spatula to remove the last trace of fig chutney from the cooking pot. I'm proud to own what I'm assured is the largest collection of spatulas in Andalucia. Many of my spatulas have been donated by friends who share my fondness for this amazing kitchen implement, particularly in its most sophisticated form – the wonderful Silicone Spatula. I have a large box in the kitchen dedicated solely to silicone spatulas. In this box, around four dozen of my most loyal spatulas reside in a warm bed of soft tissue, awaiting my next invitation to spatulate. I will often spend a good few minutes in quiet anticipation, reflecting on which spatula to select for the task in hand.

There is only one man on this earth who could possibly understand my appreciation of vital kitchen equipment, and that man is surely Ulrich Haarburste, the author of a novel I mentioned in an earlier chapter and beyond brilliance in my opinion. It's called "Ulrich Haarburste's Novel of Roy Orbison in Clingfilm". I especially commend this book to all enthusiasts of:

A/ Roy Orbison and

B/ Clingfilm

From the book's sales figures, there are clearly thousands of us enthusiasts. Fans of terrapins are also catered for in this book, in much the same way that cat enthusiasts are catered for in my book. You'll find Herr Haarburste's book easily just by googling these two hitherto unrelated words - Orbison Clingfilm. I found the book inspiring and uplifting, and I learned a lot about Dusseldorf in Germany and the magical qualities of clingfilm, or

besitzensuchenzugenmachenubergruppenschnurpenplastich

to give it its correct German name.

I would point out however that spatulas are not mentioned in Haarburste's book. Not even once. Ach !

In his excellent autobiography, Rod Stewart asks himself the question "What would it be like if I wrapped myself entirely in cling film?" While I'm delighted that he has an interest in clingfilm, I feel he may be jumping on the bandwagon. I can't say I'm impressed. Rod

Stewart dresses in tartan to look Scottish, but the man is English. Unlike Roy Orbison, he hardly ever wears dark glasses. He's rubbish.

On the subject of kitchen equipment, the Andalucians in our area simply do not understand spatulas. Our local hardware shops only sell crude wooden devices which are incapable of performing with anything like the efficiency of your modern silicone spatula. Rest assured I refuse to have such wooden products in my home. As a producer of home-made chutney, I have not come to Spain to struggle vainly to remove the last vestige of chutney from my cooking pot.

No, life in the sun is much more relaxed thanks to silicone spatulas. The best spatulas are available in the cities. My wife struggles with my addiction. On a recent trip to Seville, she found me in the kitchen department of the enormous 'El Corte Ingles' store, struggling with an armful of spatulas.

"Oh God, Jim, you've got dozens of spatulas in the kitchen. Why in God's name do you need more?"

"You exaggerate, dearest," I replied, heading for the check-out. "I have only found fifteen which interest me. Look at this one, it's a spoon spatula – half spoon, half spatula. It's quite revolutionary."

"If you say so. But why the pink one?"

"It's glow-in-the-dark, so if there's a power cut, I can still see to remove every last vestige of food from the cooking pot."

"If you say so. But why the small one with the wooden handle?"

"It's a Le Creuset spatula. It's the sexy one I was telling you about which I found on the internet."

"You seem to find a lot of sexy stuff on the internet."

"Yes, but this is the Kylie Minogue of spatulas. Look at it - stunningly beautiful, compact and petite. With this spatula I can tease out every last vestige of fig chutney from the most remote crevice of the cooking pot."

"Oh great." My wife spat out her words. "You have everything a well-matured lunatic spending his weekends bottling chutney could wish for. You have spatulas on the brain."

"That reminds me. I need to make more chutney."

"Why? There are three boxfuls in the garage and God knows how many jars in the kitchen."

"Chutney is like good wine. It matures with age."

This is true. My 3-year-old fig chutney is at its peak. I make all sorts of chutneys, from the delicate pineapple to the rich and sweet kumquat and red pepper chutney. May I reassure my readers that I am not eccentric. As evidence of this statement, may I make it absolutely clear that I refuse to make pickle!

Anyway, we were still in El Corte Ingles. Ideally, I needed nine out of the fifteen spatulas I was holding, but my other half only let me have three. One of them is included in the lovely bouquet of silicone spatulas which I have placed at the beginning of this chapter. Due to publishing restrictions on Kindle, it's not possible for you to see these examples of my collection in all their colourful glory.

My friend Stuart, who lives somewhere in the country below Scotland, shares my enthusiasm for spatulas, and it is gratifying to have found a kitchen implement soul-mate. We exchange emails with photos of spatulas and attractive cooking pots. The pot lids are often the most alluring aspect of my photos, and I do regard the pot lid as being under-valued in our daily lives. A pot without a lid is like a rose bush without rosebuds, or for enthusiasts of the French Revolution, like a guillotine without a lethally-sharp blade.

Stuart had suggested that I list all my spatulas for you with detailed descriptions. Sadly, I cannot do this for security reasons. I can, however, mention some of my favourites by name. Apart from the aforementioned Kylie, my collection includes Lily the Pink, Mr.Black, Elkie, Sky, Trivago, Julie (a spoon spatula named after Julie Andrews who sang "A Spoonful of Sugar" in the Mary Poppins movie), The White Knight, Big Blue, Wee Blue, Toni, Humph and the Beverley Spatulas (a presentation box of three pure white spatulas of slightly varying sizes but identical design).

But the daddy of all my spatulas is Sir Ian, named after the distinguished cricketer Sir Ian Botham (who has a holiday home not far away from us in the Almanzora valley). Sir Ian is that rarest of kitchen tools, a long-bodied spatula shaped very like a cricket bat. The long body makes Sir Ian ideal for spatulating large pans which may or may not have contained chutney.

Up until now Kylie has been the only Spatula in my collection capable of removing the last vestiges of sauce from small containers, as all my other spatulas have been too tight a fit. Kylie has performed with grace and great accuracy during this period.

Here's a great spatula story. One day I began seaching for Kylie to spatulate the last vestige of curry sauce from a small jug. Sadly, my search was fruitless as she was in the dishwasher which was in the middle of its cycle, so my second choice was Kathleen, a birthday gift from a friend. Kathleen is an emerald green spatula, a little bigger around the middle than Kylie but actually more flexible due to the lighter guage of the silicone at the perimeter. Kathleen and I pursued our prey with vigour and great accuracy, and after less than half a minute's spatulation, I had managed to remove the last vestige of curry sauce from the small jug with great ease, and deposit it into a small plastic freezer box. Job done!

You may consider me a tad eccentric in giving names to my spatulas, but I have so many that it's the only way I can identify them in an emergency situation. Carrie thinks I should put labels on them, but she's just being silly.

Quality kitchen equipment is simply too important to ignore in our lives. On the subject of sharp blades, I have known domestically stunted people whose kitchen does not even contain a knife sharpener. For pity's sake, what sane person would give house room to a kitchen knife without regularly sharpening it to keep it in the peak of cutting efficiency? It's nothing short of madness. Without the benefit of hard evidence, I can only imagine it's like having a beautiful nymphomaniac wife and not placing regular orders from the Ann Summers range!

- - - - - - - - - - - -

The flyer under my car's windscreen wiper looked tempting. It was titled 'Flamenco Show' and there was to be a singer cum guitarist and a dancer. It was to be held at a beach bar on the playa. I sent emails to some friends and arranged for a bunch of us to go down on a Friday night.

The performance was organised by a lady who I was told had previously expressed dissatisfaction about local flamenco concerts starting much later than advertised. Late starts are fairly normal practice in Andalucia, where you can often arrive at least half an hour late and find yourself waiting for the show to start. The start time for this particular performance was 8-30 pm and true to form, at 9pm we were still waiting for it to start.

Eventually the singer/guitarist sat down and played a really great introduction to his first song. He then sang some half-decent flamenco and strummed along. In flamenco concerts you normally hear a singer and a separate guitarist. This allows the guitar player to embellish the singer's work with improvised accompaniment. Strumming along in the manner of a pop singer is not the same thing at all and for me it was a rather boring performance.

There was a tall, elegant, English female dancer who had probably started learning flamenco a bit late in life to develop the flexibility of the traditional Spanish dancers. The Spanish start learning from early childhood - and the girls seem to have some extra hip bones. But the English lady did her level best in the circumstances. The adjustable spotlights on the walls of the beach bar had, of course, not been adjusted to shine on the performers (perish the thought), so the singer/guitarist was particularly difficult to spot in the half-light.

After half an hour or so, the two performers took a break.

They returned about 15 minutes later. The second set was much more interesting than the first. The audience were invited to sing "Oh-oh" in the chorus of the fifties pop song 'Volare'. Then we were treated to some Spanish pop songs along the lines of 'Viva España' during which the flamenco guy sat and battered his guitar and bellowed along to some mock-flamenco dancing. By now my friends were asking me what the hell was going on, so I pulled the flyer out of my pocket and passed it around - it definitely said 'Flamenco Show' at the top!

For me, the highlight of the evening was when the flamenco singer belted out the Gypsy Kings' version of 'My Way'. A few British couples got up to dance the foxtrot, and the whole room joined in the chorus, helping the singer by belting out "I did it my way" at the end.

It was just another event in Almería province when scratching your head is the only option. It's fair to say that the flamenco singer did it his way. It was a touching if somewhat deafening tribute to that distinguished flamenco performer, Frank Sinatra.

One Saturday night I was playing piano in a plush restaurant at a golf resort. I had been chatting to some folk in the restaurant and had some song requests from the diners. There was a group of male golfers directly behind me, relaxing on sofas. I'd just started my second set when a tall, stocky man from the group of golfers came up to the piano and put a £50 note on top of it. Not 50 euros, 50 quid. I quickly brought the tune I was playing to an end and looked at him quizzically.

"That's yours if you can play two requests." He said.

"R-really?" I stammered in astonishment. I get tips fairly regularly, but never in my life have I had such a massive tip. I wondered if the note was a fake and he was playing a trick on me. "What are your two requests then?"

I figured that they must be pretty challenging tunes, and that I'd have little chance of bagging the 50 quid. As it happened, both tunes were in my repertoire - the theme from 'Love Story' and the theme from 'Chariots of Fire'. Neither of them were difficult to play.

The fellow explained. "I've a bet on with my mates. They've bet me £100 that you won't be able to play both tunes. If you can, I get £100 and you get £50. The banknote stays on the piano until you've played the tunes. Deal?"

"Deal."

I played a couple of other requests while hatching a plan.

When I played the opening bars to "Love Story" there was a murmur behind me. After I'd finished the tune, I played the single note which forms he opening to "Chariots of Fire". It's not difficult, even Mr Bean could play it (at the opening ceremony for the London Olympics in 2012). As I started the tune proper, I could hear the groans from the sofa behind me as wallets were brought out to settle the bet.

I finished playing my wee medley and pocketed the £50 without further ado. It wasn't a fake!

- - - - - - - - - - -

My friends Christine and Brian have a beautiful married daughter and a lanky gay son who is in the hospitality industry. When I visited them one day they told me that Alan and his boyfriend were coming over for a holiday. I had asked about the boyfriend, and they had shown me a photo of him dressed as Shirley Bassey. My eyebrows shot up.

"Douglas does a drag act," Christine explained. "He mimes to Shirley Bassey records and he's got a fabulous dress with a feather boa."

This got my mind going. "I don't suppose he'd consider bringing his gear over and doing an interval act at one of our gigs?"

Christine shook her head. "Sorry Jim. He's only bringing over hand luggage."

A few days later, Christine phoned.

"Listen Jim, I've spoken to Douglas and he says try and stop him doing his Dame Shirley. He's paying to take a suitcase and he's bringing over all his drag clothes and shoes."

I was delighted. Jill and I often had other musicians coming to our gigs, and the venues where we played were invariably delighted if we got them up to sing or jam with us. Our audiences loved the impromptu nature of our gigs, and they never knew what daft number we might pop in, or what guests might perform with us. We often invited musicians up to jam around the piano, and we'd had guitarists, a banjo player, bass players, harmonica and sax players, and lots of singers turn up at our gigs. Fact is, my band gear of an 88-key piano and a 61-key synth can produce rather more notes than a guitar player could ever do with 6 strings.

I decided that Douglas should sing "live" and not mime to records. I'll not bore you with details of my rehearsal with him, but it was unusual. He certainly had a deep penetrating voice, but he was completely tone-deaf and had absolutely no sense of rhythm. That aside, he was God-awful.

By this time Jill and I were performing a lot of gigs as 'J & J Music'. We were having a lot of fun and gaining a lot of new fans. We have a big bunch of fans called the 'Gillettes'. They're nothing to do with razor blades, they're simply named after their leader Gillian. They're a lovely bunch who travel around and often turn up at our gigs, when we have more fun than you can shake a stick at. They include the lovely Sue Metcalf, who describes herself as our number one fan and laps up everything we do, despite living around 40 miles from our area.

Jill and I were booked to play one Saturday night, when Douglas and Alan were over, at a big bar/restaurant on the road to Albox, and a lot of our followers had booked. The place had recently been taken over by a charming American lady and her Spanish husband, and they were delighted at the idea of a Shirley Bassey impersonator doing an interval spot.

The previous week, we had played a gig in Bédar, and a very fit local builder named Harry had raved about our music. He had offered to roadie for me at our next gig for a few beers. I took him up on his offer as I knew I had a heavy solo gig the night before.

Harry and I arrived at the venue just as Jill and Simon were arriving, so I made the introductions and we started setting up our music equipment. By the time we had done our sound check and changed into our stage clothes, the venue was crammed full. I had hoped that my roadie Harry would be able to get a seat at the table with Jill's family and friends, but there was no room and as every last seat had been taken, he had to stand at the bar. But I bought him some beers and he seemed happy.

After our first set, we took a break and I went looking for Harry to buy him another beer, but he wasn't anywhere to be seen.

After our second set, I found Harry standing at the bar with a huge smile on his face.

"Jim, I just wanted a seat, so I decided to pop over to the bar across the road," he explained. "I ordered a beer then went outside for a smoke and a seat. A lady walked past me in the darkness then sat down beside me. We got talking, and we seemed to get on pretty well. Turned out she's in business, and she gave me a free sample."

"A free sample?" I enquired.

"Yes."

"A free sample of what?"

"She provided a service for me."

"What kind of service?"

"Do I have to spell it out for you, Jim?"

"Well, what kind of business is she in?" I was puzzled.

"She's a hooker. She gave me a BJ."

"I don't believe you."

Harry took her calling card out of his pocket. "She says I can phone her next time I'm up this way. But she says I have to pay next time."

I was still open-mouthed when it was time for the interval act. I got the nod that Douglas was ready. Jill gave him the big build-up and I sat at the piano ready to play a bit of 'Goldfinger' as an intro theme. The vision which arrived on stage in a red plunge dress and matching feather boa was a little different from the original Dame Shirley. Douglas is six feet five and stick thin. The high-heels with thick soles added another five inches or so. What we had here was a skinny six foot ten version of the glamorous Dame - a stretch Shirley Bassey!

Being Scottish and having just arrived from a wet and miserable Glasgow, Douglas's complexion was more than a few shades paler than Dame Shirley's. And Douglas's deep singing voice was even worse than it had been in rehearsal - think Johnny Cash on a rollercoaster.

Dame Shirley's opening song was 'Big Spender'. It wasn't a simple murder. First, she tortured it. Meanwhile, the audience were wetting themselves with laughter. So we got a result. At my suggestion, the second and absolutely last song was "Kiss Me Honey Honey, Kiss Me". The towering Dame Shirley plumped herself on the laps of several terrified gentlemen in the audience, licking their ears and snogging them violently. I did try to follow the singing, but it was no use. I tried several keys, but as soon as I found the right one, Dame Shirley changed key once again.

Our special guest was a total hoot, and 'she' left the room to bigger cheers than Jill and I got that night.

I got a phone call one Friday morning. It was one of the few occasions when my sleep was not cruelly disturbed.

"Hey, my man," Purred a cultured voice. "It's Robin the bass player. How is your lovely wife?"

"Same as usual," I replied.

"Oh." Robin hesitated for a moment. "I really enjoyed the jam session the other night. What's that noise?"

"It's the cat wanting to speak to you."

"Eh?"

"He has a thing about phones. Just ignore him."

"Ok. Jim, can you play a dinner dance on the playa tonight? I'm really, really stuck."

Although I was clearly bottom of the barrel, I had a quick word with my dearest.

"All right, yes, I'll do it. I had a gig with a blues singer but it got cancelled because he decked the restaurant owner. And my wife says she'll be busy writing Christmas cards."

"That's great. It's billed as a Candlelight Dinner Dance. The venue had a band booked, but the pianist has done a runner to Marbella with the trumpet player's wife, though Christ knows why he'd want to get off with that fat slag." Robin has a way with words. "Anyway, the venue have asked me if I can get a pianist to do the gig with me."

"Sure, Robin. I'll be glad to do it. But do we not need a wee bit of rehearsal?"

"Nonsense. Just bring along a list and maybe some chords, and we'll be fine, just the two of us. The punters are knocking on a bit down there, so don't play anything too modern."

Robin is a real English gent. He went to sea at the age of sixteen, and became a Master Mariner, then got back on dry land, went to university and got a BA Honours degree. After that he became a lecturer, and gained two MAs. In 1985 he became a professional bass player and worked with Humphrey Lyttelton and George Melly among others. Not to be outdone, he's also had twenty-odd children's books published. In 1999 he sailed to Spain in an eleven-metre sailing boat with his wife and their young son. There's an old Ian Dury song called 'There Ain't Half Been Some Clever Bastards'. For reasons I don't understand, Robin is not mentioned in the lyrics.

Robin is an absolute model of old-school courtesy and politeness -

except when he's riled, when he turns purple, stomps around and swears like a trouper. A bit like myself, really. He's in his sixties now, tall with greying swept-back hair, and rather elegant. He's an excellent double bass player and I just love the way he can bend the notes.

The double bass is a huge instrument which requires fingers like steel and a phenomenal amount of effort to play. Robin demonstrates exactly how much effort it takes by sweating profusely within minutes of starting to play, his head to one side, his eyes fixed in the distance and his mouth open for air and grunting. If Robin had told me that he had won first prize at the Spanish National Speed-Sweating Championship to add to his tally of certificates, I wouldn't have been in the least surprised!

I was first to arrive at the restaurant at a quarter to seven, and the only other car in the car park contained an elderly couple in an ancient white Peugeot. The woman wound down the window.

"The front doors don't open till seven, son - that's when they let the public in. You need to go round the back and knock on the back door. There's someone in there - I saw them when I looked through the glass. They'll open the door and let you in to set up your gear."

So, the door was duly opened and I went in to check the place out. I saw Robin arrive, and on my way back to the car, the woman called over to me in a clear and penetrating London accent.

"The Candlelight Dinner Dance costs 18 euros, but John is going to let us in for 5 euros each if we don't take the meal. This is our ticket." She showed me a tiny scrap of paper with a hand-written message. "We ate at half past five, so we don't need a meal. I got some lasagne from Lidl and we had it at home then we had a tub of their nice chocolate ice-cream for afters, so our meal only cost us five euros eighty. Malcolm's got his washboard."

"His washboard?"

"Only if you want him to play, son. You don't have to, but he's played it in New Orleans, you know. Oh, yes. And at our club in Watford. It's on the High Street. Do you know it?" I shook my head. "Oh, we had great times there, dance bands at weekends and bingo for the pensioners through the week. The prizes were great. You'll not believe this, but one time at the bingo I won a pair of crutches. They were really light, that aluminium stuff, with plastic handles and rubber feet. You could adjust them for height. I gave them to my friend Beryl when she had her mother to stay, and the old bitch never gave them back. But she died a few months later and I got them back then all right. You don't need crutches in a coffin, know what I mean? Heh heh! Malcolm used to play his washboard with some of the bands who came to the club, although one time there was a young band on and they told him to fuck off. Charming, heh heh! Isn't that right, Malcolm? Well, you go in and set up, son, and we'll see you when the doors open at seven. By the way, he's Malcolm and I'm Sadie. M and S, so you won't forget. Like Marks and Spencer, only Malcolm and Sadie. You see?"

I nodded my head to confirm that I had understood the strange simile. The old couple remained in their car until the restaurant opened their doors to the public. Wise move, I thought. If they had gone out for a drink somewhere while they waited, it would have cost them money.

Robin and I took the music equipment into the restaurant.

Seven o'clock came. The old couple hobbled in, she all of four foot ten in a lurid pink frock with a floral pattern, subtly set off by white pop socks and sandals. Her face was also pink. She had probably been quite pretty in her younger days, but her face had now become horizontal, as if she had aged in a metal vice. She had white frizzy asylum hair and a short straggly, white beard. Her husband Malcolm was a pale-looking fellow, tall and resplendent in a grey cardigan and matching cream slacks with an elasticated waistband. And a long plaster over his nose, which failed to hide a spectacularly long nasal hair curling from the base of his left nostril round to the right hand side of his nose. I thought maybe he was saving it to enter it in a competition....

They were the very first guests at the Candlelight Dinner Dance. During Malcolm's frequent toilet breaks, the elasticated waistband required careful adjustment when he went from the sitting position to the standing position.

Malcolm and Sadie (M & S) were shown to a table right next to the band, with a tablecloth but sadly lacking candlelight or crystal wine glasses. Well, what do you expect for 5 euros?

The old couple admired the music gear. Sadie threw somewhat inane questions at me while I set up, like how many keys were there on my electric piano and whether they all worked. Robin could see I was getting annoyed with the bombardment. He sighed despairingly, and asked me to come outside for a second. He sat on the wall and rolled a cigarette.

"That couple are a nightmare, Jim!" he announced in a loud

whisper. "In London a while back they followed me to every gig, and I managed to shake them off. But they're back." He took a long slow drag on his cigarette. "He's deluded and she's not right in the head."

I told Robin about the washboard and he shook his head. "This is what they did in England. They followed bands around and she got him to do guest spots with his bloody washboard."

The charming old couple came out at that point, and for once Malcolm got a word in to explain that his hip was bad that day. In fact, I got a detailed breakdown of all his ailments, while Sadie chipped in with hers. She never stopped talking, and she clearly believed I possessed the ability to listen to two simultaneous descriptions of ailments.

Robin and I played through dinner. The other guests were well-dressed, exclusively ex-pat pensioners with an average age of seventy-plus, obviously attracted to the format of a Candlelight Dinner Dance. Malcolm and Sadie (M & S) insisted on giving us a critique at the end of every tune, so I adopted the strategy of segueing one tune into the next in order to confuse and confound them.

After about an hour, Robin and I took a break. Robin (the scheming sod) made a quick getaway outdoors for a cigarette. I was slower, as my piano was further from the door, and I was collared by Sadie on the way out.

"That was lovely music, son. Malcolm thought some of the songs would be too slow to play washboard on, but we enjoyed them all. Did you know Nat Gonella at all? He played the trumpet at our club in Watford, it must have been around 1980. It was a lovely place, and when Nat Gonella came, they laid on a lovely buffet. He's maybe dead now, 'cos he was quite old back then. We had a chicken curry type thing with rice. They served it on paper plates, but I didn't mind. First you got into the queue for your chicken curry, then you moved along to the next table and got some rice. You didn't have to wait in a queue for the rice though. After a while they announced that there was plenty left in case anyone wanted seconds. I liked it, so I went back for seconds. Malcolm didn't like it that much, so he never had seconds. Well, son, I don't want to hold you back, so you have a nice break. If I know Robin, he'll be out having a cigarette, but it killed my mother you know, she only lived till she was 63 and she died on Easter Sunday 1963 - 63, same as her age. We had to put her in one of these homes for folk dying off and I've not smoked much since. It was a lovely place, though, I wouldn't have minded living there myself, except for the smell. They had a lovely garden with seats and a smoking area, and the kitchens were spotless. My mother didn't like the woman in the next bed, as she slept a lot and didn't want to talk about politics. Anyway, she had a really bad problem - she would waken up, sit on the edge of the bed and pee on the floor. She was a darkie. Not my mother, the woman on the next bed. I don't mind darkies myself, a few of them are quite nice. My brother lived with us for twelve years you know, but he died two and a half years ago after he fell off a wall on the way to Tesco's. So it's just me and Malcolm now. Well, you have a nice break, son, and just let Malcolm know when you want him to play his washboard."

I took a deep breath and went outside to join Robin. We had a nice break.

Halfway through the second set, I made an announcement on the microphone and invited Malcolm to play on my swing arrangement of "Folsom Prison Blues", figuring that if I got this out of the way, Malcolm and Sadie (M & S) might go home early too.

There was a delay between the invitation and Malcolm's performance, as firstly he had to take his washboard out of the crumpled Mercadona carrier bag on the floor, then put his collection of metal thimbles on his fingers (as aficionados of the washboard will know, this is necessary to get a clattering noise out of this redoubtable washing implement). Unfortunately, some thimbles went onto the wrong fingers (as aficionados of the washboard will know, this can be a major setback) and some re-arrangement was necessary with the help of Sadie, who asked Malcolm what the bloody hell he was doing.

The restaurant owner John also helped with the preparation by retrieving the dropped thimbles from the floor and returning them to Malcolm. As the washboard preparation ceremony took several minutes longer than expected, I played some soothing Richard Clayderman music on my piano to calm the audience's anticipation of the event, while trying to ignore the clattering noises and raised voices to my right.

Eventually, Malcolm indicated to John precisely where he wanted his chair placed in front of the band, and he sat down ready to play. For a bit of fun, I announced to the audience that we were firstly going to check if the washboard was in tune (as aficionados of the washboard will know, this is not strictly necessary). Laughter from the audience. A blank stare from Malcolm.

We kicked off our washboard tribute to Johnny Cash. I'm by no means a washboard enthusiast, but I thought Malcolm was pretty good if you like that sort of thing (aficionados of the washboard presumably relish a constant clattering racket in their eardrums).

Malcolm kept time like a real trouper, but unfortunately he was forced to stop playing about three-quarters of the way through his performance, complaining of a really, really sore hip. So Robin and I completed the tune without any further clattering, and the audience showed their appreciation for Malcolm.

I quietly suggested to Robin that it would maybe be nice to bring Malcolm back on later in the evening for a rendition of Gershwin's lovely romantic ballad 'Someone to Watch Over Me' in an arrangement for piano, double bass and washboard. We could dedicate it to his wife. However, Robin threatened to insert his double bass into a part of my anatomy which would have definitely caused me lasting damage!

The dinner dance finished early, shortly after the raffle had been drawn (raffles being a vital element around here in a proper Candlelight Dinner Dance). There were plenty of people there, but despite all our efforts, the most we got on the dance floor was two couples, the least elderly and most mobile of our audience. The dinner-dancers mostly sat and looked at us all night - some even had the strength to turn their chairs round to see us better. They mostly sat and listened to our music as if it was a concert. John said they all really enjoyed the evening, and told us they would come back again another time (if spared, of course).

Malcolm and Sadie (M & S so you won't forget) were still there at the end, having made two coca colas last all night. When we were packing up our gear, Sadie said to Robin, "You must give me your address, Robin, as we'd like to see where you've moved to and maybe come and visit you!"

Robin replied "Ah, you'd need to ask my wife, and she's not here. I can't remember the address."

I said to Sadie, "It's ok, I know where Robin lives". Robin turned sharply and gave me a menacing look which I hadn't seen on the face of a human since I told Carrie's mother that I wanted to marry her daughter....

"But actually," I continued. "Last year when I wanted to send him a Christmas card, I realised that I didn't know his postal address. I'm sorry."

Sadie then asked for my address. "Jim, it would be really nice for us to come to your house one day. Brian could bring his washboard, and we could have a nice day with you and Malcolm playing music and your wife and me listening. I could make some sandwiches and bring my knitting. Does you wife wear pop socks?"

I told her I was moving house, and had no idea of my new address. They looked a bit puzzled, then the penny must have dropped. The washboard and accessories were put back in the crumpled Mercadona carrier bag in total silence. Sadie inspected the contents to check that Malcolm had put everything in the bag the right way, Malcolm stood up and adjusted his elasticated waistband. I followed the charmingly eccentric old couple out as they shuffled off back to their ancient Peugeot, all the while Sadie heckling Malcolm.

"Watch the step. For goodness sake, Malcolm, you need to get back to that fat optician woman again! Have you got all your thimbles? Where's the car?"

CHAPTER 12 - DECEMBER

And now the end is near…..

And now I'm recalling the huge picture window at the council-run cultural centre in Garrucha. Belens (nativity scenes) are everywhere at Christmas time, and this picture window displayed a nativity scene. There's not much sign of Christmas here until early December, when many shops and buildings put up nativity scenes.

This belen in Garrucha was massive (I'm guessing at least 15 feet wide), and massively interesting. There's a clearing beneath the hills with the baby Jesus, his parents and various animals. There are sheep, goats and horses. The animals are not all to scale, and I'm sure hippos are bigger than goats. I hadn't before realised that Jesus had been born at the seaside, as there is a lighthouse at either end of the nativity scene!

It never ceases to amaze me what I find in this neck of the woods. Many of the local shops have belens - even butchers and hairdressers. One newsagents' shop had a small tent with an assortment of plastic figures. I spotted the three wise men, a camel, a unicorn, two giraffes, three tigers and a rhinoceros in the tent – but no baby Jesus. A bit like a David Attenborough version of the nativity.

Around mid-December, poinsettia plants start appearing. Every town hall sends squads of workmen out to plant these brilliant red plants on the squares and verges. Decorations are put up in all the towns and villages. Bédar's decorations are swapped around each year with other villages, so we never seem to get the same decorations twice running.

During the day in December, we can often walk around in the warmth of the sun wearing t-shirts. At night, the wonderful aroma of log-burning stoves permeates our valley. Olive wood is very hard and is a favourite for burning. There are ample prunings each year, and any amount of suppliers.

We sometimes have guests to stay and they like to try the local shops in the village. Quite a few have entered our local baker's shop then walked out again as the glass cabinets have been completely empty of bakery products. They've simply assumed there's no bread in the shop.

There is a solitary jar of honey for sale on the counter though, and some postcards of old Bédar. There is also a huge poster on the wall showing around 40 types of bread, 36 of which are not actually for sale in the shop. The correct technique to buy bread in our local baker's is to ask for a baguette or a rotunda (a round loaf). If you want brown bread, ask for integral. Once you've told the lady who runs the shop what you're looking for, she will go into the next room and bring out a loaf. It's like buying your bread from an Argos catalogue store, but without having to fill up the forms. What could be simpler?

Many of the shops run by older ladies still have pictures of either Jesus or their favourite saint. The shop is often simply a front room in their house. They don't like to have lights on, as that would cost money and may attract the wrong type of custom.

Walking around my village of Bédar, the street names often amuse me. We have a Jesus Street and we have friends on Almond Street. One of our shorter streets is Calle Medio (Half Street). The baker's shop is on Calle Horno (Oven Street). There is also a Virgin Street, something I've certainly never seen in Glasgow!

The food in the shops around here is often very rustic. The caps on my teeth cost far too much to risk biting a chunk out of a baguette from certain rustic bakers. The meals at our local restaurants are mainly rustic too, but they are always home-cooked, and we never have to worry about ordering soup or rice pudding and getting something out of a tin or packet.

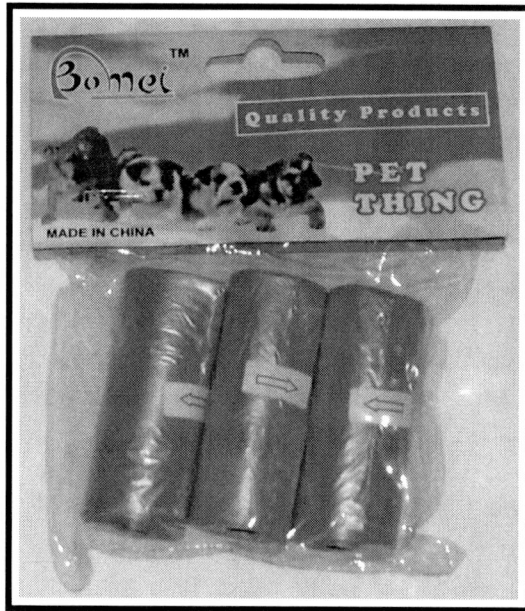

In our area, there are several Chinese shops. The signs over the doors aren't in Chinese, but the staff are Asian. Their shops are full of cheap, Chinese-made goods which are invariably manufactured to much lower standards than European-spec products. Chinese bazaars are the place to go if you want to buy:

- Masonry nails with a crumple zone. This safety feature bends the nails in two when you try to hammer them into a wall.
- A rubber plug for your sink which leaks water, with a connecting chain which will rust through and add a warm colour to your sink in a way stainless steel never could.
- A shower head bracket to replace the broken one in your bathroom, in a very attractive chromed plastic, which provides entertainment during showers as it's not quite strong enough to hold up a shower head.
- An ice cube tray which is not quite frost-proof and cracks the first time you try to get your ice cubes out.
- A bright green plastic tray clearly inspired by Rolf Harris' wobbleboard. During a summer lunch, my Spanish host's attempt to use his flexible friend to move half a dozen wine glasses from his terrace into his house resulted in an enormous crash and a grudged purchase of a new box of six wine glasses.

213

- A plastic brush and shovel set which is extremely difficult to use as the front lip of the shovel has a 45 degree angle. This causes any rubbish being brushed onto the shovel to fly straight into the air.
- An electric kettle with a heat control knob enabling you to decide the precise rate at which the kettle will boil. You may think this is completely pointless, but this brilliant control allows the kettle to take things easy in the hot summer months, then crank up the action around Christmas when you need it to really perform. I had to have it.

And I just had to have the ideal Easter-themed Christmas present for my loved one - a bright green rectangular clock with a picture of the Last Supper on the top half, a picture of a well-stocked fish tank on the bottom half, and a stick-on chromed plastic badge on the bottom right displaying the word 'Benidorm' - a mere 167 miles from the shop!

- - - - - - - - - - - -

I'd put my specs on and opened my emails one morning, when I found this message from Jill asking if I fancied doing a duet with her on 'Fairytale of New York' at out Christmas gigs. A singing duet. I thought I'd better run this past my wife.

"I'd love to do 'Fairytale', Carrie, but I've never been a singer and anyway how am I going to be able to sing like Shane McGowan? I'd need to down bucketfuls of whisky."

"You should be able to sing like him already, then," was my wife's dry retort. "And if you want to look like him too, I know someone who'd happily knock some of your teeth out," she said with a charming smile.

This amazing record by the Pogues with Kirsty MacColl is the best-loved Christmas pop song in the UK by some margin. But the interplay of voices makes it really difficult to bring off. However, I knew instinctively that Jill could nail Kirsty McColl's vocal part and she was keen to perform it with me. I had an idea to do an arrangement with a bit of John Lennon's 'War is Over' as the introduction to the Pogues' great song. And rather than the fade-out on the record, I wanted an arrangement with a proper finish. To top all that, I would have to sing the first two verses in a low key to suit my voice, then change to a higher key for Jill's fast waltz-tempo part. Basically, I needed to produce a totally new arrangement of the song.

In addition to performing Christmas songs during December, we had been asked to perform some Christmas carols at a few venues a few days before Christmas. I have this big pipe organ sound on my synth, which is perfect for 'O Come All Ye Faithful' and the like. I've devised this show of two halves, so after the carols, we perform all the cheesy Christmas dance favourites from Shakin' Stevens to Slade to send folk home tired but happy.

One morning I was deep in dreams that I was on BBC TV's 'Dragon's Den' and being grilled by the same bank manager who always pops up in my dreams. I was describing my next business venture – the 'Mourners' Munchmobile'. This was a low-cost alternative to a funeral reception. Instead of booking a posh hotel for a buffet, or a co-op hall for steak pie and potatoes, this was an on-site crematorium facility. Okay, it was only a converted ice-cream van spray-painted matt black and dispensing burgers and hot dogs, but it was all done in the best possible taste. Instead of chiming the 'Blue Danube' or 'The Happy Wanderer, my 'Mourners' Munchmobile' chimed tasteful tunes such as 'Abide With Me' and "The Lord Is My Shepherd'.

"Really?" This was the usual raised-eyebrow response from my bank manager.

I was just loading a black Kalashnikov when I was rudely awakened by the phone ringing. It was my friend Harvey.

"Jim, can you play for my group of singers on Boxing Day?"

"Now then, Harvey, you know that I came to Almería to say "YES" to everything musical."

So rather than looking forward to an easy Christmas in the sun, as the year was drawing to a close, I found myself with more than a few challenges. At least the weather was fairly mild, although the nights were becoming colder and we had to have our calor gas heater on some nights.

I was worried about singing 'Fairytale'. Singing doesn't run in our family. Noses run, for sure, but not singing. I don't sing in the bath or around the house. My wife does sing sometimes, quietly yet tunefully. We were once at a party and some people were taking turns at singing. I suggested to Carrie that she might do likewise.

"Come on, Carrie, give us a song."

"No way," came the reply.

"You sing around the house, so why not sing something here?"

"I told you no."

"Come on, just a quick wee song," I persisted.

"I'll smash your glasses."

The whole room roared with laughter at my comeuppance. To the best of my knowledge, Carrie has never sung in public, and it would probably be best if I didn't ask her.

I've written songs from an early age. Back in the seventies, I sang one of my own songs on a documentary about a paddle steamer on the old BBC Nationwide TV show. When I came down to Almería, I was inspired to write a song about the rugged landscape, the music, and the good friends I'd made. I did a big arrangement and recorded it a while back. It was played on our local Spectrum FM radio. There are several Spanish stations, but Spectrum is the only English-speaking station, and the good folk there keep the ex-pats and visitors well-informed about local news in Spain, celebrity gossip, exchange rates and local events.

The folks at the station are great supporters of local musicians, and every week they feature a local act. This could be a youngster who sings to their own guitar accompaniment, a 4-piece rock band, and very often a soloist who simply sings along to karaoke backing tracks. My own stuff has been featured, and they seem to enjoy our wacky mash-ups, like my arrangement of the old Yazoo song 'Only You' featuring Mozartian classical piano, and my reggae mash-up of Peter Sarstedt's 'Frozen Orange Juice' which has the accordion intro from 'Where Do You Go To My Lovely' and a snatch of Haircut 100's 'Fantastic Day'.

It's great having our own local radio station, and they are good enough to promote any event put up on Facebook. Like it or not, Facebook has been a godsend out here for information on local events. Many towns only promote events to local residents. One example is the Three Kings festival, when finding information is always a challenge.

The Spanish don't exchange Christmas gifts on Christmas Day – they wait until Three Kings' Day. This is traditionally the day when the three wise men visited the baby Jesus and it was not until 12 days after his birth (Twelfth Night) that they arrived at the stable in Bethlehem. I suppose getting around was slow in those days and a wise man wouldn't want to go racing around on a camel. On 5th January, the Three Kings arrive by boat at Garrucha harbour, but just try finding out what time they arrive! The town halls around here are not good at promoting events.

216

The first year we came over to spend the winter in Almería, we had heard about the Three Kings' event by word of mouth, as no posters were put up outside the town. Carrie and I turned up in Garrucha two hours early. Eventually, the Three Kings arrived, and floats drove them around town. They threw sweets to the children from their floats, something which would not be allowed in the UK of course as you could lose an eye. I'm happy to report that none of the children (or adults) at this event have ever lost an eye or had damage of any kind caused to them by small sweets in wrappers.

The staff at Spectrum FM were recently surprised to learn that there was a Three Kings' pageant and a fantastic Medieval Market at the small town of Los Gallardos, only five kilometres down the road from our village of Bédar. The local town hall had put posters up around the town, but the world outside Los Gallardos didn't know that this major event was taking place every year. It seems to be the Andalucian way. It seems that they don't want to attract people to their town who might spend money.

We only found out about the Medieval market by accident the previous year when we were on our way to Garrucha to see the arrival of the Three Kings. Our car's engine management system threw a wobbly and the computer strongly advised us against proceeding very far in case of engine shut-down. We had to turn back, and we stopped in Los Gallardos to give our car a soothing drink and a siesta. We discovered this wonderful market quite by accident, and enjoyed great Moroccan kebabs before the music started in the tent.

Roast lamb is a very popular dish down here. The Miramar restaurant in Bédar is renowned for its leg of lamb for two, roasted with onions, tomatoes and fresh herbs. The perfect accompaniment is a plate of patatas a lo pobre and trust me, one portion is more than enough for two people. If you think you can manage a starter before all that, the fish soup is fantastic - it's more like a stew, with whole chunks of fish and shellfish. Wash it down with rustic bread and alioli. The Miramar's gazpacho is great too, served in a large bowl with croutons and fresh vegetables to pour on top. Gazpacho is simply raw liquidized salad vegetables, and very good for you as none of the goodness is boiled away.

Every Christmas, the older residents of our village are invited to a festive lunch for a modest fee. Apparently I qualified, having recently hit the age of 60. This year the lunch was to be at a big hotel on Mojacar Playa. There was to be a grand buffet followed by a dance.

The music was provided by the same duo who had played at our local bar at the New Year party.

A local singer was at the lunch, a Spanish lady called Rosa with a good voice, and several people asked if we would do a song together. I was reluctant, as I knew full well that the keyboard player didn't actually play either of his keyboards. What he did was twiddle his right hand over the top keys, without actually touching them, and all the music came from a backing track. This is accepted by the Spanish, even with fiesta bands. I've seen a bass player in a 10-piece fiesta band turn round to take a swig of water, and his bass was still playing. Maybe it was in hands-free mode!

Anyway, the audience at the lunch were insistent that Rosa and I should perform. Someone spoke to the keyboard player and he agreed to let me play.

I went up to the stage with Rosa and sat at the keyboard. The 'keyboard player' explained to me that the lower keyboard didn't make any sound (no surprise there, then) and that he didn't know how to change the sound on the top keyboard. Rosa wanted to sing a popular Spanish song called 'Maria la Portuguesa' which I knew and liked. Although the tune was unmistakenly Spanish, the tempo was identical to 'Scotland The Brave'.

What the audience heard was a unique version of 'Maria'. The only sound which the 'keyboard player' could find on his top keyboard was a tinkly celeste. Imagine opening a musical jewellery box on a dressing table. That's the sound I got. It wasn't ideal for a fast-moving latino number. The audience was surprised to say the least, but we got a round of applause and I swiftly removed myself from the stage before an encore could be requested. It wasn't my finest hour.

- - - - - - - - - - - -

Every year, around a week before Christmas, there's a carol service in the big church at Mojacar Pueblo. It's what is called a "fortress church" and built in 1560 on the site of a former mosque. The church was built to deter pirates or invaders, and it looks rather austere from the outside. Inside it's more churchy, with statues of folk involved in the bible and a nice mural on a wall.

Sorry to be a bit vague, but I don't know a lot about churchy stuff. My wife was a church elder back in our village in Scotland, but I'm no good at religion. I was brought up in the Church of Scotland, but for a child it was never any fun. In the sixties, my father's favourite hymn was 'By Cool Siloam's Shady Rill'. This was all beyond me. I had no idea what a rill was, however to show my readers that I care deeply for them, I checked it out on wikipedia, which tells me ***'In geomorphology, a rill is a natural fluvial topographic feature'.***

So now we all know! But I still have no idea why Siloam was cool. The rest of the lyrics were impenetrable, and included the downright silly expression 'man's maturer age'. I could never connect with this obscure sort of stuff, musically or otherwise.

I was always envious of Catholics, as their leader in Rome is called 'The Pope' – a nice snappy title for the leader of a religion with 1.2 billion followers. The leader in Edinburgh of the rather more modest Church of Scotland with 398,000 followers is the much more grandly titled 'Moderator of the General Assembly of the Church of Scotland'. Rather less snappy.

What appealed to me about this carol service in Mojacar was this. Every year, the local Spanish priest would invite a local British church to share the service. Even in Andalucia, there are branches of different church denominations, admittedly rather small branches. Our local town of Turre has an Evangelical church which reaches out and does much good for the poor in our community whatever their land of birth. The concept of the service was that the local Mojacar catholic church members would sing a carol in Spanish, then the local Brits would sing a carol in English. To a musician like me, it was a lovely idea to integrate the two religions. After all, they were both celebrating the birth of the same child.

There was a list of the carols to be sung and the lessons to be interspersed with the carols, but no lyric sheets for the hymns - only a Spanish lad with a laptop and a projector. Unfortunately, he appeared to be afflicted with St Vitus' Dance. The name of the first hymn appeared on the projector screen. I say screen, but it was really the back wall of the church which was mainly white. It took a good few minutes to get the projector focused onto the church wall, during which time the priest greeted the congregation while a slide show of the lessons in Spanish flashed on and off behind him, and occasionally lent blasts of colour to his white robes.

The Spanish group comprised a choir of eleven plus a guitar player and a lady with a tambourine. They opened with a very jolly song not unlike the seventies' song 'Una Paloma Blanca'. The small choir was loud and enthusiastic, and a happy mood was established.

Next, the Anglican vicar announced the first carol in English, and the church organist played the intro to 'Once in Royal David's City'. Without the benefit of hymn books or song sheets, the Brits stood up and mumbled what they believed to be the words of the first verse of this classic carol, and it was more or less okay. As for the second verse, well there were several different recollections of how the verse started. And by the last verse, chaos ensued as we all looked at each other for guidance. Projector Man wasn't much help as he was setting up the translation of the first of nine lessons from the bible, only he couldn't find it among the dozens of slides on his projector.

As this first carol in English ground to a confused halt, some of the congregation were of the opinion that 'All in white shall wait around' while others were clearly thinking 'For he leads his children on'. Not that night he didn't. Divine intervention was sadly lacking!

The Spanish priest then stepped up to the podium and read the first lesson, while the English translation of the second lesson was projected onto his white robes. The Brits scratched their heads and looked quizzically at each other, then the Spanish choir attacked their next song with great gusto, guitars twanging and tambourines ringing like sleighbells.

After the second lesson had been read, the next carol was 'The First Noel' and we were asked to sing three of the five verses. As with the National Anthem, most folk are fine singing the first verse, but when it comes to that verse after the initial God Save the Queen where the anthem mentions 'Rebellious Scots to crush', well how many people can sing that verse without a song sheet? I'm guessing about as many as knew the last verse of 'The First Noel' that December night. There was a distinct lack of agreement among the congregation.

The second-last carol of the evening was 'Silent Night'. As there were some German people present, it was suggested that they should sing 'Stille Nacht' in German while the Spanish sang 'Noche de Paz' and the Brits sang 'Silent Night'. To hear a carol sung in three languages all at once was just as mixed-up as it sounds.

The most confusing part of the evening was left until last. The final lesson was read in English by a fellow who forgot to switch on his microphone. The priest came over and switched it on for him halfway through the lesson so the congregation could hear him. While this was happening, Projector Man attempted to find the Spanish translation among the dozens of slides on his laptop, which flashed back and forwards just below a statue of the Christmas hero himself.

Everyone felt rather dizzy by the time the last carol of the evening was announced - 'O Come All Ye Faithful'. Of course, neither the Brits nor the Spanish had been given the words, so the Anglican vicar helpfully announced that anyone who didn't know the carol in their own language was welcome to sing it in the original Latin – 'Adeste Fideles'. So once again we were treated to a carol sung in three different languages all at once, with various conflicting ideas in all three languages about the words of the last verse. The evening concluded in total confusion among the congregation, as Projector Man zapped through his collection of slides again to find the one which said 'Merry Christmas' while the priest and the Anglican vicar hugged each other in a brotherly way you'd certainly never witness at a Rangers and Celtic match.

After the service, everyone trooped round to the back of the church to see the nativity scene. The evening air was not cold, and we all hung around and chatted under the lights of Mojacar village. The nativity scene was nice but rather dull - sadly lacking in hippos, unicorns or lighthouses.

As I eased the car up our driveway that night, I met Sammy head-on and made an emergency stop while Carrie got out and picked him up so I could park the car. As usual, we got a bollocking for coming home at this ungodly hour. We fed and cuddled Sammy until he calmed down and forgave us our sin of leaving him all alone in an empty house.

We always know what's Sammy is thinking. On our frequent trips to the UK, we leave him in the cattery. Although he stays in a luxury suite and has his own television and personal valet, he strongly objects to being removed from his beloved home. After collecting Sammy and taking him home in his basket, he'll show his contempt for us by peeing in a corner then scurrying away before we get the chance to chastise him. He knows exactly what he's doing. And although he'll make use of our laps to relax, he'll pointedly sleep with his back to us for a good few days as further punishment.

But on the whole, Sammy has become very attached to me. If he spots me sitting in my lounge chair, he'll exclaim in delight then jump onto my lap. Next thing, his front paws will be on my stomach and his face will be nuzzling mine while he's purring in contentment. Then he'll wash himself on my lap, and when he's finished he'll examine my hands and begin washing me. It's not a pleasant experience to be washed by a cat's tongue - it's like being rubbed down with wet sandpaper. But I'm clearly being honoured, so I remain still and say nothing. Once this task has been completed, Sammy will recline on my lap in his favourite position, with his head cradled by my right arm.

The night of the church service, we had a Christmas nightcap, then I tucked Sammy up in his basket and put his favourite soft brown sheet over him. I stroked his head until he settled down into continual purring. It's like putting a baby to bed, and my other half thinks I'm going soft. He's only a cat etc etc.

After our nightcap, we rolled into bed quite late but Carrie always likes to read before she goes to sleep. I was just about to put the light out when I gasped in pain. I'd been sitting on a church pew for most of the evening and my back was complaining. So I got up, slunk out the bedroom door and closed it behind me. I went downstairs, took my usual cocktail of pain killers with a glass of water, then walked back upstairs and into the bedroom. I closed the door, got into bed and put the light out.

"Your feet are usually cold," I told Carrie "but they're warm tonight."

"What are you talking about? My feet are freezing," she replied.

"Oh, I didn't see you put in a hot water bottle."

"I didn't. What on earth are you on about?"

I pulled back the bed covers right to the bottom of the bed. There, curled up in a ball, was Sammy, quite unconcerned and pretending to be unaware of any problem.

Carrie burst out laughing. "How did he get there? Did you let him in?"

"He must have sneaked in when I went down for my painkillers."

Sammy will sometimes get up and sleep in the sofa bed outside our bedroom door. But this night he had obviously snuck in without me seeing him, then made his way silently under the bed covers to the foot of our bed. Trying to remove him wasn't easy. Nearly a year of good living has made Sammy into a bit of bruiser. He acts comatose and somehow renders himself a dead weight. It must be a cat thing. Eventually I managed to grab his shoulder and heave him out of the bed. I shoved him out the bedroom door.

"Bugger off Sammy and leave us in peace. And I'm not tucking you in again."

"AAAAAAAAAAAAAAAWWWWWWWW."

Came the night before Christmas, actually two nights before Christmas, at the fabulous Desert Springs golf resort. The resort has several events at Christmas, including Santa's Grotto for kids of all ages. I had been playing solo piano in the resort's delightful El Torrente restaurant on Sunday nights during the summer months, and there were more than a few party nights. I was booked to play background music, but I like to work a room, interacting with the audience and playing requests. Every week I did two sets - I'd behave myself in the first set then take a break and crank things up in the second and get in a bit of boogie. I usually got the audience fired up enough to give me the clap (sorry, I mean to clap) in my second set, so that we all went home tired but happy.

But now it was two nights before Christmas and the big log fire was burning brightly in the restaurant. The staff had served mulled wine and the restaurant was crammed full with a happy and lively audience. Jill and I had spent the first hour leading the audience in all the most popular carols. The audience had followed their song sheets and they had sung lustily. Now it was time to premiere my rather weird version of 'Fairytale of New York', which we hadn't told the audience about. We had told Ellie, the lovely girl who manages the restaurant, and she was all excited because like most people, she loves the song.

I played a few chords on the piano to give Jill the key, then she started 'War is Over', speaking the first few words 'So this is Christmas'. By the time we hit the chorus 'So Happy Christmas', I had joined on harmony. Then we finished our brief version of John Lennon's song and I started the piano intro to 'Fairytale'. There was an audible gasp from the audience, then as I started singing the verse, some applause - definitely not something my singing had ever attracted in the past. I spat out the words of the slow start of the song - 'It was Christmas Eve, babe', as best I could in a Shane McGowan-like sneer.

By the time of the key change for the fast part of the song, I played the Irish tune on my synth's accordion setting. Then Jill began singing Kirsty's part 'They've got cars big as bars...'. The audience went wild and started cheering and swaying in time to the fast waltz music. Wow, I hadn't expected that! Jill and I harmonized and swapped lines - it's anything but an easy song to perform. A few minutes later came the big finish I had arranged. Thank goodness, we had both nailed the song, and we were drowned in cheers.

It just shows the lasting affection the public have for this great song, which returns to the charts every year without fail. Grateful thanks Shane and Kirsty for giving this piano man such a thrill.

The next thing I know, it's Christmas Day and we're off to our friend Gail's house where she's cooking Christmas dinner. The owners of her local shop also own a pig farm, and she had ordered a leg of pork fresh from the farm. At the shop, she was presented with a piece of meat over three feet high, and the shopkeeper had to cut the bottom half of it off so the meat could fit into the oven. I'm surprised her oven was big enough even for the top part. It was massive. For a vegetarian, Gail is great at finding bloody enormous pieces of meat!

I much prefer Christmas in Almería. The previous Christmas we had gone to the UK and we had stayed in a hotel near our elder son's home in Staffordshire. In mid-September he had tried to book a restaurant for a traditional Christmas lunch. He could only find a choice of one - a pub chain. The only sitting he could get was 12 noon. We had had to give our menu choices in the middle of October. Lunch was served by secondary schoolchildren literally dripping with acne. The food was poor, the pub understaffed and the service was just as dreadful as you'd expect from such cost-cutting. After three hours, we still hadn't been served our coffee and mince pies included in the menu and we had to leave to let the next sitting into the pub. We vowed never to endure such a miserable rip-off Christmas meal again.

We arrived with friends at Gail and Gren's house in early afternoon and were greeted by some of their neighbours. We all sat outside in the sun and had drinks and nibbles. When the sun went down, around 5pm, we all went indoors to eat our Christmas dinner. This lasted several hours. Well, there was rather a lot of pork to get through. After dinner, we helped with the washing-up, then played my favourite party game 'Who's In The Bag?'. It was a wonderful day.

Next day it was time to fulfil my friend Harvey's request for me to play for his choir at the Boxing Day concert. It was held in the huge church in Vera, a real landmark if ever there was one, as it can be seen from miles away. There were no less than eighteen choirs, including a few childrens' choirs. I played for carols sung by Harvey's choir of local men and women. The best fun of the evening was a 'Las Tunas' choral group, playing traditional Spanish Christmas songs on their guitars and mandolins.

Two days later, we drove up to Huercal Overa with two lady friends to see 'The Nutcracker', the famous ballet with music by Tchaikovsky. This features the most famous ballet number of all time - the 'Dance of the Sugar-Plum Fairy' with its tinkly celeste music sounding like a music-box. And the 'Russian Dance' is also a big favourite.

When we arrived, the audience were waiting outside for the big theatre to open. The seats weren't allocated, so we decided to go up to the balcony for a good view. When we got to the top of the stairs and entered the balcony area, it was as if we'd stepped into a sauna. I suggested moving, but I was out-voted by the three ladies who needed warming up.

We couldn't see the orchestra, so we reckoned it must be behind the stage. But there was no sound of an orchestra tuning up and I was rather puzzled. The music started quietly until someone turned up the volume. Then it dawned on me - the dance company were using a backing track. Bugger me - karaoke ballet!

The dancing was fine if you like that sort of thing (I didn't) and the costumes were certainly sparkly. The interval came after a very long first act, and I hadn't really understood the story from the dancing.

"Don't worry," said Carrie. "The second half will be better and the music will be more familiar to you."

The second half was much shorter than I had expected, and I couldn't understand why the finale was upon us after about 40 minutes. It turns out that this was a unique version of 'The Nutcracker' ballet. Not only was it the karaoke version, it was also the version minus the 'Russian Dance'. And God help me, this is the absolute honest (if unbelievable) truth. It was also the version without the 'Dance of the Sugar-Plum Fairy'. The most famous piece in the entire ballet world had been left out!

That was my first-ever ballet. I have absolutely no plans to go to another.

The following evening Carrie and I went up to Bédar's lovely old church for the annual concert by the village's brass band, which seemed to be augmented on this occasion by musicians from other towns and villages. I counted forty of them, trumpets, trombones, clarinets - and possibly the biggest drum I had ever seen, a huge bass drum about five feet high. For me, this was much better entertainment than the karaoke ballet.

The band played mainly Spanish tunes, but towards the end of the concert the lights were turned off completely. There was a terrifying scream from a member of the orchestra, then the band started playing the intro to 'The Phantom of the Opera', followed by a selection of Andrew Lloyd Webber songs from his musicals. We certainly hadn't been expecting to hear that by a brass band in a Spanish village church at Christmas, but nothing ever surprises me down here.

225

Then before I knew it, New Year's Eve had arrived.

I was to fly back to Scotland in the new year to attend to business and see family and friends. When I'm away from my beloved Levante area of Almería I can't wait to get back. My song 'Almería's Shores' (which has now been translated into Spanish) has this chorus:

"For all the times the sun has warmed my face
For the music that has warmed my winter days
For all the friends who've warmed my heart and soul
I'll return again to Almería's Shores."

That's how I feel about the place.

But now it was the last day of a simply amazing year with lots of new friends, new restaurants, new adventures, and wackiness in abundance. And a loving but deranged cat to share in the coming year's fun in the sun.

I had performed many, many gigs and played piano for dozens of singers and musicians. I had played at loads of jam sessions. I had learned and played Spanish coplas, boleros, zarzuelas and operatic arias with Carlita, and her performances had resulted in several standing ovations. I had also done a lot of solo piano gigs where I just sat down and played what was in my head.

And I had received even more standing ovations with my musical pal, Jill. I can honestly say that of all the singers I've worked with in my lifetime, Jill is one of the best interpreters of a song with whom I've ever had the pleasure of working. She gets right inside the lyrics, and she can hit an audience in the solar plexus. Those who prefer phoney, overwrought fake emotion will never 'get' this in a million years. But those who lay their hearts and souls open to music are regularly moved to tears by the way Jill moulds a 'voice and piano' song with me. The way we develop these songs is totally organic, and the more we perform a song, the better it seems to get. And Jill's wonderful husband Simon and her equally wonderful parents Ruth and Ted have invariably been amongst those cheering us on.

We had ended the year by recording songs for a J & J Music CD. We called it 'J-ology'. Geddit? It includes some of my daft arrangements such as my boogie piano version of Barry Manilow's 'Mandy'. It also included a few of my own songs. In one song I had tried to encapsulate the spirit of our major local seaside resort of Mojacar in a 3-minute pop song, something no-one had ever previously done to the best of my knowledge. It's called 'I Love Mojacar' and I'm delighted that it's proved so popular.

Still breaking new musical ground, and with the encouragement of stunning young(ish) ladies, I'm one lucky old bugger. And I feel truly blessed to be living in what is, for me, probably the best place on earth. I'm in a beautiful village of several nationalities, with some great bars and restaurants in which to chill out with my local friends, and a real buzz about the place. And I'm in an area where music is truly an integral part of the way of life.

So there you have it. Although I've been successful in business, there are people here who are much, much richer than me financially. I know several very affluent men who are lonely and unhappy.

But I have something which, to me, is far more valuable than money. I have music.

At school, I was totally hopeless at maths and managed to get the grand total of 16% in my final maths exam. I've no idea how it works, but I can pull a tune from my memory banks, and even if I've never played it, I can work out the chord structure and the melody, and make a reasonable job of performing it. I guess it's just the way my brain is wired. And I can work all this out on the greatest of all musical instruments, the piano. It was the piano, not the guitar or anything else, which you'd have found in the pubs to help Britain through two world wars. With my piano, I can entertain a room full of people and send them home happy. Music has given me countless friends. People regularly come up to me in the street and thank me for giving them an evening to remember, even years after the event.

Would I prefer a shedload of money to the gift of music? No thanks.

And so, after spending the last day of the year pottering around the garden in the sun and playing football with Sammy, it was time to go upstairs and get dressed up for the New Year's Eve celebrations. Carrie had put on her red dress and her fake fur coat, I had put on a shirt and jacket (and trousers...) and we started to make our way downstairs.

"Wait for it," I said to Carrie.

"WWWWAAAAAAAAAAAAAAAAAAAA."

As usual, Sammy was right on cue. Predictably, he had figured out what was happening. He'd seen that we were dressed up, he had sniffed Carrie's perfume and he was asking us most vociferously if we were really, really going to abandon him once again.

As we headed for the front door of our house to the sound of loud feline insults, I complained yet again to anyone listening that I'd never wanted a bloody cat....

ACKNOWLEDGMENTS

My grateful thanks to all my friends, musicians, restaurant owners, in fact thanks to everyone who made this book possible. Without you, most of this stuff wouldn't have happened to me and the book simply wouldn't have been written. And my grateful thanks to each and every one of you for your enthusiastic and loyal support for my music.

I reckon that the best travel book in the history of the world was 'Round Ireland with a Fridge' by Tony Hawks. His book set the standard for which I was aiming. If my book raises you a fraction of the smiles which Tony raised for me, I'll be as chuffed as a Scotsman with something large and hairy between his legs (it's called a sporran).

Some characters in my book have been diguised to avoid hurt or embarrassment to them - and to avoid any legal actions against me! None of my friends had any objection to me using their real names. The situation with my wife is that she requested minimum involvement within the text of my book, and she also requested that I did not use her real name. I have acted precisely according to her wishes.

My special thanks must go to the wonderful Kathy Defriend for her support, enthusiasm, patience and skill in editing my book. Kathy was a commissioning editor and a publishing editor with a major publishing house before coming to Almería. I was a complete rookie as a writer, and I have learned much from Kathy. During the editing, I never actually got rapped over the knuckles with a ruler, but I'm sure it came pretty close on occasion.

A big thankyou also to a wonderful family friend of many years, Christine Eagleson, for editing my book for grammar and punctuation. This enthusiastic ex-English teacher was partly responsible for the huge number of exclamation marks you witnessed!!!! I must also thank Christine's husband Brian for really constructive help and for being of great support to me with this book.

If you're interested in finding out more about the history and terrain of our amazing wee corner of the world, I can heartily recommend my mate Kevin Borman's excellent book "Flamingos In The Desert". You can obtain it from Amazon and other sources in both paperback and kindle formats. For several years, Kevin has walked all around the area researching places and people. He's been up and down mountains, in and out of ancient ruins and he's even slept under the stars. As a result of his extensive and thoroughly detailed research, his book is full of fascinating facts. The research I did for my book, on the other hand, was done mainly in drinking establishments.

If you've enjoyed my book, I would greatly appreciate it if you could leave a review on Amazon to spread the word to other readers. This may even encourage me to write another book about my musical life!

And I'd love to hear from you. Just drop me a line at boogietastic@hotmail.com or you can send me a Facebook message at www.facebook.com/boogieman.in.andalucia

I promise to respond. But probably not in the earlier part of the day....

9 781785 106507